Perceptions of
Technological Risks and Benefits

Perceptions of
Technological Risks and Benefits

Leroy C. Gould
Gerald T. Gardner
Donald R. DeLuca
Adrian R. Tiemann
Leonard W. Doob
Jan A. J. Stolwijk

Russell Sage Foundation/New York

The Russell Sage Foundation

The Russell Sage Foundation, one of the oldest of America's general purpose foundations, was established in 1907 by Mrs. Margaret Olivia Sage for "the improvement of social and living conditions in the United States." The Foundation seeks to fulfill this mandate by fostering the development and dissemination of knowledge about the political, social, and economic problems of America. It conducts research in the social sciences and public policy, and publishes books and pamphlets that derive from this research.

The Board of Trustees is responsible for oversight and the general policies of the Foundation, while administrative direction of the program and staff is vested in the President, assisted by the officers and staff. The President bears final responsibility for the decision to publish a manuscript as a Russell Sage Foundation book. In reaching a judgment on the competence, accuracy, and objectivity of each study, the President is advised by the staff and selected expert readers. The conclusions and interpretations in Russell Sage Foundation publications are those of the authors and not of the Foundation, its Trustees, or its staff. Publication by the Foundation, therefore, does not imply endorsement of the contents of the study.

Library of Congress Cataloging-in-Publication Data

Perceptions of technological risks and benefits / Leroy C. Gould . . .
[et al.].
    p. cm.
    Bibliography: p.
    Includes index.
    ISBN 0-87154-362-1
    1. Technology—Risk assessment. I. Gould, Leroy C.
T174.5.P46 1987
363.1—dc19   88-15774
                                              CIP

Foreword

In 1973, world oil prices escalated sharply, and the United States, along with the rest of the world, suddenly faced an "energy crisis." Following as it did the Watergate crisis, the drug crisis, the civil rights movement, the environmental movement, the consumer movement, and the Vietnam War, this price escalation prompted some to wonder whether the nation's traditional institutions would survive. They did, although not without change.

This is a book about one of these changes: people's perceptions of the risks and benefits of technology and their judgments about appropriate levels of technological regulation, as revealed in surveys conducted in 1982 and 1983 in Connecticut and Arizona. (One survey in each state involved members of the general public; a second covered people who had given public testimony either supporting or opposing certain technological developments.)

The book had its conception several years ago in an interdisciplinary Energy Seminar at Yale University's Institution for Social and Policy Studies. The seminar had been organized to investigate how the social and behavioral sciences might be involved more effectively in the search for solutions to the energy crisis. The Yale Institution for Social and Policy

Studies Energy Seminar has met continuously over the years, under various names, since it was founded in 1975.

In 1978, Jan A. J. Stolwijk, Professor of Epidemiology (Environmental Health) at the Yale School of Medicine, Associate Director of the John B. Pierce Foundation Laboratory, and a member of the ISPS Energy Seminar, led a discussion in which he argued that the energy crisis was not a crisis of energy supply, but a crisis in risk-management. Stolwijk argued that there are more than adequate energy supplies to fuel an industrialized world—coal and oil shale, augmented by conservation, for the near term, and nuclear energy for the long term; the only trouble is that these alternatives have economic, social, or environmental costs that most people would just as soon avoid. The problem was not a problem of energy supplies, but of substituting more dangerous, less convenient, and more expensive energy forms for petroleum and natural gas, which until then had been abundant, cheap, and remarkably safe both to extract and to use.

The need to develop new energy systems, Professor Stolwijk continued, came at a time when traditional technology risk-management institutions were not functioning well. Conflicts between public interest groups and institutions responsible for managing technological risks had become more common and the time necessary for approving new projects longer and longer. Therefore, the most pressing policy crisis was not energy, *per se,* but managing the trade-offs between the risks and benefits of new energy technologies in such a way that these technologies can come on line sufficiently quickly and in sufficient quantities to replace the energy sources that are rapidly being depleted.

The authors of this book, each a member of the Energy Seminar, thus became interested in late 1978 and early 1979 in the technology risk-management issue. Although all were not in agreement with Professor Stolwijk's presentation of the problem, all were convinced of its importance, and thus organized a separate group to study risk-management processes, particularly those related to energy technologies. Donald De-Luca was then Director of the Roper Center Office for Teaching and Research at Yale. Leonard Doob was Sterling Professor Emeritus of Psychology and Senior Research Scholar at the Institution for Social and Policy Studies at Yale. Gerald Gardner, currently Professor of Psychology at the University of Michigan–Dearborn, was then a Visiting Research Scholar with the Yale Institution for Social and Policy Studies. Leroy Gould, now a Professor at The Florida State University and Visiting Research Scholar in the Yale Institution for Social and Policy Studies, was then a Senior Research Associate at the Institution for Social and Policy Studies and a Lecturer in Sociology. Dr. Adrian Tiemann was Sociologist for the Technology Evaluation Operation, Energy Science and Engineering, General Electric Corporate Research and Development, in Schenectady, New York. Jan Stolwijk is currently Chairman of the Department of Epidemiology and Public Health at the Yale School of Medicine.

In the early stages of our work we became convinced that the key to understanding what appeared to be a growing crisis in technology risk-management was to understand the interactions between traditional technology risk-managers (those scientists and technicians who, as members of government regulatory agencies or industrial self-regulatory bodies, set product safety and performance standards) and that relatively new category of actors that some were calling "intervenors" (members of the general public who, individually or collectively, initiate legal, legislative, or other actions in an attempt to influence or alter these standards). How one could study these interactions most effectively, however, was not at all clear.

One idea was to interview technology risk-managers to learn more precisely how they arrive at their decisions and in what ways, if any, their decision processes might more readily accommodate public values. Another idea was to survey members of the public in order to find out why so many people have come to distrust professional technology risk-managers and just how wide the gap really is between the managers and the general public. Another idea was to review various risk-management decisions to determine exactly what impact, if any, intervenors actually have in the management process. We ultimately chose the second option, the public survey, in part because we thought it would be the most feasible study to conduct and in part because we thought that traditional research agencies would be more likely to support this line of inquiry than the others.

In 1979, at Dr. Tiemann's suggestion, we submitted a request to General Electric Corporate Research and Development for funds to develop a general population survey of technological risk and benefit perceptions and attitudes. These funds were awarded and, along with an additional grant the following year from the Northeast Utilities Company, allowed us to develop and pretest survey items and test several methodological hypotheses (Stolwijk et al., 1980; Gardner et al., 1982).

With the support of General Electric Corporate Research and Development and Northeast Utilities Company, we submitted a proposal in 1981 to the National Science Foundation, Technology Assessment and Risk Analysis Division of Policy Research and Analysis, for a major field study. Our original proposal was for a general population survey of people residing in Connecticut and western Massachusetts.

NSF peer reviewers suggested two major additions to the study

(#PRA8014194): (1) a survey of the general public in another, contrasting region of the country (preferably in the Sunbelt), and (2) surveys of, or interviews with, samples of intervenors from the same two regions. We incorporated these suggestions into the research design and resubmitted the proposal. The additions increased the estimated costs of the project by approximately two-thirds and ultimately extended the completion date of the study by three years.

Although some of this added time resulted from the additional complexity of the study, nearly a year of it resulted from the unfortunate coincidence of our research proposal and a new presidential administration that reviewed many research proposals then pending at the National Science Foundation and other federal agencies. Ultimately we had to change the title and the stated objectives of the study and agree not to include questions in the survey that would, among other things, ask members of the general public what they thought appropriate levels of federal safety regulation should be. Needless to say, we found these restrictions an unwarranted political intrusion into the conduct of free academic research, and we ignored them completely.

Individual grants from the Russell Sage Foundation to Professor Gould and from the Exxon Education Foundation and the University of Michigan–Dearborn to Professor Gardner supported the completion of this book. We are grateful to these organizations, and to the National Science Foundation, General Electric Corporate Research and Development, and the Northeast Utilities Company for supporting our work.

The purposes of this volume are twofold: (1) to describe the results of our Connecticut and Arizona surveys, and (2) to interpret the relevance of these findings to changes taking place in U.S. technology risk-management institutions. Chapter 1 reviews the background of technology risk-management, the rise of modern risk-management institutions, and the growth of direct public involvement in the risk-management process. Chapter 2 describes the sociodemographic characteristics of the intervenors and members of the general public we surveyed, their perceptions of the risks and benefits of technology, and their views about current and desirable levels of technological safety regulation. Chapter 3 summarizes the results of other studies on people's perceptions of technological risks, benefits, and regulation, and outlines the major hypotheses of our work. Chapter 4 describes the questions we included in our surveys and gives an overview of the analytic procedures we used to interpret their answers. Chapters 5 and 6 present our findings about what accounts for variations in people's perceptions of technological risks and benefits and their judgments about the acceptability of current technological standards and regulations. Chapter 7 reports our findings about what accounts for variations in whether or not people take action to try to influence risk-management decisions. Chapter 8 presents our conclusions and comments on the policy implications of our findings and the relevance of our research to other social scientists working in this field.

Since the sample design, exact survey questions, and detailed analyses used in our study will probably be of interest to only a few readers, we have relegated the discussion of these matters to four technical appendices. Appendix A is a copy of the survey instrument we used, with the exact wording of the questions. Appendix B describes our sample design and the tests we performed to determine whether we should weight the data from the general public samples. Appendix C gives an account of the scales we constructed and presents reliability scores for each. Appendix D reviews some of the technical details of our statistical procedures.

Although all of the authors of this book have been actively involved in the study from the beginning, different members of the group assumed different roles at various stages of the research. As noted earlier, the initial inspiration for the work came from Professor Stolwijk. Dr. Tiemann was influential in getting the group together and in securing initial funding from General Electric Corporate Research and Development. Dr. DeLuca and Professor Gould played particularly active roles in securing funding from Northeast Utilities Company, while Professor Gardner and Dr. Tiemann assumed the major responsibility for designing and conducting the pilot research made possible by that grant. Dr. DeLuca supervised the sample design, instrument development, and data collection for the Connecticut and Arizona surveys. Professors Gould and Gardner were responsible for the majority of the data analysis and the preparation of this document; Gould had primary responsibility for Chapters 1, 2, 4, 7, and 8 and Appendices C and D; Gardner, primary responsibility for Chapters 3, 5, and 6; and DeLuca, primary responsibility for Appendix B. Professor Doob served as consultant, critic, guide, and inspiration through all stages of the research.

Contents

1

Introduction

Although a survey of the evening news might lead some to believe otherwise, most people living in the United States and other industrial nations today manage to survive a majority of the years apparently allotted them by the inherent biological limits of human existence (Gori and Richtee, 1978). Life expectancy at birth in Switzerland, the longest in the world, is 79 years, just exceeding the 78 years in Sweden (*World Almanac,* 1986). People in the United States have a life expectancy at birth of 75 years.

It has not always been thus. According to one estimate, a third of the people living in prehistoric hunting and gathering societies died by the time they were 20, and few lived beyond the age of 40 (Vallois, 1960: 196). The major threats to life then appear to have been trauma (Weidenreich, 1949); the fact that hunting and gathering peoples were so widely scattered (probably never more than one person per square kilometer of habitable earth's surface [Cipolla, 1978: 84]) appears to have limited the spread of communicable diseases. It was the increased population densities made possible by settled agriculture that made these scourges possible. Indeed, in agricultural societies plagues and famine became the leading causes of death, periodically wiping out 20, 30, or even 50 percent of the population at one time (Cipolla, 1978: 89). On average, life expectancy at birth in early agricultural societies appears to have been somewhere between 20 and 35 years (Cipolla, 1978: 90). Even today, people living in agricultural and hunting and gathering societies have shorter life expectancies than people living in industrialized nations.

Now—except in times of war—heart disease, cancer, cerebrovascular disease, and accidents are the leading causes of death of people living in industrial societies. The National Center for Health Statistics (1984: 59) reported an annual age-adjusted mortality rate in the United States in 1983 from heart disease of 188 per 100,000 population, from cancer of 132 per 100,000, from cerebrovascular diseases of 34 per 100,000, and from accidents of 35 per 100,000. The rate for motor vehicle accidents was 18, for homicide 8, and for suicide 12. The total age-adjusted mortality rate in the United States from all causes in 1983 was 550 per 100,000 population.

The Risks of Technology

Maybe because life has always been something of a risk, people seem always to have gone to considerable lengths to increase life expectancy. Medical practitioners are a part of most societies, and controlling, or attempting to control, natural hazards has long been an important element in religious ritual. Even as late as the eighteenth century, when Benjamin Franklin was discovering that lightning was electricity and would flow to the ground along a wet kite string, it was still the practice in Europe to try to drive off thunderstorms by ringing church bells. One eighteenth-century observer counted 386 lightning strikes on church steeples over a 33-year period, which resulted in the death of 103 bell ringers (Mazur, 1981: 1).

It was not until the development of modern science and technology that people could employ lightning rods and other technical devices to protect themselves from natural hazards and that public health procedures provided protection from many communicable diseases. Some risks were reduced by eliminating or reducing exposure; others by managing the results of exposure. Although lightning still kills nearly 100 persons annually in the United States, and church bells are still rung to warn hikers of approaching thunderstorms in some regions of the European Alps, most people today manage to avoid death from lightning and such other natural hazards as tornadoes, earthquakes, and volcanic eruptions. Similarly, communicable disease epidemics and famine are no longer major threats to life in industrialized nations, nor for that matter even in most agricultural societies, having been replaced by cardiovascular disease, cancer, and other diseases associated with aging as the major causes of death. To a very large exent, such changes are a result of the scientific and technological advances of the past two centuries.

Even while science and technology were eliminating or reducing some kinds of risks, and thereby dramatically lengthening life expectancy, they simultaneously introduced new risks of their own, not only to those, like Benjamin Franklin, who participated directly in the new enterprises (Franklin was fortunate not to have been killed by his kite-flying experiment), but for everyone. Harnessing natural forces in reservoirs behind man-made dams; generating and distributing electricity; manufacturing and riding in modern transportation vehicles; mining, storing, distributing, and using minerals and fossil fuels; and producing, disseminating, and using synthetic organic chemicals are only some examples of technological processes that generate risks to life and health, some of which are not even apparent until years after a technology has been introduced. As many as 300,000 people in the United States are permanently disabled each year by product-related injuries, while another 80,000 are killed in such accidents (Brodeur, 1985). Air and water pollution and food contamination take an additional toll. The automobile alone, which to many is probably one of the greatest triumphs of modern technology, is associated with approximately 50,000 deaths a year in the United States, making it the leading cause of death among people aged 5 to 44 (Baker, O'Neill, and Karpf, 1984). In addition, there are 31,000 deaths a year from gunshot wounds.

Thus, while modern science and technology are responsible for prolonging and enriching the lives of most people in the world, they are also responsible for shortening the lives of some and for threatening the lives or well-being of all. There is no little irony in the fact that the electricity that powers our video-cassette recorders and hospital operating rooms may be produced by a nuclear or fossil-fuel power plant that pollutes the air or carries a threat to large populations of catastrophic meltdown and irradiation. There is no irony at all in the fact that the nuclear devices that ended the most recent global war have now evolved into devices that could eliminate the entire world population.

Establishing Risk-Management Institutions

In the early days of the Industrial Revolution, technologists themselves assumed the primary responsibility for limiting and managing the risks associated with the technologies they were putting into place; free-market forces, along with occasional legislative intervention, sufficed to manage any trade-offs that became necessary between the risks and benefits of growing industrialization. As industrialization continued, engineering and other professional societies emerged which developed standards of performance and safety for their professions based on research and especially on the failure experience of particular products or applications. Often, such safety standards had their roots in catastrophic fires, boiler explosions, railroad accidents, or bridge failures. The standards they developed were usually a matter of consensus with representatives from relevant industries and were seldom precisely documented.

As cities became crowded and the incidence and toll of infectious disease increased during the eighteenth century, the Sanitary Movement developed and ultimately produced dramatic improvements in the health and life expectancy of city dwellers. By the first half of this century, public health officials were assuming responsibility for protecting public health in general, while other professionals, operating under explicit or implicit legislative mandate and supervision, were assigned or assumed responsibility for identifying particular risks, estimating their magnitudes, and setting safety standards. Usually these regulatory bodies, such as the Food and Drug Administration, the Environmental Protection Agency, the Federal Aviation Administration, and the Occupational Safety and Health Administration in the United States, were set up as part of the executive branch of government. Sometimes, however, as in the cases of the Underwriters Laboratory and the American Society of Heating, Refrigerating, and Air Conditioning Engineers, already existing professional or industrial organizations continued their traditional risk-management roles. Although the new government regulatory bodies promulgated many new codes and standards, it was not uncommon for them simply to adopt the standards that had already been developed by professional or trade associations. In either case, however, the safety standards they set determined, implicitly, how much society would pay to achieve given levels of benefits, or to avoid given levels of risk.

Although these regulatory bodies and industry and trade associations documented their activities more carefully than their predecessors had, they nonetheless continued to deliberate behind closed doors and to reach their decisions by establishing a consensus among experts. With but occasional exception, the public appears to have accepted these procedures as being legitimate and the decisions of these bodies as being both reasonable and appropriate. Not being able themselves to measure accurately the risks of technologies, people evidently felt comfortable, for the most part, in leaving these scientifically demanding activities to professionals. When disasters at sea, serious floods, large fires, big explosions, major mining disasters, or other highly publicized catastrophes occurred, regulatory bodies usually responded quickly with investigations and more stringent regulations. The effects, in such cases, were immediate and their connection with causes obvious.

Public Involvement

During the past several decades, however, significant numbers of people, acting sometimes as individuals but more often as members of public interest groups, have begun to make it clear that some risk-benefit decisions made by professional technology risk-managers are not acceptable and should be modified. Consumers Union, publisher of *Consumer Reports* and activist for consumer safety, was founded in 1936. The first nuclear power plant, built in Detroit in the mid-1950s, was contested, and by the mid- to late 1960s a major nuclear power controversy had emerged (Mazur, 1981: 97). In 1962 Rachel Carson published *Silent Spring*, detailing the hazards of pesticides; and in 1965 Ralph Nader published *Unsafe at Any Speed*, criticizing the Chevrolet Corvair and General Motors, in particular, and all automobile manufacturers, in general. These two very widely read works caught the imagination of many people in the United States and played a major role in expanding and legitimizing the environmental and consumer movements.

In addition to identifying, publicizing, and otherwise protesting specific risks, however, some individuals and environmental and consumer organizations also demanded that the general public be assigned a more direct and prominent role in the technology risk-management process. Frustrated by their attempts to get behind the closed doors of traditional risk-management institutions, these people and organizations fought both for access to the details of regulatory decisions and for public hearings or other mechanisms by which members of the general public could get their feelings and values on risks across to professional risk-managers and thus be included in risk-management decisions. In many instances, these demands have been granted (Draper, 1971; Otway, 1975; Lowrance, 1976; Sullivan and Fenn, 1976; Rowe, 1977; Dodge and Grier, 1978; Douglas and Wildavsky, 1982a).

Many of our society's risk-management institutions and procedures have thus been transformed markedly in the past two decades. No longer are technological risk-benefit decisions the exclusive domain of experts from government, industry, and academia; now interested citizens and public interest groups have a direct say in the risk-management process (see, in particular, Nelkin, 1984). One consequence of this change (indeed, probably also one of the reasons for it) is that public awareness of a number of risks has increased. Another consequence is that the acceptable levels of some risks, as embedded in current regulation, have been reduced, while other risks have been increased (for example, in reallowing the use of saccharin and removing seat-belt ignition interlock regulations). Overall, however, the net effect of public involvement in technology risk-management has probably been to increase, rather than reduce, the levels of protection afforded by safety standards.

Although people have been sending letters, signing petitions, and organizing protest meetings for years, the direct and large-scale involvement of the public in the risk-management process via public hearings, public forums, workshops, colloquia, and the like, and in particular the active participation of public interest groups, has presented a challenge that not a few technology risk-managers have labeled unreasonable, if not downright impossible. Faced with mounting lists of dilemmas in applying science and technology to national needs, technologists have suddenly been asked to incorporate what they often consider to be ill-founded or irrational public opinion into their scientifically based risk-management decisions (Kasper, 1980; Schwing, 1980; Raiffa, 1980; Otway and Thomas, 1982). Such intrusions, they have argued, not only slow down the decision-making process but lead to risk-benefit trade-offs that err unreasonably on the side of public safety at the expense of technological progress. Some have gone so far as to suggest that public overreaction to technological risk shows pathological "elements of phobic thinking" (DuPont, 1980).

Establishing Acceptable Safety Standards

Meanwhile, scientists and technologists with a broader perspective have acknowledged that public sentiments have a legitimate place in the risk-management process. For example, William Lowrance (1976), after a lengthy literature review, concluded that technology risk-management has always involved public values as well as scientific measurement and projection. "Measuring risks," as Lowrance labels the scientific component of risk-management, is a scientific matter, appropriately left to professional risk-managers trained in such fields as physics, chemistry, and biology. "Judging safety," as he refers to the other component of risk-management, however, is a matter of public values best left to the political process.

Some, like Jacques Ellul (1964) and Langdon Winner (1977), have argued that it is too late for society to control the course of technology, as modern technology has developed a momentum of its own that is ultimately beyond political control. Others (Woodhouse, 1982 and 1983), only slightly less pessimistically, have argued that although the political institutions of present-day democratic societies are not capable of dealing with modern technologies, which are too large, too complex, and too scientifically advanced for the average citizen to comprehend, it is not impossible to think of new institutions that might bring technology back under political control.

One of the more widely discussed, although never implemented, of these modifications is the "science court" (Kantrowitz, 1975), which would separate issues involving the measurement of risk from issues involving public values (what Lowrance referred to as judgments of safety) and would arbitrate conflicts involving the former. Thus freed from disputes among contending scientists, conflicts involving public values would have a better chance of being resolved, advocates of the science court claim (Mazur, 1981: 42).

Measuring Risks

Inherent in this and similar proposals, and in Lowrance's distinction between measuring risks and judging safety, is the notion that technological or other kinds of risk can be measured, scientifically, while values cannot. Setting aside for a moment the fact that social scientists have been "measuring" values for years (albeit with arguable levels of precision), a case can be made that risks, intrinsically, cannot be measured at all. Although it is in some respects a semantic argument, it nevertheless needs to be pointed out that the word *risks* refers to future events, while measurement is an activity of the past or present. In other words, scientists can measure past incidents of death or injury but not those that have yet to occur. Risks, therefore, may be assessed, or projected, but not measured.

There is an important logical, as well as semantic, point to be made by this distinction. The semantic point is that the term *measurement* implies greater degrees of accuracy or precision than do the terms *assessed* or *projected*. The logical point is that risk projection is at heart a theoretical, not an operational, enterprise. The accuracy of risk projections, in other words, depends on more than the accuracy of past measurements; it depends equally on the validity of all underlying assumptions that classify future events in the same categories as past events. As Malcolm Brown (1986) has observed, when a risk-manager or intervenor provides numerical estimates of risk that look too precise to be true, they probably are.

The prediction that the sun will come up tomorrow, for example, is based both on the fact that it has been observed to come up every morning that we know of in the past, and the supposition that the rotation of the earth and the luminosity of the sun will be the same in the future as they have been in the past. Not a bad supposition, most would agree, but a supposition nonetheless; after all, it is possible that the sun will not come up tomorrow morning.

Projecting specific risks in well-established, well-measured, and essentially unchanging technical systems, like the risk of tire failure on a passenger automobile, is probably not too different from projecting the probability that the sun will rise tomorrow or that one will throw a seven in a game of craps; the similarity between past events and future events is quite close. Predicting the probability of tire failure for a brand-new vehicle, however, may be much less accurate, as was demonstrated recently by several unexpected blowouts and near blowouts on space shuttles during landing. The point is, of course, that the space shuttle is very unlike any other vehicle, and projecting aspects of its performance based on the performance of other vehicles, as NASA is well aware, is done with some peril.

Predicting the overall risks of novel and complex technologies, such as the space shuttle or nuclear electric-power reactors, is a difficult, if not impossible, task. It involves the use of elaborate analytic techniques, such as "fault-tree" and "event-tree" analyses which mathematically combine past experience with the technology's many underlying parts into a prediction about the technology's future overall performance (Lewis, 1980; Slovic and Fischhoff, 1983; Perrow, 1984). A review by a National Academy of Sciences/National Research Council Committee on Risk Assessment in the Federal Government (NAS/NRC, 1983) concluded, however, that the availability of data appropriate to such analyses is a major stumbling block to such technology risk assessments.

Measuring Values

Even though measuring the risks of a technology is inherently impossible, and projecting them is only as accurate as past measurements of accidents associated with that technology or the similarity of that technology to other technologies that have been accurately measured, measuring social values associated with these risks is not impossible. Starr (1969 and 1972), for example, made one such attempt based on the premise that trial and error leads societies to optimal levels of regulation for technologies with which they have had long experience. The number of deaths now caused by railroads in this country, for example, must be acceptable to the American public as a proper price to pay for the benefits railroads provide. If it were otherwise, political pressures would have led to a different trade-off between the risks and benefits of this technology.

Using historical data, Starr plotted statistics on the risk of death and the estimated dollar value of benefits for several technologies and concluded that: (1) U.S. society tolerates greater risks from those technologies and activities that provide greater benefits (specifically, risks are accepted in proportion to the third power of benefits), and (2) risks from voluntary activities are roughly 1,000 times more acceptable, for the same level of benefit, than risks from involuntary activities. Using these standards, one could now estimate the acceptability of newer, untested technologies. As an example, Starr (1969: 1237) reckoned that commercial nuclear power must be acceptable to the public since the risks of death from this technology do not exceed the risks of death from other, older technologies that yield comparable benefits.

Other scientists and technical experts have used simplified versions of this "revealed-preference" method of assessing public values, as it has come to be called, to try to convince the public that opposition to given technologies, in particular to nuclear power, is unreasonable (Wilson, 1979). Therefore the revealed-preference approach has a normative, as well as a descriptive, purpose; that is, it is used not simply to determine public sentiments but also to decide which new technologies are acceptable (Otway and Thomas, 1982; Otway and von Winterfeldt, 1982).

Another of the attractions of the revealed-preference approach to determining the acceptability of a new technology is that it permits an elegant end-run around what is probably the most difficult moral problem facing traditional cost-benefit analysis: setting a dollar value on human life. Rather than judging a technology acceptable if the dollar value of its benefits exceeds the dollar value of its costs (including deaths), as cost-benefit analysis must do, the revealed-preference approach uses historical data to calculate the number of deaths that are "acceptable," given the dollar benefits of the technology (Howard and Antilla, 1979).

Although Starr's work has had considerable impact and has been widely cited, it has also been widely criticized (Otway and Cohen, 1975; Green, 1980; Fischhoff, Slovic, and Lichtenstein, 1979 and 1981). The approach assumes that historical values are good guides to future policy, which ignores the fact that public values may change with time, sometimes rather rapidly. It also assumes that regulatory decisions in fact truly reflect the values of an informed public, a point that most consumer advocates and busines leaders would probably disagree with, the former citing the "capture" of regulatory agencies by private industry, the latter the "undue" influence of overzealous intervenors. Other analysts, using different data and different assumptions, have arrived at revealed-preference curves that are considerably different than those derived by Starr (Fischhoff, Slovic, and Lichtenstein, 1979; Otway and Cohen, 1975).

Expressed Preferences

In part as an attempt to overcome the difficulties inherent in Starr's indirect approach to assessing public attitudes toward technology risk-benefit trade-offs, some researchers (Otway and Fishbein, 1977; Fischhoff, Slovic, and Lichtenstein, 1978 and 1979; Slovic, Fischhoff, and Lichtenstein, 1979, 1980, and 1981; Vlek and Stallen, 1979; Green and Brown, 1980; Renn, 1981) began directly asking people to rate the risks and benefits of various technologies and activities and to judge the acceptability of prevailing technology regulations. This "expressed-preference" approach is based on prevailing societal values and allows researchers to gather information bearing on aspects of risk and benefits that are not easily quantified or for which mortality and morbidity statistics are not available.

Like the revealed-preference approach, however, expressed-preference research has limitations, among which is the fact that even though people may have little or no relevant knowledge about the risks of a technology, they express opinions about its risks, benefits, and regulation anyway (Fischhoff, Slovic, and Lichtenstein, 1979). In addition, people's opinions are sometimes so vague or poorly thought-out that their responses can be affected significantly by even small variations in the wording of questions (Tversky and Kahneman, 1981). And finally, much expressed-preference research has had to be conducted on small samples of people that are not necessarily representative of the public at large.

The study we report in the following chapters is expressed-preference research. It was designed specifically to verify and extend previous expressed-preference research, especially that of Slovic, Fischhoff, and Lichtenstein, and to address and attempt to overcome some of its inherent weaknesses. We have attempted to overcome the problem of representativeness by employing relatively large, general-population samples from two different regions of the country, Connecticut and Arizona, and the problem of "salience" by including special samples of people who had already demonstrated their general concern about the risks or benefits of technology by testifying at state or federal hearings. (Details of these populations and the sampling procedures we employed are available in Appendix B.) We also chose to ask questions about technologies that were matters of some public attention (nuclear power, nuclear weapons, handguns, automobiles, commercial air travel, and industrial chemicals) and included specific questions about the salience of each to the respondents. We have also included in our study potential correlates of perceived risk and judged acceptability not included in the earlier works, a more complete measurement of the dimensions of perceived benefits, and an assessment of the relationship between people's propensity to take personal action in the risk-management process and their risk perceptions, benefit perceptions, and judgments of acceptability. Chapter 3 provides a detailed discussion of these extensions and improvements.

2

Intervenors and the General Public

Table 2.1 summarizes the sample design of our study, which included two full-probability samples of people living in Connecticut and Arizona as well as special samples of "intervenors" living in the same two states. Intervenors were chosen from lists of persons who had given testimony at federal or state hearings related to then-current technological issues. In Connecticut, hearing records were sufficiently detailed for us to choose equal numbers of intervenors from two subpopulations: intervenors who had given testimony favorable to industry, and intervenors who had spoken against current industry practices or plans. Hearing records in Arizona, however, were not as detailed as they were in Connecticut, and we were thus unable to separate intervenors from this state into two categories.

The Yale Roper Center conducted the surveys in Connecticut, and the National Opinion Research Center (NORC) selected the sample and conducted the interviews in Arizona. (Appendix B gives details of the sample design and interviewing procedures; Appendix A is a copy of the survey instrument.) The Connecticut general population sample, being drawn from a utility customer list, was simple random at the household level. The Arizona general population sample, drawn from the greater Phoenix area according to conventional area probability procedures, was also full prob-

Table 2.1
Sample Design by Region

Samples	Connecticut	Arizona	Total
General Population[a]			
Completed interviews	542	479	1,021
Response rate %	77	63	70
Intervenors	150	149	299
Pro-safety	(75)	—	—
Pro-benefits	(75)	—	—
Total completed interviews	692	628	1,320

[a]Both general population samples are full probability.

ability at the individual level, although it was not simple random at either the individual or the household level. The response rate was 77 percent in Connecticut and 63 percent in Arizona.

Table 2.2 shows some of the general characteristics of the Connecticut and Arizona residents who took part in the survey. While there were few differences in 1982–83 between the two regions in terms of average age, gender, or race, Connecticut residents were somewhat better educated and earned somewhat more money than did people living in Arizona. The most prevalent religion in Connecticut was Catholic, while more people in Arizona were Protestant than any other religion. Arizona residents were more mobile than Connecticut residents, with 21, as opposed to 12, percent having lived in another state five years earlier. Although a slightly larger percentage of Arizona residents listed themselves as being Democrat (34 percent) than did Connecticut residents (29 percent), Arizona residents considered themselves to be more conservative, and a smaller percentage indicated that they had voted in the previous presidential election.

Table 2.3 compares pro-benefits and pro-safety intervenors from Connecticut. (Since we were unable to classify all Arizona intervenors as being pro-benefits or pro-safety, we have not included Arizona intervenors in this comparison.) Pro-benefits intervenors were somewhat older, on average, then either pro-safety intervenors or the general public; much more likely to be male; better educated; and had higher incomes. They were more likely to be Protestant than any other religion, and although they were less mobile than the general public, they were more mobile than pro-safety intervenors. Although pro-safety intervenors were considerably more likely than the general public to rate themselves as "liberal," and pro-benefits intervenors more likely to list themselves as "conservative," a

Table 2.2
Sociodemographic Characteristics of General Population Samples

Demographic Characteristic	Connecticut ($n = 542$)	Arizona ($n = 479$)
Mean age	45 years	44 years
Gender		
Male	45%	48%
Female	55	52
Race		
White	94%	94%
Nonwhite	6	6
Gross family income		
Under $15,000	22%	35%
$15,000–$29,999	36	36
$30,000–$74,999	36	24
Over $75,000	6	5
Median income[a]	$24,750	$19,025
Education		
Mean years of school	13 years	13 years
High school diploma	82%	77%
College degree	31	24
Religious preference		
Protestant	37%	45%
Catholic	44	32
Jewish	3	2
Other	5	10
None	11	11
Married	68%	62%
Lived in a different state 5 years ago	12%	21%
Self-designated liberal/ conservative views		
Liberal	30%	25%
Moderate	35	35
Conservative	35	40
Political party affiliation		
Democrat	29%	34%
Republican	26	30
Independent	38	26
No preference/other	7	10
Voted in 1980 presidential election	74%	60%

[a]Median income is approximate since it was interpolated from grouped income categories ordered on a scale from 1 to 18.

Table 2.3
Sociodemographic Characteristics of Connecticut Intervenor Samples

Demographic Characteristic	Pro-Benefit Intervenors (*n* = 75)	Pro-Safety Intervenors (*n* = 75)
Mean age	50 years	46 years
Gender		
Male	92%	64%
Female	8	36
Race		
White	95%	100%
Nonwhite	5	0
Gross family income		
Under $15,000	0%	7%
$15,000–$29,999	10	23
$30,000–$74,999	72	63
Over $75,000	18	7
Median income[a]	$38,600	$33,530
Education		
Mean years of school	16 years	17 years
High school diploma	97%	100%
College degree	84%	80%
Religious preference		
Protestant	53%	43%
Catholic	31	28
Jewish	4	9
Other	3	4
None	9	16
Married	84%	81%
Lived in a different state 5 years ago	7%	4%
Self-designated liberal/ conservative views		
Liberal	26%	50%
Moderate	18	19
Conservative	56	31
Political party affiliation		
Democrat	19%	39%
Republican	51	28
Independent	29	32
No preference/other	1	1
Voted in 1980 presidential election	97%	97%

[a]Median income is approximate since it was interpolated from grouped income categories ordered on a scale from 1 to 18.

fairly large percentage (19 percent) of pro-benefits intervenors said that they were Democrats and an even larger percentage (28 percent) of pro-safety intervenors said that they were Republicans.

Figures 2.1 through 2.12 profile the responses of the two general population samples and the Connecticut pro-benefits and pro-safety intervenor samples on four of the most important variables in our study: (1) perceptions of benefits, (2) perceptions of risks, (3) perceived strictness of current technological safety standards, and (4) desired strictness of safety standards. Perceptions of benefits were remarkably similar among the four groups, although they varied considerably among the six technologies: automobile travel, commercial air travel, nuclear electric power, nuclear weapons, handguns, and industrial chemicals. Somewhat more Connecticut than Arizona residents saw none or few benefits to be had from handguns, but overall there were few differences between the general public samples from these two regions. Compared to the general public, a larger fraction of Connecticut intervenors, whether pro-safety or pro-benefits, saw great benefits from industrial chemicals. Connecticut pro-benefits intervenors, on the whole, saw more benefits than did pro-safety intervenors. Aside from the strikingly high proportion of pro-safety intervenors who saw absolutely no benefits to be gained from nuclear weapons, however, advocates on the whole saw the benefits of technology about the same as members of the general public.

There is also striking similarity among the four groups in terms of their perceptions of risk. Members of the general public in Connecticut and Arizona, and pro-safety and pro-benefits intervenors in Connecticut, were about equally likely to judge automobile travel and industrial chemicals as risky and, with a few minor variations, to judge commercial air travel as not risky. A majority in each group viewed the risk of nuclear weapons as being very great. The general public and intervenors in Connecticut, however, viewed handguns as being much riskier than Arizona residents did. Pro-benefits advocates viewed nuclear power as being much less dangerous than did pro-safety advocates.

Although each of the six technologies included in the survey has been a matter of public attention in prior years and has led to risk-management controversies, only perceptions of nuclear power and handguns differed very much between our samples: The perceptions of handguns differed between regions; the perceptions of nuclear power differed between pro-safety and pro-benefits intervenors. It is somewhat surprising that there were not larger regional differences in perceptions of nuclear power, as Connecticut residents, at the time of the survey, received more than half of their electricity from nuclear power plants while Arizona residents received the large majority of their power from non-nuclear sources.

Figure 2.1
Connecticut and Arizona Residents' Perceptions of the Benefits, Risks, Current Standards, and Desired Standards for Automobile Travel

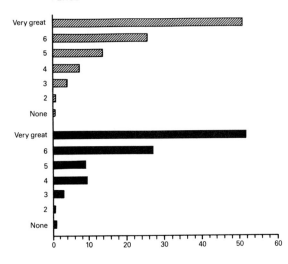

PERCEPTIONS OF BENEFIT

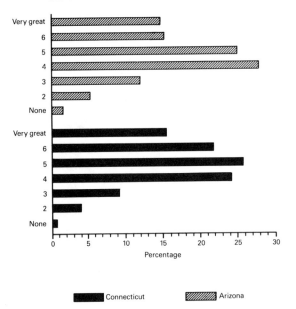

PERCEPTIONS OF RISK

Figure 2.1 (continued)

CURRENT RESTRICTIONS AND STANDARDS

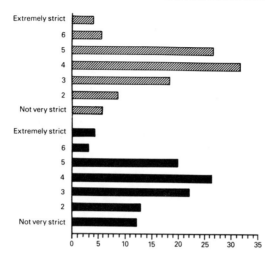

DESIRED RESTRICTIONS AND STANDARDS

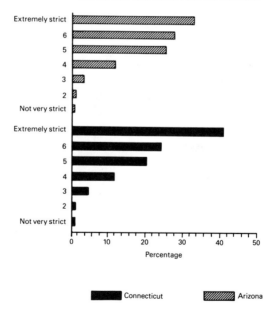

Figure 2.2
Connecticut and Arizona Residents' Perceptions of the Benefits, Risks, Current Standards, and Desired Standards for Commercial Air Travel

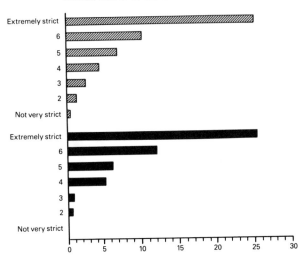

PERCEPTIONS OF BENEFIT

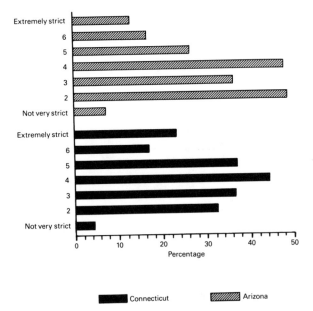

PERCEPTIONS OF RISK

Figure 2.2 (continued)

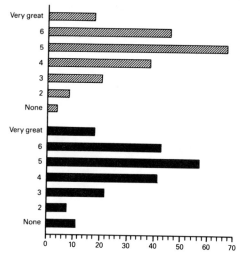

CURRENT RESTRICTIONS AND STANDARDS

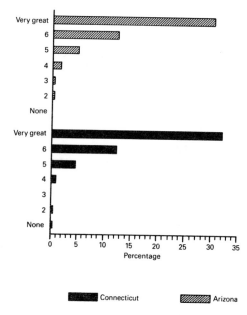

DESIRED RESTRICTIONS AND STANDARDS

Connecticut   Arizona

Figure 2.3
Connecticut and Arizona Residents' Perceptions
of the Benefits, Risks, Current Standards,
and Desired Standards for Electricity and Nuclear Power

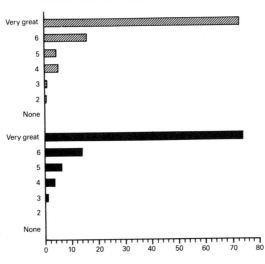

PERCEPTIONS OF BENEFIT

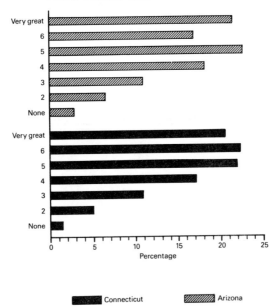

PERCEPTIONS OF RISK

Connecticut   Arizona

Figure 2.3 (continued)

CURRENT RESTRICTIONS AND STANDARDS

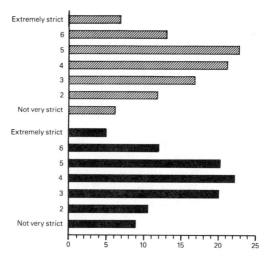

DESIRED RESTRICTIONS AND STANDARDS

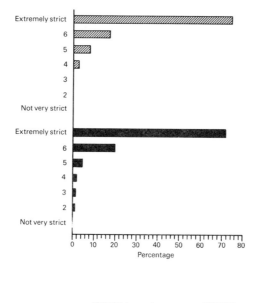

Connecticut   Arizona

Figure 2.4
Connecticut and Arizona Residents' Perceptions of the Benefits, Risks, Current Standards, and Desired Safeguards for Nuclear Weapons

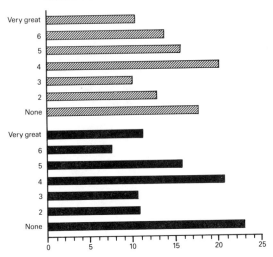

PERCEPTIONS OF BENEFIT

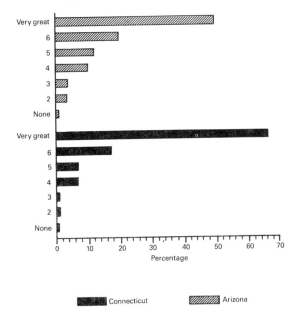

PERCEPTIONS OF RISK

Figure 2.4 (continued)

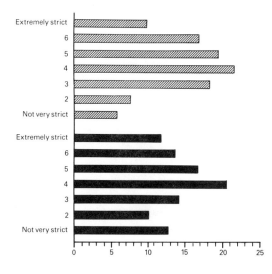

CURRENT SAFEGUARDS

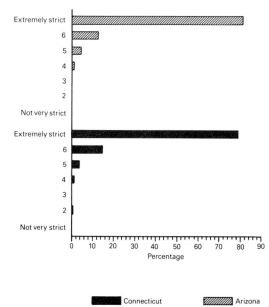

DESIRED SAFEGUARDS

Connecticut   Arizona

Figure 2.5
Connecticut and Arizona Residents' Perceptions of the Benefits, Risks, Current Restrictions, and Desired Restrictions for Handguns

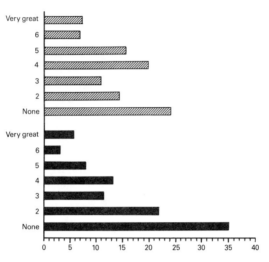

PERCEPTIONS OF BENEFIT

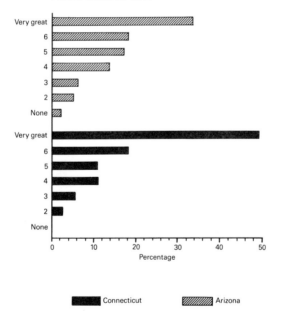

PERCEPTIONS OF RISK

Percentage

■ Connecticut   ▨ Arizona

Figure 2.5 (continued)

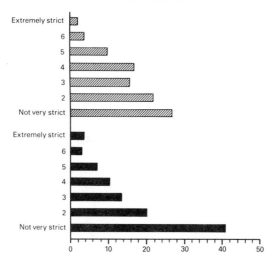

CURRENT RESTRICTIONS

DESIRED RESTRICTIONS

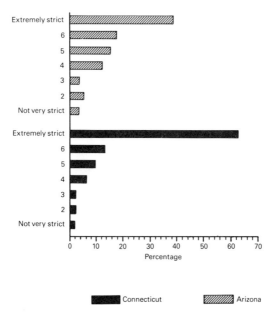

Figure 2.6
Connecticut and Arizona Residents' Perceptions of the Benefits, Risks,
Current Standards, and Desired Standards for Industrial Chemicals

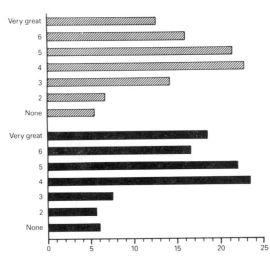

PERCEPTIONS OF BENEFIT

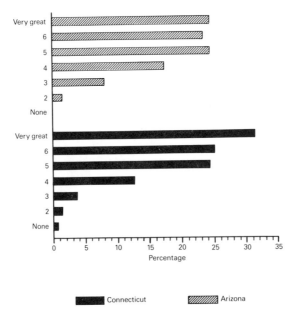

PERCEPTIONS OF RISK

Figure 2.6 (continued)

CURRENT RESTRICTIONS AND STANDARDS

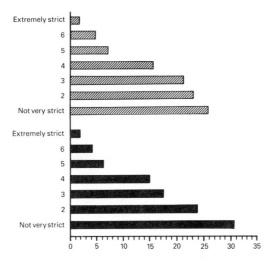

DESIRED RESTRICTIONS AND STANDARDS

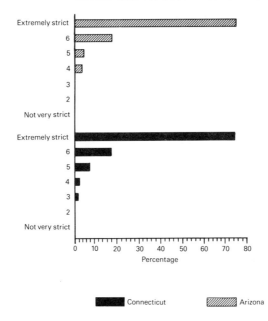

27

Figure 2.7
Connecticut Pro-Safety and Pro-Benefit Intervenor Perceptions
of the Benefits, Risks, Current Standards,
and Desired Standards for Automobile Travel

PERCEPTIONS OF BENEFIT

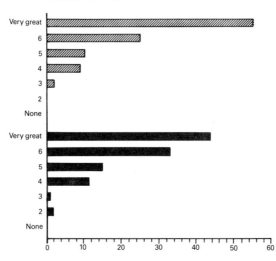

PERCEPTIONS OF RISK

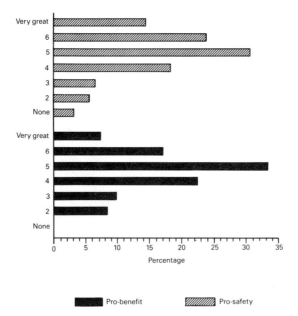

Figure 2.7 (continued)

CURRENT RESTRICTIONS AND STANDARDS

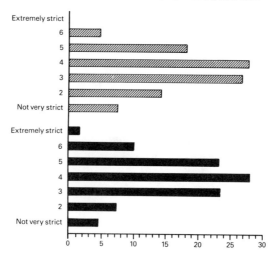

DESIRED RESTRICTIONS AND STANDARDS

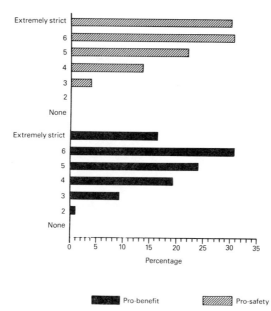

Figure 2.8
Connecticut Pro-Safety and Pro-Benefit Intervenor Perceptions
of the Benefits, Risks, Current Standards,
and Desired Standards for Commercial Air Travel

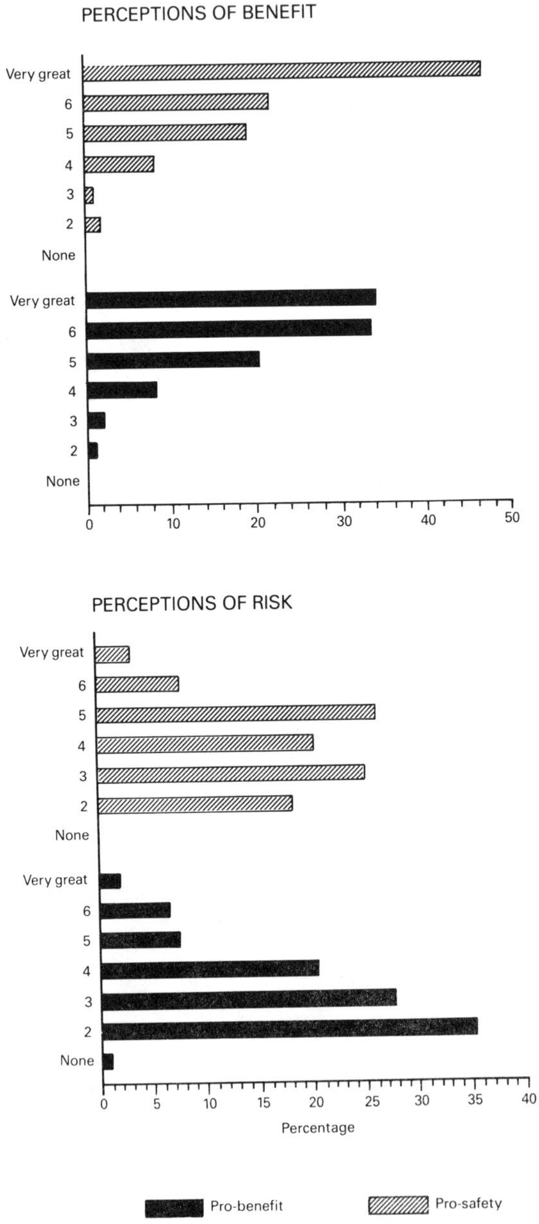

PERCEPTIONS OF BENEFIT

PERCEPTIONS OF RISK

Percentage

Pro-benefit   Pro-safety

Figure 2.8 (continued)

CURRENT RESTRICTIONS AND STANDARDS

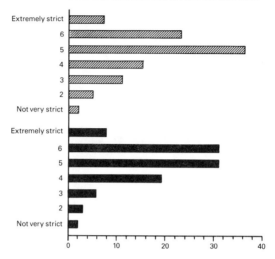

DESIRED RESTRICTIONS AND STANDARDS

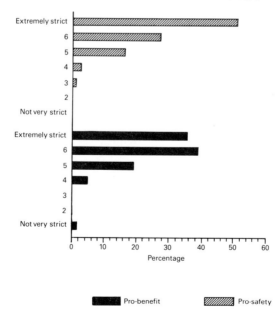

■ Pro-benefit   ▨ Pro-safety

Figure 2.9
Connecticut Pro-Safety and Pro-Benefit Intervenor Perceptions of the Benefits, Risks, Current Standards, and Desired Standards for Electricity and Nuclear Power

PERCEPTIONS OF BENEFIT

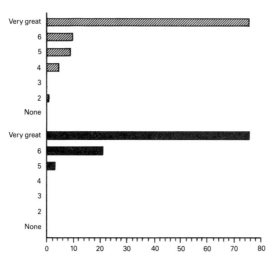

PERCEPTIONS OF RISK

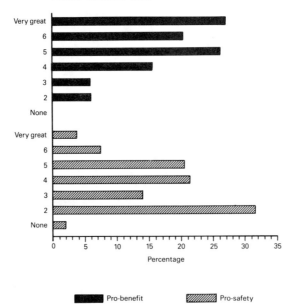

Percentage

Pro-benefit   Pro-safety

Figure 2.9 (continued)

CURRENT RESTRICTIONS AND STANDARDS

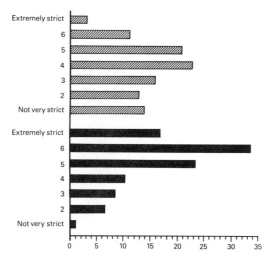

CURRENT RESTRICTIONS AND STANDARDS

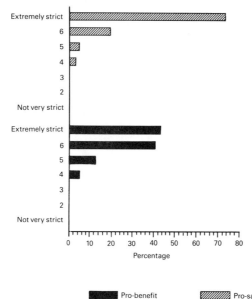

■ Pro-benefit ▨ Pro-safety

33

Figure 2.10
Connecticut Pro-Safety and Pro-Benefit Intervenor Perceptions
of the Benefits, Risks, Current Safeguards,
and Preferred Safeguards for Nuclear Weapons

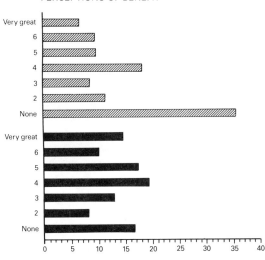

PERCEPTIONS OF BENEFIT

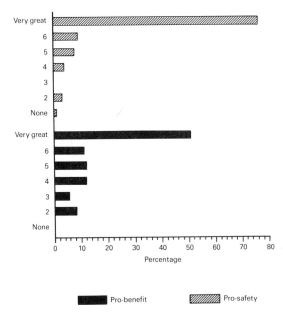

PERCEPTIONS OF RISK

Percentage

Pro-benefit   Pro-safety

Figure 2.10 (continued)

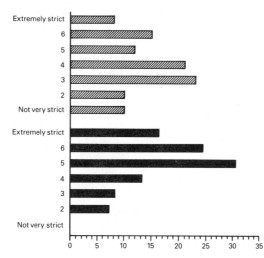

CURRENT SAFEGUARDS

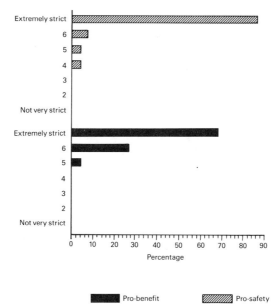

DESIRED SAFEGUARDS

Percentage

Pro-benefit   Pro-safety

Figure 2.11
Connecticut Pro-Safety and Pro-Benefit Intervenor Perceptions
of the Benefits, Risks, Current Restrictions,
and Desired Restrictions for Handguns

PERCEPTIONS OF BENEFIT

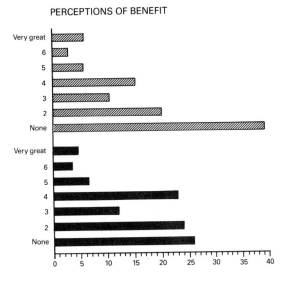

PERCEPTIONS OF RISK

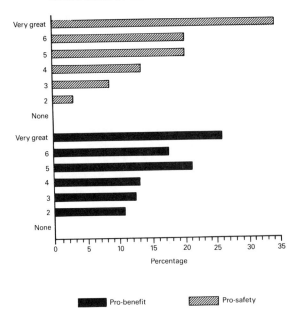

Percentage

Pro-benefit   Pro-safety

Figure 2.11 (continued)

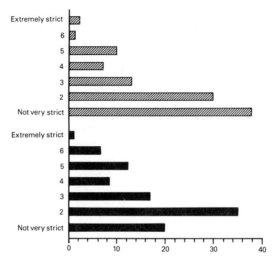

CURRENT RESTRICTIONS

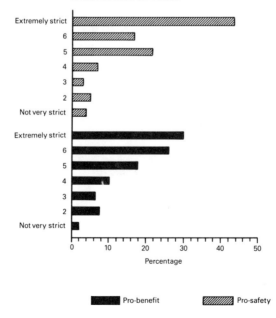

DESIRED RESTRICTIONS

Percentage

■ Pro-benefit   ▨ Pro-safety

Figure 2.12
Connecticut Pro-Safety and Pro-Benefit Intervenor Perceptions of the Benefits, Risks, Current Standards, and Desired Standards for Industrial Chemicals

PERCEPTIONS OF BENEFIT

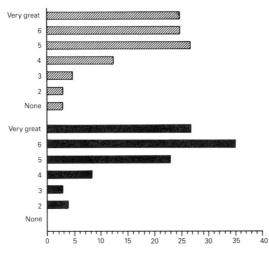

PERCEPTIONS OF RISK

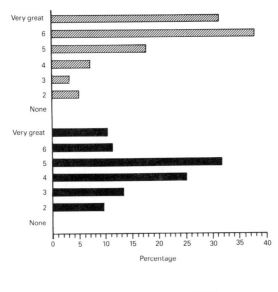

Percentage

■ Pro-benefit   ▨ Pro-safety

Figure 2.12 (continued)

CURRENT RESTRICTIONS AND STANDARDS

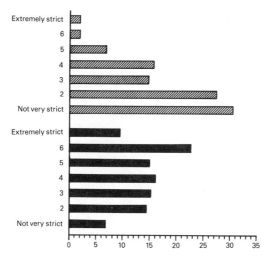

DESIRED RESTRICTIONS AND STANDARDS

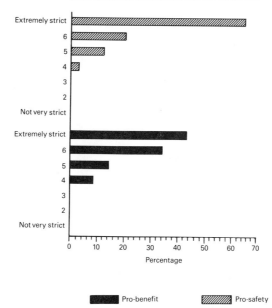

Percentage

■ Pro-benefit   ▨ Pro-safety

With the exception of members of the general public in Connecticut, who were somewhat more likely than Arizona residents to see handgun restrictions as not being very strict, people in both regions had a similar view of prevailing restrictions, standards, or safeguards that apply to technologies. They viewed the restrictions and standards governing handguns and industrial chemicals as not being very strict and the regulations of the other four technologies as being only moderately strict (i.e., a majority of respondents chose responses somewhere in the middle between "not very strict" and "extremely strict"). However, in every case except handguns, pro-benefits intervenors, by and large, saw prevailing safety standards as being stricter than did pro-safety intervenors. This difference is particularly noticeable in the case of industrial chemicals.

In terms of the restrictions and standards that should prevail with respect to industrial chemicals, however, a majority of the respondents in each group thought that they should be quite strict. Indeed, "extremely strict" was the most frequently chosen response for each group, although the percentage choosing this category was smallest for pro-benefits advocates (just over 40 percent) and largest for the two general population samples (over 70 percent). This same general pattern also prevailed for the other technologies. The two general public samples chose "extremely strict" more often than any other category for every technology, although Arizona residents were noticeably less likely to choose this extreme response for handguns than were residents of Connecticut. Members of the two Connecticut intervenor samples also thought that the standards, restrictions, or safeguards on technology should be strict, although in the case of automobile travel both pro-safety and pro-benefits intervenor groups chose the category next to "extremely strict" more often than the most extreme response. In every case, smaller percentages of pro-benefits than of pro-safety activists chose the "extremely strict" alternative.

In general, then, the similarities among these samples are more striking than the differences. The views of Connecticut and Arizona residents about technological risks and benefits and current and desired safety regulations were almost the same for automobile and commercial air travel, nuclear power, nuclear weapons, and industrial chemicals. They differed only on their views of handguns, which Arizona residents saw as more beneficial, less risky, less stringently controlled, and in need of less control than did Connecticut residents. Pro-safety and pro-benefits intervenors, although differing from each other and from the general public more than Arizona and Connecticut residents differed from each other, showed response patterns for most technologies that were quite similar. In general it might be said that pro-benefits intervenors saw current standards and restrictions to be more severe than did other groups, and pro-safety intervenors thought that they should be more severe. Only in the cases of nuclear power and industrial chemicals, however, did the two groups diverge greatly, with pro-benefits activists perceiving the risks of these two technologies as being markedly lower, and current restrictions and standards as being decidely more strict, than did pro-safety activists.

Acceptability of Current Restrictions and Standards

It will not have gone unnoticed that more people indicated that restrictions, standards, and safeguards on technologies *should be* very strict than indicated that they *are* very strict. Table 2.4 shows the percentages of general population respondents in Connecticut and Arizona that indicated, by these two ratings, that current standards should be made stricter, less strict, or left unchanged.

More than two-thirds—in the case of industrial chemicals, 92 percent—of the residents of Arizona and Connecticut were of a mind that current restrictions, standards, or safeguards on the six technologies we studied were not strict enough; that is, their "should be" ratings of the standards and restrictions on these six technologies were higher than their estimates of "current" strictness. Ten or fewer percent thought that current standards were too strict; that is, they had "should be" ratings that were lower than their "current" ratings. There were few differences, moreover, between the residents of the two regions on this issue, although significantly more Connecticut residents thought that handgun and automobile travel restrictions should be more stringent than did Arizona residents.

Too Much Regulation and Too Few Regulations

Ronald Reagan ran for the presidency in 1980 in part on the promise that his administration would "get the government off people's backs." Reagan asserted that people are tired of government regulations. Public opinion polls support this interpretation of the public mood regarding regulation; indeed, opposition to government regulation has increased steadily since at least 1949 (Lipset and Schneider, 1983: 221).

What happened to the people we interviewed in Connecticut and Arizona? Were they not aware of the national mood against regulation? The answer is that they probably were (although we did not ask them specifically) but that they, like other people, make a distinction between

Table 2.4

Acceptability of Current Restrictions and Standards on Six Technologies

Standards with Respect to	Should be	Connecticut	Arizona
Automobile travel	Stricter	75%*	68%*
	No change	15**	22**
	Less strict	10	10
	Number of cases	541	478
Air travel	Stricter	70%	68%
	No change	29	31
	Less strict	1	1
	Number of cases	539	479
Nuclear power	Stricter	77%	81%
	No change	20	18
	Less strict	3*	1*
	Number of cases	540	479
Nuclear weapons	Stricter	79%	81%
	No change	20	18
	Less strict	1	1
	Number of cases	438	479
Handguns	Stricter	85%**	74%**
	No change	9**	17**
	Less strict	6	9
	Number of cases	539	479
Industrial chemicals	Stricter	92%	92%
	No change	7	7
	Less strict	4**	1**
	Number of cases	438	479

Difference in proportions between Connecticut and Arizona general population samples statistically significant (two-tailed test) at:
*$p < .05$;
**$p < .01$.

"regulation" and "regulations," being opposed, for the most part, to the former, but in favor of the latter.

Even in 1935, in the depths of the Great Depression, Gallup found a majority of the people living in the United States answering "no" to the question: "Do you think the government regulation of business and industry should be increased?" (Lipset and Schneider, 1983: 223). Throughout the intervening years, national polls consistently found those who favored

Table 2.5

*Public Ratings of Consumer Protection Activities
by Federal Regulatory Agencies*

*"As you know, the federal government includes several regulatory
agencies charged with protecting the American consumer. I'd like to
ask you about some of the areas of consumer protection with which
these government agencies are involved. For each area, please tell me
whether you think the federal government is now doing too much,
about the right amount, or too little to protect the consumer."*

	Doing Too Much	Doing About the Right Amount	Doing Too Little
		(Percentage)	
Truthful and informative advertising	8	39	49
Tasteful and decent advertising	7	42	44
Packaging that is not deceptive	6	46	40
Products or services that are priced fairly	16	40	39
Fulfillment of product or service warranties and guarantees	8	50	35
Enough information for customers to make own purchasing decisions	8	51	35
Products or services that are dependable	11	51	32
Products or services that are safe	11	53	31
Vigorous and open competition with other companies	17	50	24

Number of people surveyed: 1,011.
Source: S. M. Lipset and W. Schneider, *The Confidence Gap: Business, Labor, and Government
in the Public Mind* (New York: Free Press, 1983), 232.

more regulation to be in a minority which by 1980 had reached a low of 19 percent, according to one Opinion Research Corporation poll (Lipset and Schneider, 1983: 227). The same poll also reported that 54 percent of the people living in the United States favored "less government regulation of business."

In the same year, however, the same polling agency asked questions pertaining to specific areas of consumer protection, with considerably different results. As Table 2.5, which summarizes these results, shows, people generally thought that federal regulatory agencies were either doing about the right amount or were doing too little in specific areas of consumer protection. Never did even a plurality of these respondents think that the agencies were doing too much.

When it comes to specific areas of consumer protection regulation, then, people in the United States appear either to be satisfied with current regulatory levels or in favor of more regulation. Our surveys (although conducted only in Connecticut and Arizona) indicated that people were not satisfied with current safety regulations on automobile and air travel, nuclear power, nuclear weapons, handguns, and industrial chemicals. Seventy-five percent of those living in Connecticut and 68 percent of those living in Arizona indicated that standards and restrictions on automobile travel should be stricter; 70 percent of the Connecticut sample and 68 percent of the Arizona sample were in favor of stricter standards and regulations on air travel; 77 percent of the Connecticut respondents and 81 percent of Arizona respondents were in favor of stricter regulations and standards on nuclear power; 79 percent of those from Connecticut and 81 percent of those from Arizona favored more stringent safeguards on nuclear weapons; 85 percent of those surveyed in Connecticut and 74 percent of those surveyed in Arizona favored stricter regulations on handguns; and 92 percent of the respondents in both states favored stricter standards and regulations for industrial chemicals.

What people favor in general, then, and what they favor in particular may be two different things. Although we have no reason to believe that residents of our two study regions were any different than other people in the United States in opposing government *regulation* in general, they were uniformly in favor of government *regulations* in particular, at least insofar as these regulations would improve safety standards on automobile and air travel, nuclear power, nuclear weapons, handguns, and industrial chemicals.

3

Research on Perceptions
of Technology:
An Overview

Respondents in our study perceived the risks of nuclear weapons, industrial chemicals, and nuclear electric power as being considerably greater than the risks of automobile or commercial air travel. Death statistics would indicate either that these perceptions of risk are inaccurate, or that they are based on something other than the risk of death; no one in the United States has ever been killed by nuclear weapons or nuclear power generation, and few operators or bystanders are killed by accidents at chemical plants (Perrow, 1984).

Many technological risk-managers have concluded, therefore, that the public simply does not know what the risks of technology are. Opposition to many technologies, they contend, arises not from the actual risks involved, but from overestimates of what the risks really are (Kasper, 1980; Schwing, 1980; Raiffa, 1980; Otway and Thomas, 1982). Indeed it has become common in discussions of technology risk-management for technologists to distinguish between "real," "objective" (or "scientific"), and publicly "perceived" risk.

Real versus Perceived Risks

Other observers have concluded, however, that the distinction between "real" and "perceived" risks cannot survive close scrutiny (Renn, 1981; Otway and Thomas, 1982; Otway and von Winterfeldt, 1982; Slovic and Fischhoff, 1983; Perrow, 1984). The risks of nuclear war, for example, are no less real just because such a war has never occurred. Indeed, one of the problems with what technologists like to call "objective" or "scientific" risk assessments is that such assessments, perforce, must be based on prior mishaps.

This, of course, as discussed in Chapter 1, is one of the inherent limitations of "objective" risk assessment. The probability of certain kinds of catastrophic events, like nuclear war, can only be guessed at, and others, like nuclear reactor core meltdowns (at least until detailed data concerning the recent episode at Chernobyl become available) can only be approximated by piecing together accident experience from other, more or less similar, technologies.

Perhaps lay people sense this. At least they are generally more concerned about infrequent, but potentially "catastrophic," events, like nuclear reactor malfunctions, than they are about "chronic" events, like automobile accidents, that kill many people, but do so with little concentration in one time or one place. As several expressed-preference research studies have concluded, the risk ratings of lay people are influenced not only by their estimates of the total number of individuals who will die as a result of a technology but also by several "qualitative" aspects of the technology, including its catastrophic potential (Slovic, Fischhoff, and Lichtenstein 1979, 1980, and 1981; Otway and Fishbein, 1977; Vlek and Stallen, 1979; Green, 1980; Renn 1981). Other qualitative aspects include: the degree of perceived disagreement in the scientific community concerning the risks, the degree to which benefits are equitably distributed among those at risk, and the degree to which risks affect future, as well as current, generations.

In other words, lay people appear to use a broader and more complex definition of "risk" than do technologists, who, for the most part, define the risk of a technology as the probable number of deaths that that technology will cause. In addition, lay people also appear to use these qualitative characteristics when making political judgments about whether a new technology is "societally acceptable." Technologists, in contrast, have been inclined to assume that the deaths associated with a new technology will be "acceptable" if they are similar in number to the deaths associated with other, better-established technologies that afford similar benefits (usually measured in monetary terms).

Thus, expressed-preference research suggests that, when it comes to technological risk, lay people and members of the technical community might be said to be speaking different languages. They use different definitions of "risk" and of "societally acceptable" technology. These differences, moreover, appear to reflect differences in values and philosophy, rather than differences in education or rationality. The next two sections of this chapter will review the expressed-preference research studies from which these conclusions first emerged.

Prior Research on Perceived Risks

Perceived Risks of Death.   Lichtenstein et al. (1978) had college students and League of Women Voters members estimate the frequency of death from 41 different causes for which historical fatality statistics were extant. Overall, estimated frequencies of death correlated highly with statistical frequencies (approximately 0.90). Renn (1981) found similar correlations (0.78 to 0.87) in a study in West Germany. The contention of technologists that the public is not "rational" in its perceptions of risk, therefore, would appear to be incorrect; that is, lay people's estimates of fatalities appear, in fact, to be in line with actual fatality statistics.

A positive correlation, however, does not always indicate a perfect fit. The studies by Lichtenstein et al. and by Renn also found that lay people tend to overestimate the likelihood of rare causes of death, like lightning strikes (consonant with claims that lay people overestimate risks), and underestimate common causes of death, like heart attacks. While the overall correlation between lay estimates and historical statistics is high, the magnitudes of the two differ considerably at the extremes.

Lay people's estimates of the probability of death also appear to be susceptible to how dramatic or sensational a particular risk is. The probability of being mauled by a grizzly bear, for example, is overestimated, while the probabilities of more prosaic causes of death, like drowning, are underestimated.

Lichtenstein et al. (1978) have called the tendency of people to overestimate the likelihood of rare events and to underestimate the likelihood of common events "primary bias," and the tendency to overestimate the likelihood of sensational events and to underestimate the likelihood of prosaic events "secondary bias." Lichtenstein et al., further, suggest that both of these biases may be traced to people's use of a mental technique or process which Tversky and Kahneman (1974) call the "availability heuristic": a tendency for people to judge an event as likely or frequent if instances of it are easy to imagine or recall.

A study by Combs and Slovic (1979) found that the estimates of death made by the subjects in the Lichtenstein et al. (1978) study closely paralleled the frequency of newspaper coverage of 41 causes of death. (One of two newspapers studied was published in the same city in which the Lichtenstein subjects lived.) This suggests that imbalances in newspaper coverage might account for inaccuracies in public perceptions of the probabilities of death from different causes. On the other hand, it is also possible, of course, that newspaper editors and the public simply share the same "availability heuristic." In either case, rare causes of death in general, and dramatic causes of death in particular, appear to be both overreported by the press and perceived as more likely by the public, while more common and less sensational causes of death are overlooked by the press and taken for granted by the public.

Qualitative Characteristics. Research by Slovic, Fischhoff, and Lichtenstein (1979, 1980, 1981) also found, however, that lay people appear to consider more than just the number of fatalities when judging the risks of a technology. In the 1979 study, subjects rated the overall risks of several technologies and activities as well as various "qualitative characteristics" of these technologies and activities. The subjects included groups of college students, League of Women Voters members, and business people who were members of a community service organization. Although lay people's estimates of the probability of death from several technologies and activities had been found previously to correlate strongly and positively with historical death statistics, the "overall risk" ratings of the subjects in this study did not correlate highly with such statistics. To see if these subjects equated "risk" with "number of fatalities," but were inaccurate in their fatality estimates, the subjects' risk ratings were correlated with their own estimates of the annual fatalities caused by the technologies and activities in the study; these correlations were only moderately strong. Further analyses made it clear that the subjects' "overall risk" ratings were influenced not just by their perceptions of fatalities but also by various qualitative characteristics, particularly the potential for catastrophic accidents, severity, and dread. Renn (1981) reported similar findings from his research in West Germany.

Subsequent studies by Slovic, Fischhoff, and Lichtenstein (1980 and 1981) discovered additional qualitative characteristics that appear to affect people's ratings of risk, including: the degree to which the risks of a technology affect future generations, the degree to which risks have increased over time, and the degree to which risks are equitably distributed among those who enjoy a technology's benefits. Factor analysis of up to 18 different qualitative risk characteristics suggested, however, that there are probably no more than three fundamental, underlying qualitative factors, or dimensions, to people's perceptions of risk. Qualitative characteristics that clustered on one factor include: catastrophic potential, controllability, dread, threat to future generations, and equitability of risk-benefit distributions. Characteristics that clustered on another factor include: delay of effects, observability, novelty, and knowledge to science (see also Vlek and Stallen, 1979, and Renn, 1981).

Prior Research on the "Acceptability" of Technological Regulation

As noted in Chapter 1, the earliest study on the "acceptability" of technological risk and regulation in this country involved comparing fatality statistics with economic estimates of the benefits for various technologies. Such revealed-preference research (Starr, 1969) suggested that society tolerates greater risks from technologies that provide greater benefits (more specifically, risks are acceptable in proportion to the third power of benefits) and that risks from voluntary technologies are approximately 1,000 times more acceptable than risks from involuntary technologies.

The first attempt to corroborate these findings through expressed-preference research in this country was reported by Fischhoff, Slovic, Lichtenstein, Read, and Combs in 1978. This research involved 76 subjects who rated the risks, the benefits, and the acceptability of 30 different technologies or activities, as well as several qualitative characteristics of the technologies and activities. The results showed that respondents were willing to accept more risk from those technologies that they perceived as providing more benefits, as Starr had predicted.

The same subjects, however, judged that current risk-management arrangements had *not* created this positive relationship; rather, there was a moderate, negative correlation between rated levels of current risks and benefits; that is, the riskiest technologies tended to provide the fewest benefits. This was contrary to Starr's conclusions. Furthermore, these subjects judged (as did the subjects in our Connecticut and Arizona surveys reported in Chapter 2) that technologies are generally underregulated in the United States and that more rigorous restrictions and standards should be placed on them. Ratings of desired changes in regulatory strictness (the number of times safer or riskier a technology would have to be in order to be considered acceptably safe) were strongly correlated with perceived current risk levels; the greater the judged risk, the greater the desire for more regulatory strictness. Similar findings have been reported in European studies by Green and Brown (1980) and Renn (1981), and in subsequent studies involving different U.S. samples by Slovic, Fischhoff, and Lichtenstein (1980 and 1981).

The Effects of Qualitative Characteristics. Fischhoff et al. (1978) found also that their subjects applied a double standard to technologies with voluntary and involuntary risks; they were willing to accept greater risks from the former than the latter, as Starr (1969) had concluded. Similar results emerged in research by Slovic et al. (1980 and 1981), Vlek and Stallen (1979), and Renn (1981). However, these researchers found that additional qualitative characteristics of technologies also created double standards. Thus, respondents' ratings of several characteristics, including catastrophic potential, equity, dread, and threat to future generations correlated with their judgments concerning the acceptability of the technology (that is, their desired changes in regulatory strictness), even when overall ratings of perceived risk were held constant by means of partial correlations. In other words, it would appear that the qualitative characteristics influence not only people's perceptions of risk itself, as noted above, but also their judgments about the acceptability of current technological safety regulations.

Several studies suggest that different groups of lay subjects emphasize different qualitative characteristics when making their ratings of risk and judgments of acceptability. The risk ratings of Slovic et al.'s (1981) business people, for example, were more highly correlated with "delay of harmful effect" and "risk unknown to those exposed" than were the risk ratings of student subjects or League of Women Voters members. Similarly, Otway and Fishbein (1977) found that members of the public who were against nuclear power placed greater emphasis on catastrophic potential, voluntariness, and the controllability of the risks in their overall ratings of that technology than did those who were in favor of nuclear power.

In summary, although expressed-preference research has found that people will tolerate greater risk from technologies that yield greater benefit and technologies that are voluntary rather than involuntary, it has not found that people perceive these preferences reflected in existing regulations. Therefore, Starr's (1969) use of existing regulations as a guide to future policy would presumably not please subjects who have so far taken part in expressed-preference research. This research suggests that acceptability judgments and desires for changes in regulatory strictness are influenced by a host of qualitative risk characteristics not included in Starr's work.

Judgments by Technical Experts

A major finding to emerge from expressed-preference research to date, then, is that lay people seem to consider a variety of qualitative characteristics, not just number of fatalities, in their definitions of "risk" and their judgments about the "acceptability" of current industrial safety standards. Scientists, engineers, and other technical experts, in contrast, appear to take only fatalities into account. One subject group in the Slovic et al. (1979 and 1981) research cited earlier, for example, was made up of professional technology risk-assessors ("persons selected nationwide for their professional interest and expertise in risk assessment"). The risk ratings of these subjects were very highly correlated with historical fatality statistics, but were only weakly or moderately correlated with their ratings of the technologies on various qualitative characteristics.

Additional evidence that scientists and engineers rely primarily on fatality estimates appears in the methods such experts use to determine the societal acceptability of a technology, including the revealed-preference approach (Starr, 1969) discussed above, the "risk compendium" approach (e.g., Wilson, 1979), and several types of risk-benefit analyses (Cohen, 1985). In each of these methods, the risk of a technology is indexed exclusively by the number of fatalities it produces, while societal acceptability is judged by comparing this number with the number of fatalities caused by other technologies or activities (for the risk compendium approach), or by the degree to which the risks and economic costs are balanced by the dollar value of the benefits. (A more detailed discussion of these procedures may be found in Green, 1980, Fischhoff et al., 1981, and Otway and Thomas, 1982.)

Differences Between Experts and the Public

Technical experts and members of the general public thus appear to define the "risk" and "acceptability" of technology in fundamentally different ways. These differences are likely to contribute to miscommunication and controversy, as the following example illustrates (Slovic et al., 1981): A number of scientists and engineers (e.g., Wilson, 1979; Sowby, 1965; Cohen and Lee, 1979) have attempted to assuage public concerns about the risks of such technologies as nuclear power by constructing risk compendia—lists of risks of death due to a variety of hazards. Harvard physicist Richard Wilson (1979), for example, calculated that each of the following creates equal increases in the probability of a person's death: (1) smoking 1.4 cigarettes; (2) traveling six minutes in a canoe; (3) traveling 300 miles in an auto; and (4) living 50 years within five miles of a commercial nuclear reactor. The intended conclusion, of course, was that since the risk of death from nuclear reactors is low, relative to conventional and currently accepted technology, commercial nuclear power should be accepted. The results of expressed-preference risk research would suggest, however, that such figures would do little to assuage public concerns about nuclear power. From the point of view of the general public, these analyses are too narrow and simplistic. They ignore many of the qualitative properties of technology that the public appears to deem important in judging risks and the acceptability of current safety standards, including the degree of scientific uncertainty concerning the risk, the maximum number of fatalities that could be caused by a single accident, and the degree of intergenerational equity.

Difference in Values. What accounts for the differences between lay and expert definitions of "risk" and "acceptability"? The major source of variation appears to be fundamental differences between lay and expert values, priorities, and philosophy. Certainly, there is no a priori reason why decisions concerning the risks of technology must be restricted to the number of fatalities involved, and doing so is itself a value judgment (Green, 1980; Fischhoff et al., 1984). As Colin Green (1980: 10) has so aptly pointed out:

> Any measure of risk involves making some moral decisions: is it worse to have 1,000 people die [catastrophically] in one accident or the same number one at a time, or doesn't it matter? Is one death of a child by leukemia as bad as 100 lives shortened by chronic bronchitis? Any measure of risk involves making value judgments such as these.

Dimensions of Risk. Hohenemser, Kates, and Slovic (1983) have argued on other grounds that "number of fatalities" is an excessively narrow index of technological risk, and have proposed a taxonomy of technological risk based on a multistage model of hazard. The model is premised on the assumption that hazards result from "a sequence of causally connected events leading from human needs and wants, to the selection of a technology, to the possible release of materials and energy, to exposure, and eventual harmful consequences" (1983: 379). Using this model, they postulated twelve logical "descriptors" or properties of hazards, including: the persistence of the released materials or energy, the delay of consequences following release, and the number of resulting human and nonhuman fatalities. After evaluating 93 hazards with these descriptors and performing factor analyses, Hohenemser et al. arrived at a seven-class taxonomy of hazards. A key feature of the basic approach and resulting taxonomy is that "only one descriptor, annual human mortality, is closely related to the traditional idea of risk as the probability of dying; the others considerably expand and delineate the quality of hazard-ousness" (1983: 379).

As an example of the usefulness of their approach, Hohenemser et al. have shown that although coal-fired power plants are likely to kill more humans (and nonhumans as well) in an average year than are nuclear power plants, coal-fired plants are more desirable on several other hazard descriptors. Thus, two technologies may differ from each other on a number of different hazard dimensions, making unidimensional comparisons between the two misleading.

Finally, Hohenemser et al. had a group of lay subjects rate 81 different technologies on overall risk as well on the various descriptors or properties in their taxonomy. Results indicated that the descriptor ratings accounted for much of the variance in overall risk ratings. This should not be surprising, as the descriptors that Hohenemser et al. developed are similar to the qualitative characteristics that earlier expressed-preference research indicated the public uses in making risk judgments. The fact, however, that Hohenemser et al. used "explicit methods, a scientific framework, and deliberate efforts to control bias," and came to similar conclusions as the earlier, more subjective, expressed-preference research, provides justification for the risk criteria and considerations used by lay people and raises questions about the narrow definition of "risk" employed by most technical experts.

Acceptability of Technology. The discussion in the preceding section has centered on definitions of "risk"; similar issues are involved in definitions of "acceptability." In the revealed-preference and risk compendia approaches favored by technical experts, a technology is judged to be socially acceptable if the risks of death associated with it do not exceed the risks of death associated with comparable technologies. These approaches, therefore, yield an absolute number of "acceptable" fatalities (a so-called "acceptable risk" level). There are many other considerations, however, that could, in principle, enter into acceptability judgments, as Otway and von Winterfeldt (1982), von Winterfeldt and Edwards (1984), and others have pointed out. Based on an examination of 162 technological controversies, von Winterfeldt and Edwards argued that societal debates about the acceptability of technology are, in fact, not just debates about the acceptability of fatality risks but, as Otway and von Winterfeldt put it, intrinsically, and legitimately, debates involving "concerns related to morals, religion, political ideologies, power, . . . and psychological well-being"

(1982: 247). Otway and von Winterfeldt concluded that efforts to base acceptability judgments exclusively on the magnitude of risks to human life are simplistic and misleading. To provide an extreme example, they point out that the "physical risks [of a technology] could in principle be essentially zero but the technology still be judged unacceptable (and subject to opposition) for other social reasons." Thus "the resolution of conflicts about technologies requires that they no longer be treated as simple technical disagreements centering on the single issue of [the level of] acceptable risk" (1982: 254).

Conclusions

Several lines of research, then, have converged on the following points: (1) fatality estimates are excessively narrow indices of the risks of technology; (2) many nonrisk considerations are, and should be, part of political debates concerning the acceptability of a technology; and (3) the different participants in these debates have fundamentally different values and priorities which shape their definitions and judgments of risk and acceptability (Pearce, 1978; Slovic, Fischhoff, and Lichtenstein, 1981 and 1984; Otway and Thomas, 1982; Otway and von Winterfeldt, 1982; Perrow, 1982; Hohenemser, Kates, and Slovic, 1983; Wynne, 1983; von Winterfeldt and Edwards, 1984; Otway, 1985; Slovic, 1986). Explicit or implicit in these authors' works is the conclusion that the public is not misguided, miseducated, or irrational in its opposition to certain technologies.

Although these conclusions have appeared often in recently published works, they were not common in the earlier works of either expressed-preference researchers or other behavioral and social scientists interested in the public's role in hazard management. The authors of these earlier works tended to assume, and thus to support, the notion that the "public misperceives the true risks of new technologies." By showing discrepancies between historical risk statistics and lay people's fatality estimates; by demonstrating problems people have in evaluating rare, probabilistic events; and by having subjects rate the risks of novel technologies, the "statistical risks" of which must be assessed by fault-tree and event-tree analyses, early researchers inadvertently gave ammunition to those who argued that "scientists are objective while lay-people are uninformed or irrational." In other words, the early work provided partisan ammunition in what is now coming to be seen as primarily a value-laden, political debate (Otway and Thomas, 1982).

Limitations of Prior Work

Representativeness of Subjects. The degree to which the conclusions of the expressed-preference research just reviewed may be applied to the U.S. population in general, however, as mentioned in Chapter 1, is open to question. The work by Slovic and his colleagues, for example, was conducted on small, nonrandomly selected groups of volunteers: students at the University of Oregon, members of the Eugene, Oregon, League of Women Voters and their spouses, business people from Eugene, and a small national sample of risk experts. Despite the fact that the authors were careful to point out the limitations of their samples, other authors, both at home (e.g., Upton, 1982) and abroad (e.g., Renn, 1981) have cited their work, not only as established fact but as typical of the perceptions of technological risks by the public everywhere.

The degree to which European expressed-preference research is representative of the European general public is similarly questionable. The research by Green (1980), for example, involved small, atypical subject samples: architectural and planning students at the University of Dundee, Scotland. The work of Otway and his colleagues (e.g., Otway and Fishbein, 1977) was limited to 224 respondents residing in various parts of Austria. The Vlek and Stallen (1979) research involved residents of the Rotterdam harbor basin and was marred by a low response rate. And finally, subjects in the Renn (1981) study were drawn from five towns in Westphalia, West Germany, four of which were sites of nuclear facilities in operation or under construction.

One major objective of the study we are reporting, therefore, was to test whether the findings of these earlier, small-scale investigations, in fact, hold among larger, more representative samples of the U.S. public. Although our surveys were not national in scope, they did involve a large number of respondents from two quite different locations in the United States: Connecticut and the Greater Phoenix area of Arizona.

Additional Correlates of Perceived Risks and Judged Acceptability. Early expressed-preference research (Slovic, Fischhoff, and Lichtenstein, 1979 and 1980; Green and Brown, 1980; Vlek and Stallen, 1979) aggregated individual-level data to compute such technology-level variables as mean perception of risks, mean perception of benefits, and mean judgment of acceptability. The unit of analysis, therefore, was technology, not person. Although this mode of analysis allowed correlations to be computed between such things as the perceived riskiness and the acceptability of technologies, it did not allow analyses of whether such things as individual persons' attitudes or sociodemographic positions correlate with individual persons' perceptions of the risks or benefits of technologies, or their ratings of the acceptability of current safety standards.

Several studies (Hendee et al., 1968; Tognacci et al., 1972; Hornback, 1974; Ostheimer and Ritt, 1976) have found that people who favor "low growth," or "appropriate technology" tend more than the general population to be middle class and young—what Webster (1975) called the "upper-middle-class counterculture." Such people are also more likely than others to join goal-oriented organizations and, through them, to seek social change. It is also the case that the better-off and the better-educated people are, the more likely they are to support nuclear power (Melber et al., 1977; Farhar et al., 1979). This suggests that judgments about the acceptability of technology safety standards and the propensity to translate these judgments into action probably vary with socioeconomic position, and also that these variations are probably quite complex.

Fleming (1972), Stallings (1973), Schnaiberg (1973), and Dunlap (1975) also report that the attitudes, values, and beliefs of those who join environmental groups or support the environmental movement are different than those of the public in general. Others report significant correlations between people's attitudes and their perceptions of the energy crisis, and between people's attitudes and their perceptions of nuclear power risk (Farhar et al., 1979).

In more recent, and more relevant, research, Renn (1981), Buss and Craik (1983), and Harding and Eiser (1984) found that such personal characteristics as gender, political orientation, and attitude toward technological growth and economic development were correlated with perceptions of risk and judgments about the acceptability of current technology safety regulations. The magnitudes of these correlations, however, were generally small. In light of these findings, and the others reviewed here, the study we report in this volume evaluates the role played by a large number of attitudinal and sociodemographic variables.

"Qualitative" Aspects of Perceived Benefits. Although expressed-preference research has examined lay people's perceptions of technological risk in great detail, discovering several qualitative risk characteristics that appear to influence lay people's risk perceptions and their judgments of acceptability, this research has not examined in a similar manner people's perceptions of technological benefits. This is somewhat curious as revealed-preference research, which expressed-preference researchers have so criticized, is just as simplistic in its assumptions about benefits as it is in its assumptions about risk. In other words, just as

revealed-preference research has assumed that the risks that count are the risks of death, so also has it assumed that the benefits that count are economic benefits. While this is an understandable, and perhaps even reasonable, assumption given the importance of things economic in Western culture, it is not for that reason alone necessarily a correct assumption. Therefore, in addition to economic benefits, we have included three other qualitative aspects of benefits in our research: (1) safety and security, (2) pleasure and satisfaction, and (3) contribution to basic human needs. These are discussed in detail in Chapter 4.

Action. Both revealed-preference and expressed-preference research have been designed to determine social values regarding the acceptability of technological safety standards. Although the two approaches have arrived at some similar and some divergent conclusions, neither has addressed very carefully the questions of how these values get incorporated into risk-management decisions or what relationship, if any, these values have with direct public involvement in the risk-management process.

The revealed-preference approach developed by Starr (1969, 1972) and others presumes that social values regarding technological risks and benefits find their way into risk-management decisions over time via institutionalized political and social processes. (Otherwise the approach could not reveal public values.) The exact mechanisms by which they get there, however, are never made explicit, although two mechanisms are implied: (1) legislative control of regulatory agencies, and (2) the fact that regulators are themselves members of society (and thus share its values).

In criticizing the assumption that the revealed-preference method depicts social, risk-benefit values accurately, expressed-preference researchers have also criticized the implicit assumption that the risk-management process, historically, has been open to these values. Expressed-preference researchers have not, however, examined current risk-management institutions carefully to determine whether these institutions have changed in this regard, nor have they examined whether those who intervene in the risk-management process today express the dominant values of the public on risk-management matters. Unless people's beliefs about the acceptability of current technological safety regulations are reflected in personal actions designed to influence risk-management decisions, public judgments about the acceptability of current technological regulations will tell us little about what these regulations are likely to be in the future.

Many social-psychological studies (Deutscher, 1966; Wicker, 1969; Brannon, 1973, 1976) have found little correlation between people's attitudes or beliefs and their actions, although others (Liska, 1975) have found relatively close correspondences in some cases. The degree of correspondence between people's beliefs about the adequacy of current technological safety standards and their propensity to take action to influence technological risk-benefit decisions, therefore, is a subject for empirical investigation.

Additional Research

The political and policy implications of the expressed-preference results reviewed in this chapter are considerable. Since these results were obtained in many cases with small, unrepresentative, or foreign samples, however, replication using more representative samples of U.S. residents became the first priority of the study reported in the remaining chapters of this book. In particular, we wished to test the following hypotheses derived specifically from previous revealed-preference or expressed-preference research.

> *Hypothesis 1.* People's overall perceptions of the risk of a technology are a function of: (a) their estimates of the number of deaths the technology will cause, and (b) several additional qualitative characteristics of the technology, including: the perceived degree of scientific disagreement concerning risks, perceived catastrophic potential, and the degree to which the risks induce dread.

> *Hypothesis 2.* The acceptability of technological safety standards is a function of: (a) people's perceptions of the overall benefits to be derived from the technology, and (b) the perceived overall risks the technology affords.

> *Hypothesis 3.* In addition to the effects of overall perceived benefits and overall perceived risks, the acceptability of technological safety standards is also a function of: (a) estimated number of deaths, and (b) the several qualitative characteristics listed in Hypothesis 1.

In addition to these hypotheses derived directly from previous expressed- or revealed-preference research, we also wished to test the following hypotheses.

> *Hypothesis 4.* People's overall perceptions of the benefits of a technology are a function of: (a) their estimates of the economic importance of the technology, and (b) several qualitative aspects of benefits, including the

contribution the technology makes to people's safety and security, pleasure and satisfaction, and basic needs.

Hypothesis 5. In addition to the effects of overall perceived benefits, overall perceived risks, fatality estimates, and the qualitative aspects of risk (as discussed in Hypotheses 2 and 3), the acceptability of technological safety standards is also a function of: (a) the perceived economic benefits of the technology, and (b) the several qualitative aspects of benefits listed in Hypothesis 4.

Hypothesis 6. In addition to the effects of overall perceived benefits, overall perceived risks, fatality estimates, qualitative aspects of risk, perceived economic benefits, and qualitative aspects of benefits, the acceptability of technological safety standards is also a function of various attitudinal and sociodemographic variables.

Hypothesis 7. The propensity for people to take action aimed at changing existing technological safety standards is a function of: (a) their judgments concerning the acceptability of current standards, (b) their perceptions of the risks and benefits of the technology, and (c) various attitudinal and sociodemographic variables.

Chapters 5 and 6 describe our tests of Hypotheses 1 through 6; Chapter 7 describes our tests of Hypothesis 7. Chapter 4 outlines the study procedures and the methods of analysis we employed.

4

The Study

The Surveys

Trained interviewers posed approximately 300 questions to each of the 1,320 respondents in the two Arizona and the two Connecticut samples of our study during a one- to two-hour personal interview (Appendix A). The majority of these questions concerned six technologies: automobile travel, air travel, nuclear weapons, nuclear power, handguns, and industrial chemicals. In addition to being asked about their perceptions of the risks, benefits, and safety standards currently regulating these technologies, and their judgments of how strict these standards ought to be, as described in Chapter 2, respondents were also asked to rate three qualitative aspects of the risks associated with each technology (Questions 46-B, 46-D, and 46-E): (1) their catastrophic potential, (2) how much people dreaded them, and (3) the degree to which they were understood by scientists and technologists.[1] They were also asked to estimate the number of deaths that would likely result from each technology (Question 46-C) and to rate four specific aspects of the benefits each technology provides (Question 44-B through 44-E): (1) economic benefits, (2) contribution to basic human needs, (3) contribution to people's safety and security, and (4) contribution to personal pleasure or satisfaction.[2]

Then, respondents were asked whether they had ever done any of ten different things to express their views on the restrictions and standards that apply to the safety of each technology (Questions 9 through 14): (1) written a letter, telephoned or sent a telegram to an editor, public official, or company; (2) signed a petition; (3) circulated a petition; (4) voted for or against a candidate for public office in part because of his or her position on the issue; (5) attended a public hearing or a meeting of a special interest organization; (6) spoken at a public hearing or forum; (7) boycotted a company; (8) joined or contributed money to an organization; (9) attended a public demonstration; or (10) participated in a lawsuit.[3] And finally, respondents were asked four questions designed to assess the salience of the risks posed by each technology (Questions 39 through 42): (1) how often they discussed issues of safety with friends or family; (2) how firm their position was on safety issues; (3) how involved they were in the issue; and (4) whether they felt that they needed more information about the safety of the technology.[4]

In addition to these questions asked about each technology, respondents were also asked questions about their confidence in those who run several organizations, including those responsible for technology risk-management (Question 2); their sources of information about technological risks (Questions 24 through 29); their attitudes toward technology and the environment (Question 45); their orientation toward risk in general (Question 43); their views about government support of various industries (Question 36); and their memberships in voluntary organizations (Question 63). Standard questions about each respondent's social and demographic position ended the interview (see, for example, Table 2.2).

Scales

Although some of these questions, like the perceived risk of a technology, served as discrete measure of individual variables, many questions had to be combined into multi-item scales. These scales, which are detailed in Appendix C, include measures of: action (continuous and discrete action scales for six technologies); acceptability of current restrictions and standards for six technologies; environmental attitudes ("pastoralism" and "urbanism"); attitudes toward technology; cognitive risk orientation; confidence in organizations ("establishment" institutions and environmental and consumer groups); attitudes concerning government support of (energy) technology; salience of technological issues (with subscales for six technologies); membership in voluntary organizations; and socioeconomic class.

Acceptability of Safety Standards

Although most of these single-item measures and scales are reasonably straightforward, having for the most part been derived from previous expressed-preference or other research, one variable, the acceptability of technological safety standards, deserves special attention. Expressed-preference researchers have tried to measure this variable in several different ways. In their early work, Slovic and his colleagues (Fischhoff et al., 1978) divided respondents' mean risk ratings by their mean risk adjustment ratings (the number of times safer or riskier than now a technology would have to be in order to be deemed acceptable). They also asked respondents to indicate both "current" and "acceptable" levels of risk on discrete graphic continua (Slovic, Fischhoff, and Lichtenstein, unpublished). Green and Brown (1980) used a variant of this method in their research. The purpose of both methods was to measure the *absolute* level of risk that respondents would find acceptable, so that "acceptable risks" could be plotted against perceived benefits for various technologies, producing functions that could then be compared to Starr's (1969) revealed-preference functions.

Slovic (1980) discovered, however, that estimates of "acceptable risk," as determined by these two different expressed-preference methods, did not correlate with each other. This meant, of course, that one, the other, or both estimates were invalid. Other researchers (see, for example, Green and Brown, 1980) have come to the conclusion that the "absolute level of acceptable risk" is not a salient or meaningful psychological dimension for respondents. Rather than accepting or rejecting risks, society accepts or rejects technologies as a whole, weighing such other considerations as the benefits, the degree of equity in the distribution of risks and benefits, available alternative technologies, and institutional arrangements for managing risks. Thus absolute levels of acceptable risk, which are the intended outcomes of revealed-preference and risk compendium approaches as discussed above, cannot be meaningfully defined.

Expressed-preference researchers, therefore, have attempted to measure the acceptability of technology in several additional ways. Otway and Fishbein (1977) and Renn (1981) assessed respondents' overall attitudes toward different technologies by means of a standard semantic differential test. Vlek and Stallen (1979) had respondents use a Q-sort procedure to rank-order different technologies and activities according to their "acceptability" (defined as the degree to which the benefits outweighed possible risks). Slovic, Fischhoff, and Lichtenstein (1980) and Buss and Craik (1983) used the "risk adjustment" ratings described above (i.e., the number of times safer or riskier than now each rated technology would have to be in order to be judged acceptable) in their final analyses, rather than attempt to derive an "absolute" level of acceptable risk.

All of these measures of the acceptability of technological risk, however, suffer a major practical shortcoming: They are hard to interpret or to apply to the process of setting risk-benefit policy. As Fischhoff et al. (1978: 151) point out in the case of their own measure:

> If people assert that motor vehicles should be five times safer [to be acceptable], does this mean that they would accept any immediate Draconian step designed to attain that goal? Does it mean that a five-fold reduction in risk is a long-term goal for society and that meaningful (but not necessarily drastic) steps should be taken until that goal is reached, or does it mean that the adjustment ratios . . . only measure relative concerns about the risk levels of various activities? A more behaviorally relevant scale of acceptability should be developed, with clearer implications for regulatory actions.

The measures of acceptability used by Vlek and Stallen (1979) and by Otway and Fishbein (1977) are similarly difficult to interpret and apply.

In an attempt to overcome these drawbacks, Slovic, Fischhoff, and Lichtenstein (1981) had respondents evaluate both current and desired regulatory actions with a six-category rating scale that ran from "monitor the risk," through increasing degrees of restriction, to "total ban" on the technology. We used a somewhat similar question in our survey. For each technology, respondents rated both "current" and "desired" regulatory strictness on a 1- to 7-point scale ranging from "not very strict" to "extremely strict" (Questions 3 through 8). Each rating was later analyzed separately and then combined into a composite measure of the "acceptability of current technological safety regulations" by subtracting each respondent's "desired strictness" rating from his or her "current strictness" rating.

Then we tailored additional, specific acceptability questions for each technology. (Otway and Thomas, 1982, have argued for this kind of specificity.) In the case of nuclear power, for example, we asked about the appropriate degree of government support for alternative sources of energy, including solar energy and conservation (Question 36-A through 36-E). Another question (Question 33) asked about the deployment of additional nuclear plants. (This question was motivated by pretest data, Gardner et al., 1982, which showed that desired regulatory strictness for nuclear power and desired level of deployment are not perfectly correlated.) Two final questions (Questions 23-B and 23-C) asked respondents if they agreed or disagreed that "the profit motive of private companies makes it difficult for the safe operation of nuclear power plants," and that "nuclear electric power plants should be operated by the government, rather than by private industry." Other questions (Question 30 through 32 and 34 through 35) addressed specific policy issues concerning the other five technologies.

Analysis Design

The basic design of our analysis is different from that of the earliest expressed-preference research (e.g., Slovic, Fischhoff, and Lichtenstein, 1979, 1980; Green and Brown, 1980; Vlek and Stallen, 1979) and similar to that of more recent research (Renn, 1981; Buss and Craik, 1983; Harding and Eiser, 1984). Even though data for all expressed-preference research have been gathered from individual persons, the earlier research aggregated these data. The geometric means of respondents' perceptions of the risks and benefits of several technologies, for example, were correlated with such other aggregate measures as the average rating each technology received on a scale of "acceptability." Because correlations were computed across technologies—rather than across persons—technology, technically, became the statistical unit of analysis even though the person remained the theoretical unit of analysis. In our study, and in the studies of Renn (1981), Buss and Craik (1983), and Harding and Eiser (1984), analyses were based not on aggregate measures but on ratings made by individual respondents for single technologies.

Although each mode of analysis has its own particular strengths and weaknesses, the mode we chose has the following advantages. First, by using the same theoretical and statistical levels of analysis, it eliminates the "ecological fallacy" (Robinson, 1950) and avoids problems of aggregation bias (Orcutt et al., 1968; Renn, 1981). Second, it allows conditional theoretical statements; to what types of technologies, for example, does the theory apply, or apply only weakly (Renn, 1981). And third, it permits correlations between such characteristics of persons as attitudes and sociodemographic status, and people's perceptions of benefits or risks, their judgments of acceptability, or their actions.

Descriptive Statistics. Although a few of the variables in our study, such as age, are measured with interval scales, and a few others, such as work status, are measured with nominal scales, most variables are measured with ordinal scales. This is not at all unusual for survey research.

Nevertheless, the mixture of measurement levels presents analytic problems since most descriptive and inferential statistics are designed for data of a particular measurement level.

The usual solution to this problem is to restrict analyses to simple bivariate associations described by percentage tables and to simple first-order partials (e.g., Zeisel, 1968). If more elaborate multivariate analyses are called for, certain scales are modified so that all variables can be analyzed with product-moment statistics; nominal variables are reclassified as one or more dichotomies (if they are not already dichotomies), and ordinal variables are transformed, where necessary, so that their univariate distributions and patterns of relationship with dependent variables meet the distributional and linearity assumptions of the product-moment system of statistics.

There is much to recommend this approach, as product-moment statistics are, without a doubt, the most powerful, most thoroughly developed, and most familiar multivariate statistics available to the survey researcher. There were, however, several reasons not to use product-moment statistics in our analysis.

Product-moment measures of association (zero, partial, and multiple correlation and regression coefficients) are sensitive to a very specific (namely, linear) form of relationship. Relationships that are monotonic, but not linear, as well as relationships that are curvilinear (i.e., that describe curves that change sign) are not described properly with product-moment statistics (Achen, 1982). Therefore, when using product-moment statistics, one must plot each variable against each other variable to make sure that all relationships are linear. When they are not, one or both variables in the relationship must be transformed so that the relationship approximates linearity.

When analyzing a limited number of variables, measured on interval scales that cover a reasonably large range and form reasonably strong correlations with other variables, this procedure is altogether practical. However, when most variables are measured on ordinal scales that employ only a few measurement categories and are only weakly correlated with other variables, as is often the case in our study, it becomes almost impossible to determine whether a particular scatter plot would be described best by a line that is straight or by one that is curved. Given further that we must analyze many relationships, involving several dependent variables, for four samples and six technologies, it is virtually impossible to choose transformations that are appropriate for each variable in each situation.

Therefore, we chose an ordinally based, nonparametric system of zero-order and multivariate statistics based on Kendall's tau-B (1962) and partial Somers's D_{yx} (1962a and 1962b) for the analysis of variables that are interval, ordinal, or dichotomous-nominal classifications (Hawkes, 1971; Ploch, 1974), and Goodman and Kruskal's tau-b (1954) for analyzing nominal variables with more than two categories. (To distinguish between the two tau measures, we have adopted a convention of referring to the Goodman and Kruskal tau measure as tau-b and to the Kendall measure as tau-B.) In the few cases involving nominal by ordinal comparisons we used theta (Freeman, 1965: 108–119). These statistics, although lacking some of the power of the product-moment system, have the advantage of avoiding many of that system's more demanding assumptions. Since these statistics may be less familiar to some readers than the more common, product-moment statistics, we have described them in some detail in Appendix D. Table 4.1 is a short guide to interpreting each of the statistics used.

Inferential Statistics. Inference tests for tau-b and zero-order tau-B are available (see Appendix D). Inference tests for multiple tau-B or the standardized regression coefficient used in the ordinally based regressions we have computed, however, are not available. This lack is a price that must be paid for using the nonparametric regresson model. Since most of the samples we are analyzing are quite large, however, this price is quite small. That is, with sample sizes of over 400, any descriptive statistic that is "substantively" significant will be "statistically" significant as well. A zero-order (tau-B)^2 of 0.01, for example (which accounts for only 1 percent of the variation in the dependent variable),[5] will be "statistically significant" at $p < .01$ for samples of this size. Testing the "statistical significance" of our results, therefore, is not very meaningful.

Samples. Although our general population samples are full probability (see Appendix B), they are not simple-random (although the Connecticut sample is nearly so). Neither are our samples of intervenors. Strictly speaking, therefore, we do not meet the assumptions for tests of statistical significance with any of our samples (Morrison and Henkel, 1970: 305–313).

Since the two general population samples are full probability, however (even though they are not simple-random), and thus subject to sampling variability, we have followed the common practice of treating them as if they were simple-random. For some purposes, however, it was useful to combine general population and intervenor samples. These combined samples do not meet the assumptions of inference tests at all, and thus we have treated them as complete enumerations.

With two good general population samples to work with, one might ask, why combine samples at all? The answer is that the variation of one of

Table 4.1
Descriptive Statistics Used in the Analyses and Their Interpretations

	Symbol	Function	Interpretation	Inferential Test Available	Product-Moment Analogue
Zero-order measures of association					
tau-b	t_b	Measures association between two nominal variables.	Proportional reduction in error.	Yes	None
[tau-B]²	t_B^2	Measures association between two ordinal variables.	Proportional reduction in error or variation explained.	Yes	r^2
theta	Θ	Measures association between nominal independent and ordinal dependent variables.	Proportional reduction in error.	No	None
Regression statistics					
Multiple [tau-B]²	T_B^2	Measures combined effects of several independent variables.	Proportional reduction in error or variation explained.	No	R^2
Ordinal regression coefficient	B_o	Measures relative effect of one independent variable.	Relative importance in explaining variation in dependent variable.	No	B

our most important dependent variables, action, was so small among members of the general public that meaningful analyses of this variable were virtually impossible unless we augmented the general population samples with intervenors who were known to have taken action with respect to the risks or benefits of at least one technology. This strategy was absolutely crucial for the analyses reported in Chapter 7, and, to keep Chapters 5 and 6 comparable, we adopted the same strategy for the analyses reported there.[6]

Using these combined samples not only eliminated the probability nature of the samples, but in the case of the dependent variable—action—also destroyed the assumption of normal distributions upon which product-moment statistics are based. This, therefore, was a final reason for choosing nonparametric, rather than parametric, descriptive statistics for our analyses.

Analysis Strategy. Our first analytic task was to compute zero-order measures of association between each independent and each dependent variable for both the Arizona and Connecticut combined samples. When both variables were ordinal (or nominal dichotomies and ordinal) we used (tau-B)^2 to measure these associations. (Ordinal dependent variables included action, acceptability, perceived risks, and perceived benefits of the six different technologies.) When the dependent variable was nominal, as it was with activist status, described in Chapter 7, we used tau-b. Each of these statistics can be interpreted as the proportional reduction in error in predicting the dependent variable from knowledge of the joint distribution of the independent and dependent variables, over what could be done knowing only the distribution of the dependent variable (Costner, 1965). (Tau-B)^2, like r^2, can also be interpreted as the proportion of the variation in y (the dependent variable) that is "explained," or accounted for, by the covariation of x and y (Hawkes, 1971).

We then eliminated from further consideration all independent variables that accounted for less than 1 percent of the variation in any dependent variable (i.e., with [tau-B]^2 values of less than 0.01) and constructed ordinal regression equations for the dependent variables acceptability, perceived risk, perceived benefits, and action for both the Connecticut and Arizona combined samples (general public plus intervenors). We computed these regressions (eight each for each technology) in a two-stage process with the computer program SPSS (Nie et al., 1975). First we constructed matrices of zero-order tau-B coefficients, using the subprogram NONPAR CORR, and then we fed these matrices into the subprogram REGRESSION, which computed multiple (tau-B)^2 and standardized regression coefficients (standard Somers's D_{yx}).[7] This required a different matrix for each technology in each region.

These equations showed that several of the independent variables that had had significant zero-order relationships with one or another of the dependent variables in the analysis (i.e., they accounted, overall, for at least 1 percent of the variation in the dependent variable) had very small standardized regression coefficients. This meant, of course, that while they had some overall effect (direct and indirect effects combined), they had very little direct effect. Since we could not compute the statistical significance of our ordinal regression coefficients, and thus use statistical significance as a criterion for eliminating variables from the equations, we decided to include all variables in the final equations that had a zero-order relationship (tau-B)^2 of 0.01 or greater, even though the effects of some independent variables, controlling for the others, is sometimes quite small.

Multiple (tau-B)^2 for these regressions may be interpreted just like multiple R^2 in ordinary-least-squares regressions, that is, as the proportion of the variation in y that is explained, or accounted for, by the combined effects of all the independent variables in the equation. The standardized regression coefficients, as in the product-moment system, may be interpreted as indicating the relative importance of each independent variable in explaining the total variation that is explained. (Since the concept of "slope" has no meaning for variables measured on ordinal scales, unstandardized, ordinal regression coefficients would have no meaning.)

Although most of the dependent variables we worked with are ordinal, the variable action status, reported in Chapter 7, is nominal, consisting of three discrete categories: those who took pro-benefits action, those who took pro-safety actions, and those who took no action. Regression analyses, either of the product-moment or ordinal varieties, are not appropriate for this type of variable. Analyses of this variable, therefore, was restricted to zero-order tau-b coefficients between each independent variable and "action status," within each of the two combined samples. (Nominal independent variables were analyzed at this stage without collapsing categories; ordinal and interval variables were segmented into not fewer than three categories each.)

Summary

This study, then, has several unique characteristics. It is the first expressed-preference research in this country to employ large representative samples of the general public from two contrasting regions of the country, as well as comparative samples of people from the same regions who had given public testimony concerning the risks or benefits of technology. One of its primary purposes was to verify results from earlier studies that did not employ representative samples or that were done in Europe.

With large representative samples of unaggregated data, we were able to include many personal-level independent variables in the analysis and to employ regression analysis. (Earlier expressed-preference research relied, for the most part, on simpler, zero-order statistics.) These analyses allowed us to measure not only the total amount of variation in each dependent variable accounted for by several independent variables, but also to calculate the relative contribution made by each independent variable in explaining this variation.

And finally, this is the first expressed-preference research, so far as we are aware, to go beyond an assessment of people's judgments about the acceptability of current safety regulations and the antecedents of these judgments; we also investigated the effects of these "acceptability" judgments on people's propensity to take actions designed to influence safety regulations. In the end, then, this is more than an expressed-preference study; it is also a study of intervention.

NOTES

1. Due to the limitations of the survey format, we included only 3 of 18 qualitative risk characteristics studied earlier by Slovic, Fischhoff, and Lichtenstein (1981). We selected these three because Slovic et al.'s work showed them to be correlated strongly with overall risk ratings and "risk-adjustment" estimates, and because they loaded strongly on the main factors of factor analyses reported by these authors.

2. Although some earlier research (Otway and Fishbein, 1977; Renn, 1981) included a few questions about the benefits of technology, expressed-preference research in general has explored the determinants of perceived risk in far greater detail than the determinants of perceived benefit (Starr and Whipple, 1980). We chose the four qualitative benefits characteristics included in our survey from a list of five included in a prior unpublished study by Slovic and his colleagues (Study 6).

3. Prior research indicated that attitudes about general objects (e.g., nuclear power, the environment) predispose people to perform a variety of different acts with respect to those objects rather than any specific act (Fishbein and Ajzen, 1975;

Weigel and Newman, 1976; Otway and Fishbein, 1977). Therefore, we included questions about ten different kinds of actions in the questionnaire.

4. Yankelovich and Keene, who developed these questions, refer to them collectively as a "mushiness index" (Keene and Sackett, 1981).

5. Since it is not meaningful to talk about the mean of distributions measured with nominal or ordinal scales, the concept *variance,* which refers to the spread of a distribution about the mean, has no meaning in these cases. The concept *variation,* in contrast, refers only to how spread-out a distribution is in general, without reference to a mean, and thus is equally appropriate for nominal, ordinal, and interval scales. (For interval variables, the variation and the variance are arithmetically identical.) See Appendix D for more details on these two concepts.

6. Separate analyses of the acceptability of current regulations, perceived risks, and perceived benefits of technology using only the general population samples indicate that combining the samples made little difference in the conclusions regarding these variables reported in Chapters 5 and 6. Similar analyses for action, however, yielded noticeable differences, as would be expected, since the augmented, or combined, samples included people who were selected precisely because they were known to have taken action.

7. Since readers will be more familiar with ordinary-least-squares regressions than with ordinal regressions, we have also reported R^2 for each of the regressions discussed in Chapters 5, 6, and 7.

5

Risks, Benefits, and Regulation

This chapter reports the findings of our study relevant to Hypotheses 1 through 6 listed in Chapter 3. It begins with a discussion of acceptability and then examines the correlates of our respondents' views on the acceptability of current technology safety regulations. First the analysis looks at the influence of perceived risks and perceived benefits, and then it explores the influence of various attitudes and sociodemographic variables.

The Acceptability of Current Regulations

Data we presented in Chapter 2 showed that a majority of the general public in our Connecticut and Arizona samples favored stricter safety standards and regulations for the six technologies we investigated. Table 5.1 shows the same thing, by listing the median acceptability ratings for these two samples and, in addition, lists the median acceptability ratings for intervenors.[1] On average, every group, even pro-benefits intervenors, indicated that they thought technology safety regulations should be stricter than they then perceived them to be. The people surveyed in Arizona differed little from those surveyed in Connecticut; the only major difference between the two general population samples was that the Arizona residents saw less need for increased handgun regulation than did the residents of Connecticut. Pro-benefits intervenors, however, as might have been expected, favored smaller increases in regulatory strictness than did pro-safety intervenors. Pro-benefits intervenors were also more favorable toward technology, in general, than either general population sample, while pro-safety intervenors were somewhat less favorable. These differences were consistent across the six technologies in the study.

Measuring Acceptability

The acceptability of current safety standards and restrictions reported in Table 5.1 were calculated by subtracting respondents' ratings of how strict they thought the regulations "should be" from their ratings of the strictness of "current" regulations (Questions 3 through 8). A positive score on the resulting 12-point scale (which we call "regulation" in the analyses to follow) indicates that the respondent felt that regulations should be more lenient; a negative score, that they should be stricter; and a score of zero, that there should be no change.

It should be noted that we did not directly ask respondents whether they thought current safety standards should be tightened, eased, or left as they are; rather, we reached this conclusion via the two-step process described in the preceding paragraph. Since it was possible that our results might have been affected by the roundabout way we measured acceptability, we conducted a small experiment in which we asked 94 college undergraduates to fill out a short questionnaire containing the two regulation questions we used in our survey, and another 105 students to fill out a

Table 5.1
Median Acceptability Ratings of Current Safety Regulations
for Six Technologies

	General Population		Intervenors[a]	
	Connecticut	Arizona	Pro-Safety	Pro-Benefits
Automobile travel	−2.3	−1.8	−2.2	−1.1
Air travel	−1.5	−1.4	−1.4	−0.6
Nuclear power	−2.5	−2.4	−2.8	−0.6
Nuclear weapons	−2.6	−2.4	−2.9	−1.6
Handguns	−4.2	−2.8	−3.8	−2.8
Industrial chemicals	−3.9	−3.9	−4.2	−1.5

[a]Includes all intervenors from Connecticut and those intervenors from Arizona whose pro-safety or pro-benefits status could be determined from their public testimony.

questionnaire containing a single question that directly asked whether current regulations should be made stricter, more lenient, or left as they are. (Which questionnaire a student received was determined by random number.) The differences between the two groups were small, and such differences as did occur indicated that the single-question version elicits a greater desire for increased regulatory strictness than does the two-question version. (Details of the experiment are described in Appendix C.) We concluded, therefore, that our two-step procedure for measuring regulation was appropriate.

Risks and Benefits

As reported in Chapter 3, most researchers, whether employing revealed-preference or expressed-preference research procedures, have assumed that people's views on technology safety regulation are a function of their views on the risks and benefits provided by particular technologies. Table 5.2 reports the median perceptions of overall risk and overall benefit for the six technologies we studied. Responses are listed separately for the Connecticut and Arizona general public and intervenor samples. (Ratings were made on seven-point scales; the higher the number, the higher the perceived risk or benefit.) Aside from the fact that people in Arizona considered the overall benefits of handguns to be greater, and the risks fewer, than did Connecticut residents, the differences were small between the two general public samples. As might have been expected, pro-safety intervenors perceived greater risks, in the main, than did pro-benefits intervenors, but they did not, as might also have been expected, always perceive greater risks than the general public; Connecticut residents, on average, perceived the risks of handguns and of air travel as being greater than did the pro-safety intervenors.

Qualitative Aspects of Risk

One of the most important contributions of expressed-preference research to the general risk literature has been the discovery that people consider many things besides the risk of death when arriving at overall judgments about the riskiness of particular technologies. Table 5.3 reports the median ratings, for each respondent group and each technology, on three qualitative risk characteristics and on the relative number of fatalities that might be expected "in this country in the next year." Like overall risk, these ratings were based on a seven-point response scale, higher scores

Table 5.2
Median Perceived Overall Risks and Benefits for Six Technologies

	General Population		Intervenors[a]	
	Connecticut	Arizona	Pro-Safety	Pro-Benefits
Automobile travel				
Risks	5.0	4.7	5.1	4.7
Benefits	6.5	6.5	6.6	6.3
Air travel				
Risks	4.0	3.6	3.8	3.0
Benefits	6.5	6.5	6.4	6.0
Nuclear power				
Risks	5.1	5.0	5.4	3.6
Benefits[b]	6.8	6.8	6.8	6.8
Nuclear weapons				
Risks	6.7	6.4	6.8	6.5
Benefits	3.8	4.0	2.8	4.1
Handguns				
Risks	6.5	5.6	5.7	5.2
Benefits	2.2	3.5	2.0	2.5
Industrial chemicals				
Risks	5.7	5.4	6.0	4.6
Benefits	4.7	4.5	5.5	5.8

[a] Includes all intervenors from Connecticut and those intervenors from Arizona whose pro-safety or pro-benefits status could be determined from their public testimony.
[b] Of electricity.

indicating greater catastrophic potential, greater dread, less scientific understanding of the risks, and a greater number of deaths.

Median ratings made by the two general population samples were similar, although the median values for the Arizona respondents were somewhat lower than those of Connecticut respondents. Median ratings by pro-benefits intervenors were lower (and hence more "pro-technology") than pro-safety intervenors. The qualitative risk ratings of pro-safety intervenors were not, however, as might have been expected, always higher than those made by members of the general public.

It is worth noting that the qualitative risk characteristic ratings of Connecticut and Arizona residents (Table 5.3) are similar to those obtained earlier by Fischhoff et al. (1978, Table 2) from League of Woman Voters members; the one notable exception is that our general population respondents rated nuclear power lower on both catastrophic potential and dread than did Fischhoff et al.'s subjects. Fischhoff and his colleagues

Table 5.3
Median Fatality Estimates and Qualitative Risk Judgments
for Six Technologies

	General Population		Intervenors[a]	
	Connecticut	Arizona	Pro-Safety	Pro-Benefits
Automobile travel				
Number of deaths	6.6	6.2	6.7	6.5
Risks understood	2.0	1.9	1.8	1.7
Catastrophic potential	3.0	2.6	2.3	2.4
Dread	2.2	1.9	2.0	1.8
Air travel				
Number of deaths	3.3	3.0	2.6	2.1
Risks understood	2.3	2.2	2.2	2.1
Catastrophic potential	6.5	6.0	5.5	5.2
Dread	2.8	2.2	2.2	2.1
Nuclear power				
Number of deaths	2.4	2.3	1.6	1.2
Risks understood	4.4	4.2	3.9	3.2
Catastrophic potential	4.6	4.9	5.1	3.5
Dread	4.0	4.2	3.9	2.3
Nuclear weapons				
Number of deaths	2.1	2.2	1.4	1.2
Risks understood	4.2	4.2	2.4	2.5
Catastrophic potential	6.9	6.8	6.9	6.9
Dread	6.6	5.8	6.7	5.9
Handguns				
Number of deaths	6.4	5.6	5.7	5.3
Risks understood	1.9	2.1	1.9	1.8
Catastrophic potential	2.4	2.0	1.7	1.6
Dread	5.0	4.1	4.3	4.1
Industrial chemicals				
Number of deaths	4.1	4.0	4.3	2.7
Risks understood	4.7	4.3	4.9	4.0
Catastrophic potential	4.5	4.2	4.9	3.1
Dread	4.2	4.1	4.9	2.9

[a] Includes all intervenors from Connecticut and those intervenors from Arizona whose pro-safety or pro-benefits status could be determined from their public testimony.

found nuclear power, more than any other technology, to be rated at the unfavorable end of most qualitative risk scales—a fact, they suggested, that probably accounted for its extremely low acceptability rating. The general population respondents in our survey, in contrast, did not universally rate the qualitative risk characteristics of nuclear power at the bottom of the scale. Industrial chemicals, for example, were rated as more poorly understood than nuclear power; commercial air travel was rated as having greater catastrophic potential; and handguns were rated, on average, as more dreaded. Commensurately, fewer of our respondents rated nuclear power as needing more stringent safety regulation. Specifically, subjects in our study rated nuclear power as being less in need of increased regulation than either industrial chemicals or handguns, while respondents in the Fischhoff et al. study rated nuclear power, by a wide margin, as the technology most in need of increased risk regulation. Whether these differences are due to differences in samples (Fischhoff et al. used small, unrepresentative samples) or time periods (the Fischhoff et al. study was conducted a decade before our surveys) we cannot say. It is worthy of note, however, that the respondents in our surveys in the 1980s did not universally perceive nuclear power as the most dreaded, most catastrophic, or least understood technology, not did they universally perceive nuclear power as the technology most in need of stricter safety standards.

Components of Perceived Risk

Current literature, as discussed in Chapter 3, suggests not only that there are several qualitative dimensions to people's perceptions of technological risk, but that people's overall judgments of technological risk are a composite of these qualitative dimensions and their perceptions of the number of deaths the technology might cause (Hypothesis 1 of our study). Table 5.4 shows the degree to which each of these factors was correlated (t_B^2) with our respondents' ratings of overall risk. (Correlation values are shown separately for Connecticut and Arizona combined samples—the general public plus intervenors.) Although the estimated number of deaths shows the highest correlation with overall risk for three of the six technologies (auto travel, air travel, and industrial chemicals), even these correlations are not very strong, ranging from a very low 0.08 to a mere 0.18. The correlations between overall risk and the three qualitative risk characteristics are also low, ranging from -0.01 to 0.26.[2]

Even though these zero-order correlations are low, it is possible that the perceived risk of fatalities and the three qualitative aspects of risk, combined, might account for a more reasonable proportion of people's overall risk judgments. Multiple regression analyses, summarized in Table

Table 5.4
Zero-Order Correlations (t_B^2) Between Perceived Overall Risks,
Relative Numbers of Deaths, and Qualitative Risk Characteristics
for Six Technologies (Connecticut and Arizona Combined Samples)

Overall Risks of	Number of Deaths	Risks Understood	Catastrophic Potential	Dread
Auto travel				
Connecticut	.08	.00	.02	.04
Arizona	.08	.01	.02	.07
Air travel				
Connecticut	.18	.04	.04	.13
Arizona	.16	.03	.02	.16
Nuclear power				
Connecticut	.11	.04	.10	.17
Arizona	.11	.07	.10	.23
Nuclear weapons				
Connecticut	.00	.00	.07	.12
Arizona	.01	.01	.08	.21
Handguns				
Connecticut	.22	−.01	.03	.26
Arizona	.21	.01	.04	.27
Industrial chemicals				
Connecticut	.14	.02	.09	.14
Arizona	.15	.04	.10	.15

5.5, showed, however, that this is only marginally the case. Multiple T_B^2 values for the overall perceived risk of the six technologies ranged from a small 0.12 (for the overall risk of auto travel in Connecticut) to 0.34 (for the overall risk of handguns in both regions). Although the three qualitative risk characteristics and relative number of fatalities, combined, accounted for more of the variation in overall perceived risk than any single factor alone, the total amount of variation explained is not very impressive.

The relative magnitudes of the standard regression coefficients (B_o) in the multiple regression equations reported in Table 5.5 are quite similar to the relative magnitudes of the zero-order t_B^2 correlations reported in Table 5.4. This indicates that the zero-order correlations reported in Table 5.4 are for the most part measuring direct effects of the estimated numbers of deaths and the three qualitative risk characteristics on overall perceived risk; had particular regression coefficients been relatively smaller than their corresponding zero-order correlation coefficients, some combina-

Table 5.5

Multiple Regressions of Overall Risks, Relative Number of Deaths, and Three Qualitative Risk Characteristics for Six Technologies (Connecticut and Arizona Combined Samples)

	Connecticut		Arizona	
Dependent Variable: Overall Risks of Auto Travel				
Variation of dependent variable	.40		.40	
Independent variables	B_O	Var.	B_O	Var.
Number of deaths	.26	.31	.24	.35
Risks understood	a	.37	a	.36
Catastrophic potential	.07	.41	.06	.39
Dread	.17	.39	.23	.37
T_B^2 (R^2)	.12 (.19)		.13 (.20)	
Number of cases	652		590	
Dependent Variable: Overall Risks of Air Travel				
Variation of dependent variable	.41		.40	
Independent variables	B_O	Var.	B_O	Var.
Number of deaths	.31	.41	.29	.41
Risks understood	.11	.40	.03	.38
Catastrophic potential	.08	.36	.05	.38
Dread	.20	.41	.27	.39
T_B^2 (R^2)	.24 (.37)		.23 (.31)	
Number of cases	640		582	
Dependent Variable: Overall Risks of Nuclear Power				
Variation of dependent variable	.41		.42	
Independent variables	B_O	Var.	B_O	Var.
Number of deaths	.19	.38	.16	.38
Risks understood	.08	.43	.11	.43
Catastrophic potential	.18	.42	.14	.42
Dread	.26	.43	.32	.43
T_B^2 (R^2)	.25 (.32)		.29 (.39)	
Number of cases	647		578	
Dependent Variable: Overall Risks of Nuclear Weapons				
Variation of dependent variable	.27		.35	
Independent variables	B_O	Var.	B_O	Var.
Number of deaths	a	.37	.08	.37
Risks understood	a	.42	.05	.43
Catastrophic potential	.18	.17	.17	.23
Dread	.30	.33	.39	.39
T_B^2 (R^2)	.15 (.15)		.24 (.26)	
Number of cases	653		589	

Table 5.5 (continued)

	Connecticut		Arizona	
Dependent Variable: Overall Risks of **Handguns**				
Variation of dependent variable	.36		.40	
Independent variables	B_o	Var.	B_o	Var.
Number of deaths	.31	.36	.31	.40
Risks understood	a	.37	a	.38
Catastrophic potential	.03	.40	.01	.37
Dread	.35	.41	.37	.43
$T_B^2 (R^2)$	.34 (.41)		.34 (.45)	
Number of cases	642		587	
Dependent Variable: Overall Risks of **Industrial Chemicals**				
Variation of dependent variable	.39		.40	
Independent variables	B_o	Var.	B_o	Var.
Number of deaths	.24	.41	.25	.41
Risks understood	.06	.42	.09	.42
Catastrophic potential	.13	.42	.14	.42
Dread	.23	.42	.24	.42
$T_B^2 (R^2)$	.23 (.29)		.25 (.33)	
Number of cases	646		576	

[a]Not entered in the regression because zero-order correlation was less than 0.01.

tion of direct and indirect effects would have been indicated. Put another way, the relative effect of each of these independent variables appears to have been essentially unaffected by its simultaneous correlations with other independent variables in the equations.

The zero-order correlations reported in Table 5.4 are smaller by far, however, than similar correlations reported by Slovic and his colleagues (e.g., Slovic, Fischhoff, and Lichtenstein, 1979). Although these differences may be due in part to differences in time and samples, they are most likely due to the fact that the Slovic et al. correlations were based on aggregate rather than individual-level data, and thus overestimate individual-level correlations.

Although the correlations we found are small, they are consistent for all six technologies and both geographic regions. They indicate that the perceived number of deaths is not the only, or even the most important, component of people's perceptions of risk; three qualitative characteristics of risk (in particular, dread) also played a role in determining people's overall estimates of the risk of technology in our two study regions. This is consistent with the results reported in other expressed-preference studies and with Hypothesis 1 of our study, which stated that people's perceptions of the risk of a technology are a function of: (1) their estimates of the number of deaths the technology will cause, and (2) several additional qualitative aspects of the risk, including the perceived degree of scientific disagreement concerning the risk, the risk's perceived catastrophic potential, and the degree to which the risk induces dread.

A close examination of Tables 5.4 and 5.5 indicates, however, that there were considerable differences among technologies as to how important the relative number of deaths, or the three qualitative risk factors, are in defining overall risk. Number of deaths, for example, was a relatively important factor for air travel, nuclear power, handguns, and industrial chemicals; of only moderate importance for auto travel; and essentially irrelevant to the overall risks of nuclear weapons. Dread was an important factor in defining the overall risks of every technology except auto travel. Catastrophic potential was moderately important in the cases of nuclear power, nuclear weapons, and industrial chemicals, but virtually irrelevant to auto travel, air travel, and handguns. Whether or not the risks were perceived as being understood played little or no part in defining the overall risks of any technology.

Qualitative Aspects of Benefits

Just as early revealed-preference risk research measured the risks of technology in simple terms of risk of death, so it measured the benefits of technology in simple economic terms. As in the case of perceived risks, however, we hypothesized that people's perceptions of the benefits of a technology will extend beyond their perceptions of the economic importance of the technology (Hypothesis 4). Table 5.6 shows the median ratings of each technology in terms of four qualitative benefit characteristics: economic benefits, benefits to basic human needs, safety and security, and personal pleasure and satisfaction. These ratings, like the ratings of the qualitative risk characteristics, were based on seven-point scales; the higher the score, the greater the perceived benefit characteristic.

As might have been expected, pro-benefits intervenors tended to rate the qualitative aspects of benefits higher than did the other groups. Pro-safety intervenors, however, did not rate the benefits of the technologies lower than did the general public. Indeed, overall, there were no large or consistent differences among the four samples.

The patterns of benefit characteristic ratings we found, however, do not match the patterns found by Slovic et al. in earlier research (unpublished, Study 6). In particular, ratings of "pleasure" and "benefits to basic human needs" were uniformly lower, relative to the other benefit characteristics, in the Slovic et al. study than in ours. To make much of the comparison of the two studies, however, probably would be misleading as

Table 5.6
Median Ratings of Qualitative Benefit Characteristics
for Six Technologies

	General Population		Intervenors	
	Connecticut	Arizona	Pro-Safety	Pro-Benefits
Automobile travel				
Economic benefits	6.5	6.5	6.5	6.6
Basic needs	6.0	6.0	5.1	5.6
Safety and security	4.3	4.6	3.3	3.9
Pleasure	6.3	6.3	5.8	5.8
Air travel				
Economic benefits	6.4	6.3	6.1	5.8
Basic needs	5.3	4.9	3.8	4.4
Safety and security	4.4	4.5	3.4	3.5
Pleasure	5.5	5.5	5.4	5.2
Electricity				
Economic benefits	6.7	6.7	6.7	6.8
Basic needs	6.7	6.6	6.4	6.6
Safety and security	6.1	6.1	6.0	5.9
Pleasure	6.7	6.7	6.6	6.4
Nuclear weapons				
Economic benefits	3.9	4.2	3.5	3.4
Basic needs	2.0	2.3	1.3	1.8
Safety and security	4.4	4.8	3.8	5.6
Pleasure	(not measured)		(not measured)	
Handguns				
Economic benefits	2.4	2.7	2.2	1.9
Basic needs	1.4	1.8	1.3	1.4
Safety and security	3.0	4.2	2.4	3.4
Pleasure	1.2	1.6	1.2	1.5
Industrial chemicals				
Economic benefits	5.1	4.9	5.9	6.1
Basic needs	4.3	4.1	5.0	5.3
Safety and security	4.3	4.2	4.3	5.2
Pleasure	2.7	3.0	2.9	3.8

there were major differences in response scales, sample sizes, and sample representativeness.

Components of Perceived Benefits

Table 5.7 reports zero-order (t_B^2) correlations between respondents' perceptions of overall benefits and the four qualitative benefit characteristics: economic benefits, basic needs, safety and security, and pleasure and satisfaction. (We did not ask respondents if they derived pleasure or satisfaction from nuclear weapons.) As with overall risks, the results for overall benefits were quite similar in Connecticut and Arizona. Correlations between overall benefits and the four qualitative benefit factors were generally stronger, however, than the correlations we found between overall risks and relative number of deaths or the three qualitative risk characteristics, ranging from a low of 0.01 (for safety and security benefits of auto

Table 5.7

Zero-Order Correlations (t_B^2) Between Perceived Overall Benefits and Four Qualitative Benefit Characteristics for Six Technologies (Connecticut and Arizona Combined Samples)

Overall Benefits from	Economic Benefits	Basic Needs	Safety and Security	Pleasure
Auto travel				
Connecticut	.29	.14	.03	.15
Arizona	.25	.08	.01	.08
Air travel				
Connecticut	.31	.13	.08	.14
Arizona	.40	.09	.06	.19
Electricity				
Connecticut	.32	.25	.09	.19
Arizona	.39	.19	.12	.20
Nuclear weapons				
Connecticut	.15	.21	.20	*a*
Arizona	.15	.23	21	*a*
Handguns				
Connecticut	.22	.32	.30	.25
Arizona	.26	.34	.30	.31
Industrial chemicals				
Connecticut	.35	.28	.14	.15
Arizona	.34	.29	.18	.15

*a*Not asked.

travel in Arizona) to a high of 0.40 (for economic benefits of air travel in Arizona).

As Table 5.8 demonstrates, these qualitative benefit characteristics, taken together, also accounted for a reasonably large proportion of the variation in overall benefit ratings for each of the six technologies; T_B^2 values ranged from 0.33 (for overall benefits of nuclear weapons in Connecticut) to 0.51 (for overall benefits of handguns in Arizona). As with the qualitative risk characteristics, the relative magnitudes of the regression coefficients for the qualitative benefit characteristics were quite similar to the relative magnitudes of zero-order correlations between these factors and overall benefits. It appears, therefore, that the effects of each qualitative benefit factor on overall benefits was direct and that there were no major confounding interactions among the qualitative benefit factors themselves.

The relative importance of each qualitative benefit characteristic differed considerably, however, from technology to technology and from region to region. While economic benefits was important in defining the overall benefits of all technologies in all regions (and the most important for every technology except nuclear weapons and handguns), basic needs was only moderately important in most cases and was completely unimportant for air travel in Arizona. Safety and security played a role in defining the overall benefits only of nuclear weapons and handguns. Pleasure and satisfaction was important in every case (except nuclear weapons).

Risks, Benefits, and the Acceptability of Current Regulations

Hypotheses 2, 3, and 5 of our study state that the acceptability of technology safety regulations will be a function of people's perceptions of the overall risks and benefits of a technology, their perceptions of the number of deaths that are likely to occur because of the technology, and several qualitative aspects of the risks and benefits of the technology. Table 5.9 reports zero-order measures of association (t_B^2) between regulation and each of these variables as well as the results of multiple regression analyses using these same variables.

The data in Table 5.9 confirm Hypothesis 2 only in part. We hypothesized that public acceptability of prevailing technology safety regulations would be negatively related to perceived overall risks of technology and positively related to perceived overall benefits. Although a strong negative relationship between regulation and overall risks was apparent

Table 5.8
Multiple Regressions of Overall Benefits, and Four Qualitative Benefit Characteristics for Six Technologies
(Connecticut and Arizona Combined Samples)

	Connecticut		Arizona	
Dependent Variable: Overall Benefits of Auto Travel				
Variation of dependent variable	.33		.32	
Independent variables	B_o	Var.	B_o	Var.
Economic benefits	.41	.33	.43	.33
Basic needs	.17	.39	.13	.38
Safety and security	.02	.43	[a]	.42
Pleasure and satisfaction	.21	.36	.10	.36
T_B^2 (R^2)	.36 (.40)		.28 (.29)	
Number of cases	652		590	
Dependent Variable: Overall Benefits of Air Travel				
Variation of dependent variable	.34		.34	
Independent variables	B_o	Var.	B_o	Var.
Economic benefits	.45	.35	.57	.35
Basic needs	.08	.42	−.01	.42
Safety and security	.03	.42	.01	.43
Pleasure and satisfaction	.20	.41	.20	.40
T_B^2 (R^2)	.36 (.40)		.46 (.53)	
Number of cases	640		582	
Dependent Variable: Overall Benefits of Electricity				
Variation of dependent variable	.21		.21	
Independent variables	B_o	Var.	B_o	Var.
Economic benefits	.38	.27	.49	.26
Basic needs	.24	.30	.08	.31
Safety and security	−.03	.37	.02	.37
Pleasure and satisfaction	.17	.31	.18	.29
T_B^2 (R^2)	.40 (.43)		.43 (.43)	
Number of cases	647		578	
Dependent Variable: Overall Benefits of Nuclear Weapons				
Variation of dependent variable	.42		.42	
Independent variables	B_o	Var.	B_o	Var.
Economic benefits	.17	.42	.17	.42
Basic needs	.29	.37	.30	.39
Safety and security	.31	.42	.29	.42
Pleasure and satisfaction	(not asked)		(not asked)	
T_B^2 (R^2)	.33 (.43)		.34 (.44)	
Number of cases	653		589	

Table 5.8 (continued)

	Connecticut		Arizona	
Dependent Variable: Overall Benefits of **Handguns**				
Variation of dependent variable	.39		.42	
Independent variables	B_o	Var.	B_o	Var.
Economic benefits	.18	.40	.17	.41
Basic needs	.22	.32	.27	.37
Safety and security	.28	.41	.24	.43
Pleasure and satisfaction	.19	.25	.24	.36
T_B^2 (R^2)	.46 (.59)		.51 (.65)	
Number of cases	643		587	
Dependent Variable: Overall Risks of **Industrial Chemicals**				
Variation of dependent variable	.41		.41	
Independent variables	B_o	Var.	B_o	Var.
Economic benefits	.41	.40	.38	.40
Basic needs	.25	.42	.25	.42
Safety and security	.09	.42	.11	.42
Pleasure and satisfaction	.10	.41	.10	.41
T_B^2 (R^2)	.45 (.56)		.44 (.57)	
Number of cases	646		576	

[a] Not entered in the regression because zero-order correlation was less than 0.01.

for all six technologies in both geographic regions, overall benefits played a significant role for only three technologies: nuclear weapons, handguns, and industrial chemicals.

One reason why overall benefits played little or no role in determining people's judgments about the acceptability of nuclear power or automobile or air travel is that there was relatively little variation in people's perceptions of the overall benefits of these three technologies (most people rated the overall benefits as being very high). Since a correlation represents the amount of variation in a dependent variable that can be accounted for by covariation between the independent and dependent variables, a correlation cannot be high when the variation in the independent variable is relatively small, compared to the variation in the dependent variable.

The variations in our samples' perceptions of some qualitative benefit characteristics were also low, particularly for the qualitative benefits of electricity (rated high by everyone). This explains, in part, why these characteristics contributed so little to explaining the variation in regulation, and thus why Hypotheses 4 and 5 were also confirmed only in part. Although safety and security benefits somewhat affected our samples'

Table 5.9

Table 5.9
Multiple Regressions of Regulation, Risks, and Benefits for Six Technologies (Connecticut and Arizona Combined Samples)

	Connecticut			Arizona		
Dependent Variable: Auto Safety Regulation						
Variation of dependent variable	.43			.42		
Independent variables	t_B^2	B_o	Var.	t_B^2	B_o	Var.
Overall risks	−.04	−.14	.40	−.02	−.10	.40
Number of deaths	−.03	−.12	.31	−.01	[a]	.35
Risks understood	−.00	[a]	.37	−.00	[a]	.36
Catastrophic potential	−.02	−.06	.41	−.00	[a]	.39
Dread	−.02	−.10	.39	−.02	−.11	.37
Overall benefits	−.00	[a]	.33	−.00	[a]	.32
Economic benefits	−.00	[a]	.33	−.00	[a]	.33
Basic needs	−.00	[a]	.39	−.02	−.11	.38
Safety and security	.00	[a]	.43	−.01	[a]	.42
Pleasure	−.00	[a]	.36	−.02	−.11	.36
T_B^2 (R^2)	.07 (.10)			.05 (.06)		
Number of cases	652			590		
Dependent Variable: Air Safety Regulation						
Variation of dependent variable	.40			.38		
Independent variables	t_B^2	B_o	Var.	t_B^2	B_o	Var.
Overall risks	−.05	−.09	.41	−.05	−.15	.40
Number of deaths	−.05	−.10	.41	−.04	−.10	.41
Risks understood	−.02	−.08	.40	−.10	−.05	.38
Catastrophic potential	−.01	−.05	.36	−.02	−.10	.38
Dread	−.06	−.16	.41	−.02	−.04	.39
Overall benefits	.00	[a]	.34	.00	[a]	.34
Economic benefits	.00	[a]	.35	.00	[a]	.42
Basic needs	.00	[a]	.42	.00	[a]	.42
Safety and security	.00	[a]	.42	−.01	[a]	.43
Pleasure	.00	[a]	.41	.00	[a]	.40
T_B^2 (R^2)	.10 (.14)			.08 (.13)		
Number of cases	640			582		
Dependent Variable: Nuclear Power Regulation						
Variation of dependent variable	.42			.42		
Independent variables	t_B^2	B_o	Var.	t_B^2	B_o	Var.
Overall risks	−.11	−.22	.41	−.12	−.25	.42
Number of deaths	−.04	−.05	.38	−.04	−.09	.38
Risks understood	−.02	−.06	.43	−.03	−.07	.43
Catastrophic potential	−.03	−.03	.42	−.02	−.00	.42
Dread	−.09	−.18	.43	−.07	−.09	.43

Table 5.9 (continued)

	Connecticut			Arizona		
Overall benefits[b]	.00	[a]	.21	.00	[a]	.21
Economic benefits	.00	[a]	.27	.00	[a]	.26
Basic needs	.00	[a]	.30	.00	[a]	.31
Safety and security	.00	[a]	.37	.00	[a]	.37
Pleasure	.00	[a]	.31	.00	[a]	.29
T_B^2 (R^2)	.15 (.25)			.14 (.22)		
Number of cases	647			578		

Dependent Variable: **Nuclear Weapons Regulation**

	Connecticut			Arizona		
Variation of dependent variable	.42			.41		
Independent variables	t_B^2	B_o	Var.	t_B^2	B_o	Var.
Overall risks	−.04	−.13	.27	−.06	−.15	.35
Number of deaths	−.02	−.11	.37	−.03	−.11	.37
Risks understood	−.01	[a]	.42	−.01	−.05	.43
Catastrophic potential	−.01	[a]	.17	−.00	[a]	.23
Dread	−.03	−.11	.33	−.04	−.05	.39
Overall benefits	.04	.05	.42	.04	.09	.42
Economic benefits	.00	[a]	.42	.01	[a]	.42
Basic needs	.02	.05	.37	.02	.00	.39
Safety and security	.05	.13	.42	.04	.09	.42
Pleasure	(not asked)			(not asked)		
T_B^2 (R^2)	.10 (.16)			.10 (.15)		
Number of cases	653			589		

Dependent Variable: **Handgun Regulation**

	Connecticut			Arizona		
Variation of dependent variable	.42			.44		
Independent variables	t_B^2	B_o	Var.	t_B^2	B_o	Var.
Overall risks	−.16	−.20	.36	−.16	−.13	.40
Number of deaths	−.12	−.14	.36	−.11	−.09	.40
Risks understood	.00	[a]	.37	−.01	[a]	.38
Catastrophic potential	−.01	−.05	.40	−.03	−.04	.37
Dread	−.09	−.04	.41	−.19	−.20	.43
Overall benefits	.12	.11	.39	.15	.11	.42
Economic benefits	.04	.00	.40	.06	−.01	.41
Basic needs	.08	.04	.32	.09	.03	.37
Safety and security	.08	.05	.41	.10	.08	.43
Pleasure	.12	.13	.25	.15	.13	.36
T_B^2 (R^2)	.27 (.38)			.29 (.41)		
Number of cases	643			587		

Table 5.9 (continued)

	Connecticut			Arizona		
Dependent Variable: **Industrial Chemicals Regulation**						
Variation of dependent variable		.42			.42	
Independent variables	t_B^2	B_o	Var.	t_B^2	B_o	Var.
Overall risks	−.08	−.18	.39	−.06	−.13	.40
Number of deaths	−.04	−.05	.41	−.06	−.17	.41
Risks understood	−.01	−.04	.42	−.01	−.02	.42
Catastrophic potential	−.03	−.05	.42	−.03	−.04	.42
Dread	−.07	−.12	.42	−.03	−.04	.42
Overall benefits	.02	.03	.41	.03	.07	.41
Economic benefits	.01	.01	.40	.02	.02	.40
Basic needs	.02	.04	.42	.02	.03	.42
Safety and security	.01	.03	.42	.02	.02	.42
Pleasure	.02	.06	.41	.02	.03	.41
T_B^2 (R^2)		.13 (.20)			.12 (.18)	
Number of cases		646			576	

[a] Not included in the regression because zero-order correlation less than 0.01.
[b] Of electricity.

judgments about nuclear weapons regulation, and pleasure and satisfaction contributed some to their judgments about handgun regulations, it is apparent from the data in Table 5.9 that regulation, for the six technologies, two regions, and in the time period we studied, was primarily a function of overall risk, relative number of deaths, whether the risks were understood, the risk's catastrophic potential, and dread. All together, overall risks, overall benefits, number of deaths, and the three qualitative risk and four qualitative benefit variables accounted for a small to moderate proportion of the variation in regulation, with T_B^2 values ranging from 0.05 (for auto safety regulation in Arizona) to 0.29 (for handgun regulation in Arizona). The similarities between the relative magnitudes of the regression coefficients and the zero-order, t_B^2, correlation coefficients indicate, further, that the effects of each of these variables were essentially unconfounded by intercorrelations among the independent variables.

The Additional Effects of Attitudes, Beliefs, and Social Position

If no more than a third of the variations in our respondents' judgment concerning the acceptability of technology safety regulations can be attributed to variations in their perceptions of a technology's overall risks and benefits, the relative number of deaths that might be expected from it, and the several qualitative risk and benefit factors we investigated, what could account for the rest? We attempted to answer this question by including several attitude questions and sociodemographic items in our surveys (see Hypothesis 6), in particular: attitudes toward the environment, attitudes toward technology in general, cognitive risk orientation, political orientation (liberalism/conservatism), education, age, and gender (see Appendixes A and C for details).

As it turned out, most of these variables were not correlated with regulation at the 0.01 level of substantive significance we had established for the study. Those that were (i.e., with $t_B^2 \geq 0.01$) we added to the regressions reported in Table 5.9. Table 5.10 gives the results.

As with the various risk and benefits factors, the relative influence of these additional variables differed by technology and by geographic region. In addition to various aspects of risks and benefits, auto safety regulation in Connecticut, for example, turned out to be a function of attitude toward govenment support of energy technology, attitudes toward technology, political orientation, and gender, while the additional variables in the regression for Arizona were: attitude toward government support of energy technology, gender, and education. The additional variables raised the value of T_B^2 from 0.07 to 0.10 for Connecticut, and from 0.05 to 0.09 for Arizona.

The addition of attitude toward government support of energy technologies and political orientation in Connecticut, social class and education in Arizona, and attitudes toward technology and gender in both regions increased the variation of air safety regulation accounted for from 0.10 to 0.14 in Connecticut, and from 0.08 to 0.12 in Arizona. These and other independent variables raised the value of T_B^2 by comparable amounts for the other technologies in the two regions.

These attitudinal and sociodemographic variables contributed less to the regressions than overall risk, overall benefits, number of deaths, and the seven qualitative risk and benefit characteristics included in the regression reported in Table 5.9. Indeed, the additional variables increased the total variation in regulation accounted for by an average of only three percentage points.

The acceptability of technology safety regulations, then, would appear to be more a matter of the perceived risks and benefits of a technology (including qualitative factors) than respondents' sociodemographic positions or of their attitudes toward the environment or technology. This is in accord with the work of Renn (1981), which found that gender, age, social class, and political party affiliation had less influence on overall ratings of technologies (semantic differential and risk-benefit trade-off ratings) than did the properties of the technologies themselves (e.g., impacts on social

Table 5.10

Multiple Regression of Regulation, Risks, Benefits, Attitudes,
and Social Position for Six Technologies
(Connecticut and Arizona Combined Samples)

	Connecticut			Arizona		

Dependent Variable: Auto Safety Regulation

Independent variables	t_B^2	B_o	Var.	t_B^2	B_o	Var.
Variation of dependent variable		.43			.42	
Overall risks	−.04	−.11	.40	−.02	−.09	.40
Catastrophic potential	−.02	−.03	.41	−.00	a	.39
Dread	−.02	−.07	.39	−.02	−.08	.37
Number of deaths	−.03	−.12	.31	−.00	a	.35
Basic needs	−.00	a	.39	−.02	−.08	.38
Pleasure	−.00	a	.36	−.02	−.07	.36
Attitude toward government support of energy	−.02	−.08	.45	−.01	−.04	.45
Attitude toward technology	.01	.04	.46	.00	a	.46
Liberalism/conservatism	.02	.07	.40	.00	a	.40
Education	.00	a	.40	.01	.07	.40
Gender[b]	−.03	−.09	.25	−.05	−.17	.25
T_B^2 (R^2)		.10 (.15)			.09 (.12)	
Number of cases		652			590	

Dependent Variable: Regulation of Air Safety

Independent variables	t_B^2	B_o	Var.	t_B^2	B_o	Var.
Variation of dependent variable		.40			.38	
Overall risks	−.05	−.06	.41	−.05	−.12	.40
Number of deaths	−.05	−.05	.41	−.04	−.06	.41
Risks understood	−.02	−.08	.40	−.01	−.04	.38
Catastrophic potential	−.01	−.03	.36	−.02	−.07	.38
Dread	−.06	−.15	.41	−.02	−.03	.39
Attitude toward government support of energy	−.02	−.01	.45	−.00	a	.45
Attitude toward technology	.02	.06	.46	.03	.11	.46
Social class	.00	a	.27	.02	.06	.27
Liberalism/conservatism	.02	.10	.40	.02	a	.40
Education	.00	a	.40	.02	.05	.40
Gender[b]	−.05	−.14	.25	−.05	−.13	.25
T_B^2 (R^2)		.14 (.19)			.12 (.17)	
Number of cases		640			582	

Table 5.10 (continued)

	Connecticut			Arizona		

Dependent Variable: Nuclear Power Regulation

	t_B^2	B_o	Var.	t_B^2	B_o	Var.
Variation of dependent variable		.42			.42	
Independent variables						
Overall risks	−.11	−.18	.41	−.12	−.21	.42
Number of deaths	−.04	−.03	.38	−.04	−.06	.38
Risks understood	−.02	−.06	.43	−.03	−.06	.43
Catastrophic potential	−.03	−.03	.42	−.02	−.02	.42
Dread	−.09	−.15	.43	−.07	−.06	.43
Attitude toward government support of energy	−.02	.00	.45	−.01	−.01	.45
Environmental attitudes (pastoralism)	−.01	−.05	.46	−.02	−.06	.46
Attitude toward technology	.06	.12	.46	.04	.07	.46
Social class	.00	a	.27	.01	.05	.27
Liberalism/conservatism	.03	.09	.40	.03	.12	.40
Gender[b]	−.02	−.00	.25	−.02	−.05	.25
T_B^2 (R^2)		.18 (.29)			.18 (.16)	
Number of cases		647			578	

Dependent Variable: Nuclear Weapons Regulation

	t_B^2	B_o	Var.	t_B^2	B_o	Var.
Variation of dependent variable		.42			.41	
Independent variables						
Overall risks	−.04	−.12	.27	−.06	−.14	.35
Number of deaths	−.02	−.06	.37	−.03	−.05	.37
Risks understood	−.00	a	.43	−.01	−.03	.43
Dread	−.03	−.09	.33	−.04	−.03	.39
Overall benefits	.04	.04	.42	.04	.08	.42
Basic needs	.02	.06	.37	.02	.01	.39
Safety and security	.05	.11	.42	.04	.07	.42
Attitude toward government support of energy	−.00	a	.45	−.02	−.06	.45
Attitude toward technology	.03	.06	.46	.04	.08	.46
Social class	.00	a	.27	.01	.05	.27
Liberalism/conservatism	.02	.08	.40	.00	a	.40
Gender[b]	−.03	−.12	.25	−.03	−.13	.25
T_B^2 (R^2)		.13 (.19)			.13 (.18)	
Number of cases		653			589	

93

Table 5.10 (continued)

	Connecticut			Arizona		

Dependent Variable: **Regulation of Handguns**

	t_B^2	B_o	Var.	t_B^2	B_o	Var.
Variation of dependent variable		.42			.44	
Independent variables						
Overall risks	−.16	−.19	.36	−.16	−.13	.40
Number of deaths	−.12	−.15	.36	−.11	−.08	.40
Catastrophic potential	−.01	−.04	.40	−.03	−.02	.37
Dread	−.09	−.03	.41	−.19	−.18	.43
Overall benefits	.12	.12	.39	.15	.10	.42
Economic benefits	.04	.00	.40	.06	.00	.41
Basic needs	.08	.05	.32	.09	.03	.37
Safety and security	.08	.04	.41	.10	.07	.43
Pleasure	.12	.12	.25	.15	.11	.36
Cognitive risk orientation	.00	[a]	.46	.01	.06	.46
Environmental attitudes (urbanism)	−.00	[a]	.47	−.02	−.06	.47
Attitude toward technology	.00	[a]	.46	.02	.04	.46
Liberalism/conservatism	.00	[a]	.40	.03	.05	.40
Age	−.02	−.09	.36	−.00	[a]	.36
Gender[b]	−.02	−.05	.25	−.04	−.05	.25
T_B^2 (R^2)		.28 (.39)			.30 (.43)	
Number of cases		643			587	

Dependent Variable: **Regulation of Industrial Chemicals**

	t_B^2	B_o	Var.	t_B^2	B_o	Var.
Variation of dependent variable		.42			.42	
Independent variables						
Overall risks	−.08	−.16	.39	−.06	−.10	.40
Number of deaths	−.04	−.02	.41	−.06	−.15	.41
Risks understood	−.01	−.05	.42	−.01	−.01	.42
Catastrophic potential	−.03	−.04	.42	−.03	−.03	.42
Dread	−.07	−.11	.42	−.03	−.02	.42
Overall benefits	.02	.00	.41	.03	.06	.41
Economic benefits	.01	.01	.40	.02	.02	.40
Basic needs	.02	.02	.42	.02	.01	.42
Safety and security	.01	.02	.42	.02	.02	.42
Pleasure	.02	.06	.41	.02	.03	.41
Attitude toward government support	−.02	−.05	.45	−.00	[a]	.45
Environmental attitudes (pastoralism)	−.00	[a]	.46	−.02	−.09	.46
Attitude toward technology	.03	.05	.46	.03	.06	.46
Liberalism/conservatism	.02	.05	.40	.02	.08	.40
Gender[b]	−.03	−.09	.25	−.02	−.05	.25
T_B^2 (R^2)		.15 (.22)			.14 (.22)	
Number of cases		646			576	

[a] Not in the regression because zero-order correlation less than 0.01.
[b] Male = 1; female = 2.

justice, the environment, quality of life, and democratic rights); and the work of Buss and Craik (1983), which found that respondents' general "worldviews" (overarching attitudes toward economic growth, technological advancement, free enterprise, and material wealth) had only a modest impact on their perceptions of technological risks; and the work of Harding and Eiser (1984), which found that personal characteristics such as age and gender had relatively less influence on perceived risks than did several qualitative characteristics.

Summary

In general, then, we found that variations in the acceptability of current technology safety standards among Connecticut and Arizona residents were more a function of perceived risks than of perceived benefits. Although overall perceptions of benefits, and certain qualitative benefit characteristics, played a small role in explaining these variations, most of the variation for most technologies was explained by the five variables: overall risk, relative number of deaths, risks understood, dread, and catastrophic potential.

It should not be concluded from this, however, as some might be inclined to do, that Americans are concerned only about the risks of technologies while they ignore their benefits. Most of the respondents in our surveys rated rather highly the benefits of most of the six technologies we studied. The trouble was that so many rated the benefits of some of these technologies (in particular, auto travel, air travel, and electric power) so highly that their benefit ratings became essentially irrelevant in predicting their judgments about technology safety regulation. Since their perceptions of benefit were already very high, in other words, people had nothing else on which to base their judgments about safety regulations except their perceptions of risk.

It is also noteworthy that people's attitudes toward risk in general, their attitudes toward technology, and their attitudes toward the environment played only a very small and inconsistent role in determining their judgments about the acceptability of current safety regulations. The same was true of age, gender, socioeconomic class, income, education, religion, political persuasion, and exposure to the media. Although the absence of correlations in these cases is consistent with prior research in the technology risk field, it is nevertheless somewhat puzzling; one would have expected something as important, topical, and seemingly controversial as industrial safety regulations to have been much more strongly related to traditional ideological and social divisions than we found in our study.

Indeed, one of the more interesting findings of our research is the surprising similarity of views on risks, benefits, and regulation among the members of our four samples. Although our pro-benefits intervenors universally rated current safety standards as being more acceptable than did any of the other three groups, they, along with everyone else, felt that the standards should be more stringent than they were at the time of our interviews. In addition, although pro-benefits intervenors also rated the risks of the technologies we studied lower than did pro-safety intervenors, they did not consistently rate the benefits higher, nor, in general, were the median risk and benefits ratings of the two intervenor groups nearly as different from the median ratings made by members of the general public as one might have expected. And finally, except for handgun regulation, which has traditionally been a regional issue in the United States, there were few differences between the general public samples from Connecticut and Arizona when it came to perceptions of risks or benefits or the acceptability of current industrial safety standards. Although our samples are regional in nature, the differences between these two very different regions of the country are so small that one can only suspect that members of the lay public in the United States in general probably do not differ much when it comes to views on technology.

This does not mean, however, that members of the lay public view the risks of technology the same as do technical experts. They evidently do not. Unlike technologists, who view technological risks in terms of the risks of injury or death, members of the general public, at least to the extent that our general population samples are representative of the public at large, place equal importance on such qualitative factors as dread, whether the risks are understood, and the potential for catastrophic deaths.

NOTES

1. Since public hearing records in Arizona were seldom complete enough for us to determine whether intervenors in that state were pro-safety or pro-benefits, we had to include some intervenors in our final sample whose pro-safety or pro-benefits orientations were unknown. These intervenors have not been included in the intervenor data included in Tables 5.1 to 5.3.

2. The comparable values using the more conventional (unsquared) t_B coefficient would be -0.10 and 0.51. Like the more conventional r, as opposed to r^2, however, t_B does not have a "variation-accounted-for" interpretation, like t_B^2 has.

6

Intervenors, Technology, Nuclear Power, and Salience

Chapter 5 reported on various aspects of Connecticut and Arizona residents' perceptions of technological risk and benefits and their ideas about technology safety regulation. Chapter 6 extends this analysis in four ways. First, it further explores the views of pro-safety and pro-benefits intervenors, separate from members of the general public. Second, it examines whether the attitudes of individual respondents toward technology are the same or different for different technologies. Third, it considers the possibility of going beyond the relatively simple notion of "acceptability of current safety regulations," used in previous research and presented in Chapter 5 of this volume, by examining respondents' answers to several additional questions about the deployment and operation of nuclear power plants. And fourth, it examines how salient the issue of technological risk was to our respondents and whether the findings reported in Chapter 5 might have been affected by this factor.

Views of Pro-Safety and Pro-Benefits Intervenors on Technological Risks, Benefits, and Regulation

We chose our pro-safety and pro-benefits intervenor samples from among people in Connecticut and Arizona who had given testimony at state or federal hearings. These hearings usually concerned nuclear plant siting or air or water quality. It seemed most relevant, therefore, to analyze further our intervenor samples' views on nuclear power and industrial chemicals, the two technologies in our survey most likely to have been involved in the hearings at which they testified.

Table 6.1 shows the correlations, for pro-benefits and pro-safety intervenors from the two study regions, between overall perceived risk of nuclear power and industrial chemicals, and number of deaths, risks understood, catastrophic potential, and dread. Table 6.2 shows the correla-

Table 6.1

Correlates (t_B^2) of Overall Perceived Risks and Benefits of Nuclear Power and Industrial Chemicals—Intervenor Samples

Dependent variable	Overall Risks of Nuclear Power		Overall Risks of Industrial Chemicals	
Intervenor sample	Pro-Safety	Pro-Benefits	Pro-Safety	Pro-Benefits
Independent variables				
Number of deaths	.14	.12	.28	.13
Risks understood	.03	.08	.02	.12
Catastrophic potential	.14	.04	.15	.04
Dread	.34	.08	.26	.10
Number of cases	101	105	101	105

Dependent variable	Overall Benefits of Nuclear Power		Overall Benefits of Industrial Chemicals	
Intervenor sample	Pro-Safety	Pro-Benefits	Pro-Safety	Pro-Benefits
Independent variables				
Economic benefits	.42	.47	.29	.31
Basic needs	.24	.28	.23	.17
Safety and security	.06	.04	.10	.14
Pleasure and satisfaction	.17	.24	.06	.14
Number of cases	101	105	101	105

Table 6.2

Correlates (t_B^2) of Acceptability of Current Regulations of Nuclear Power and Industrial Chemicals—Intervenor Samples

Dependent variable	Regulation of Nuclear Power		Regulation of Industrial Chemicals	
Intervenor sample	Pro-Safety	Pro-Benefits	Pro-Safety	Pro-Benefits
Independent variables				
Overall risks	−.26	−.22	−.09	−.11
Number of deaths	−.17	−.11	−.04	−.06
Risks understood	−.02	−.09	−.03	−.05
Catastrophic potential	−.17	−.01	−.04	−.06
Dread	−.27	−.07	−.06	−.10
Overall benefits	.00	.01	.02	.03
Economic benefits	.02	.03	.04	.04
Basic needs	.03	.02	.03	.05
Safety and security	.04	.00	.02	.05
Pleasure and satisfaction	.04	.01	.04	.07

tions, for the same respondents, between regulation of nuclear power and of industrial chemicals and the various risk and benefit variables listed in Table 6.1. Since there were only 101 pro-safety and 105 pro-benefits intervenors, multiple regression analyses of these data were not appropriate.[1]

The data in Table 6.1 suggest clear differences between the two intervenor samples in terms of qualitative characteristics emphasized when rating the risks of nuclear power. For pro-safety intervenors, overall risk of nuclear power was most strongly associated with dread and, to a lesser extent, with catastrophic potential and number of deaths. This pattern of correlations is similar to the pattern produced by the total population samples (Table 5.4). In contrast, overall risk of nuclear power for pro-benefits intervenors was most strongly associated with number of deaths, and was associated to a lesser extent with dread and with risks understood. This argues that pro-benefits intervenors, compared to pro-safety intervenors, define "risk" in a manner more like that of scientists and engineers, as discussed in Chapter 3, and less like that of the general public.

Although the patterns are not quite as distinct, the results for industrial chemicals were generally similar to those for nuclear power. The t_B^2 values for overall risk indicate that pro-safety intervenors placed somewhat greater emphasis on catastrophic potential and on dread than did pro-benefits intervenors, while pro-benefits intervenors placed greater emphasis on knowledge to science.

In contrast to the results for overall risks, the patterns of correlations for pro-safety and pro-benefits intervenors were quite similar for the overall benefits of nuclear power (or more precisely, the overall benefits of "electricity"). Both groups emphasized economic benefits and, to a lesser extent, basic needs and pleasure and satisfaction in their overall benefits ratings. The t_B^2 values for the overall benefits of industrial chemicals were similar for the two groups, although the pro-safety intervenors appear to have placed slightly greater emphasis on basic needs and slightly less emphasis on safety and security and pleasure and satisfaction. Overall, the results for industrial chemicals were different from those for nuclear power in that pleasure and satisfaction was less important in defining the overall benefits of industrial chemicals for both types of intervenors than it was for the overall benefits of nuclear power.

Table 6.2 shows t_B^2 values for correlations between nuclear power and industrial chemical regulation and the various aspects of risk and benefits discussed above. As was the case for overall risks, the pattern of correlations was quite different for the two types of intervenors. Although members of both groups appear to have considered overall risks and number of deaths when judging the acceptability of current nuclear-power safety regulations, pro-safety intervenors placed significantly greater emphasis on dread and on catastrophic potential than did pro-benefit intervenors, while the latter placed greater emphasis on knowledge to science. In the case of industrial chemicals regulation, pro-benefits intervenors appeared to have placed relatively greater emphasis on number of deaths and dread in their ratings.

These results suggest, then, that pro-benefits intervenors, probably like technical experts in general, define technological "risks" and "benefits" differently from pro-safety intervenors and from the general public. Similar differences appear to occur in definitions of the "acceptability" of safety regulations, and may well be one source of the miscommunication and controversy over the management of technological risk that have disrupted many public hearings on technological issues in recent years. These conclusions are similar to those reached by Otway and Fishbein (1977) and by Slovic, Fischhoff, and Lichtenstein (1981), as discussed in Chapter 3.

Differences in Attitudes Toward Different Technologies

Mazur has argued that:

The public cannot be regarded [as] an amorphous mass society which gives the same undifferentiated response to every technological innovation. . . . To the contrary, the public's response to each technology is highly specific. It seems likely that this [response] is a reaction to particular features of the technology . . . rather than to some generalized image of technological change. [1981: 51]

In support of this hypothesis, Mazur noted that there has not been a consistent relationship in national public opinion polls between demographic variables and the degree of expressed opposition to water fluoridation, nuclear power plants, and anti-ballistic missiles. Those respondents who were most opposed to these technologies were not always of the same age, level of education, or gender. Older respondents, for example, were particularly opposed to water fluoridation but not to the other two technologies, and women were particularly opposed to nuclear power but not to the other technologies.

The data from our study follow a similar pattern. No sociodemographic or attitudinal variable was strongly and consistently associated with regulation across all six technologies and two regions (see Table 5.10). Those respondents, in other words, who wanted the greatest increases in the regulatory strictness were not consistently of the same age, gender, level of education, or degree of liberalism/conservatism, nor did they have the same attitudes toward the environment or technology in general. Indeed, only in one case did a single demographic variable— gender—show a consistently strong degree of association with regulation for even three technologies: nuclear weapons, auto safety, and air safety.

Additional support for the hypothesis that people differ in their views about the safety of different technologies comes from the pattern of intercorrelations among regulation ratings for the six different technologies. Table 6.3 shows these intercorrelations (t_B^2) based on data from all respondents (i.e., from the general population and intervenor samples from both regions). The correlations are relatively modest, ranging from 0.04 to 0.17, averaging 0.08. A reliability analysis of these intercorrelations (Appendix C) yields a standardized-item alpha reliability score of 0.69.

Table 6.3
Intercorrelations (t_B^2) Between Regulation Ratings for Six Technologies

Technology	1	2	3	4	5	6
1. Nuclear power	—					
2. Nuclear weapons	.14	—				
3. Auto travel	.07	.06	—			
4. Handguns	.04	.03	.09	—		
5. Industrial chemicals	.17	.12	.07	.04	—	
6. Air travel	.08	.08	.08	.04	.07	—

And finally, it should be remembered that those qualitative risk and benefit characteristics that were most strongly associated with overall risk and regulation (Tables 5.5, 5.8, and 5.10) varied significantly from technology to technology, suggesting that the specific properties that people most emphasize in their risk and acceptability judgments depend on the technology they are evaluating. Several aspects of our data, therefore, support Mazur's contention that members of the general public react to the risks and benefits of specific technologies rather than to risks and benefits in general.

Deploying and Managing Nuclear Power

Although the index "regulation," derived by subtracting "desired regulatory strictness" from "current strictness," probably represents an improvement over earlier measures of the acceptability of current technology safety regulations, it is nonetheless unidimensional and fairly abstract. The questions, "How strict do you think the restrictions and standards are *now* on nuclear electric power," and "How strict do you think the standards on nuclear electric power *should be*," overlook much of the subtlety and complexity of the real-world issues concerning a technology like nuclear power, ranging from the citing of individual power plants to developing a coherent national strategy for managing radioactive waste. People's attitudes toward one controversial aspect of a technology, in other words, may not correlate highly with their attitudes toward other controversial aspects of the technology.

Therefore, we included in our survey at least one additional acceptability question for each technology we studied, and, in the case of nuclear power, several additional questions. The rest of this section focuses on seven of these items pertaining to nuclear or alternative forms of electric power.

Deployment of New Power Plants. The first additional item was suggested by our pre-test data (Gardner et al., 1982), which indicated that people's opinions about regulatory strictness and level of deployment are not always highly correlated. Not an insignificant number of people, for example, favored increasing the strictness of nuclear power safety standards *and* building more nuclear power plants. To assess respondents' attitudes toward deploying new nuclear-electric power plants, we included Question 33, asking respondents if they favored: (1) building more nuclear power plants as more electricity is needed, (2) a freeze on new construction until more is known about safety risks, or (3) closing existing plants.

Table 6.4
Attitudes Toward Nuclear Power Plant Deployment

Sample	General Population		Advocates	
	Connecticut	Arizona	Pro-Safety	Pro-Benefits
Shut all plants	10%	13%	17%	3%
No new plants	66	56	57	36
Build more plants	24	31	26	61
Total	100%	100%	100%	100%
Number of cases	541	478	103	107

Table 6.4 shows the percentages of each sample that chose each alternative. The majority of the general population respondents and pro-safety advocates chose the second alternative—build no new plants for the time being—and only a small percentage of all three groups favored closing existing plants (alternative 3). Only pro-benefits intervenors, as a group, were in favor of building new plants now.

Who Should Operate Nuclear Power Plants? Another issue is the question of who should operate nuclear power plants. We included two items (Question 23) on this subject which asked respondents how much they agreed with the statements: "The profit motive of private companies makes it difficult for the safe operation of nuclear electric power plants," and "Nuclear electric power plants should be operated by the government, rather than by private industry." Table 6.5 lists the percentages of each sample that agreed with, disagreed with, were neutral toward, or were not sure about these two statements.

Approximately half of the general population respondents, in both regions, as well as of pro-safety intervenors, agreed that the "profit motive" interferes with plant safety, while only 18 percent of the pro-benefits intervenors took this position. In contrast, almost half of the general population sample respondents, in both regions, disagreed with the statement that the "government should operate nuclear plants," as did even larger percentages of pro-safety (57 percent) and pro-benefits (86 percent) intervenors. Thus, despite their concern about the incompatibility of the profit motive and safe plant operation, only a minority of respondents indicated that they would prefer that the government operate nuclear power plants.

Government Support. Another two items assessed attitudes toward solar energy—a potential alternative to nuclear power. These items (Question 36) asked respondents to indicate the preferred level of govern-

Table 6.5
Operation of Nuclear Power Plants

Sample	General Population		Advocates	
	Connecticut	Arizona	Pro-Safety	Pro-Benefits
Item: Profit motive makes safe operation difficult.				
Strongly agree or agree	46%	47	54%	18%
Neutral or unsure	23	26	7	10
Disagree or strongly disagree	31	27	39	72
Total	100%	100%	100%	100%
Number of cases	541	478	104	108
Item: Government should operate nuclear plants.				
Strongly agree or agree	33%	32%	18%	10%
Neutral or unsure	19	20	24	4
Disagree or strongly disagree	48	48	58	86
Total	100%	100%	100%	100%
Number of cases	539	476	103	108

ment funding for solar energy research and development and for installing and operating solar energy devices. Two other items assessed attitudes toward government funding for nuclear power research and development and for installing and operating nuclear power plants. Table 6.6 shows response percentages for these items.

While only a little over a third of the general population respondents favored a high level of government funding for nuclear power research, well over half favored such funding for research on solar energy. Although general population respondents in general were not enthusiastic about government funding for the installation and operation of power-generating equipment of any type, slightly more were in favor of such funding for solar power than for nuclear power.

Percentages of pro-safety and pro-benefits intervenors that favored government funding of nuclear power research and plant operation were much more similar to each other than they were to response patterns of the general population samples; intervenors, for the most part, did not favor government funding. In the case of solar power, however, the intervenor groups differed sharply from each other; fewer pro-benefits than pro-safety intervenors favored government support. In general, the responses of pro-safety intervenors were more like the responses of the general population samples than were the responses of pro-benefits intervenors.

Table 6.6
Support for Government Involvement in Solar and Nuclear Energy

Sample	General Population		Advocates	
	Connecticut	Arizona	Pro-Safety	Pro-Benefits
Item: Government should fund nuclear power research.				
Little (1 to 3)	37%	42%	64%	50%
4 or unsure	25	23	16	26
Much (5 to 7)	38	35	20	24
Total	100%	100%	100%	100%
Number of cases	541	478	104	108
Item: Government should fund the operation of nuclear plants.				
Little (1 to 3)	50%	50%	82%	82%
4 or unsure	19	23	7	7
Much (5 to 7)	31	27	11	11
Total	100%	100%	100%	100%
Number of cases	541	478	104	108
Item: Government should fund solar power research.				
Little (1 to 3)	16%	25%	17%	35%
4 or unsure	18	19	10	16
Much (5 to 7)	66	56	73	49
Total	100%	100%	100%	100%
Number of cases	541	478	104	108
Item: Government should fund the operation of solar power.				
Little (1 to 3)	38%	42%	46%	71%
4 or unsure	20	21	18	14
Much (5 to 7)	42	37	36	15
Total	100%	100%	100%	100%
Number of cases	541	478	104	108

The results reported in Table 6.6 are consistent with a common finding in public opinion polls concerning energy (e.g., Marsh and Mc-Lennan, 1980): When given alternatives to choose from, the general public consistently prefers a national commitment to non-nuclear forms of elecric power (e.g., solar, coal, and conservation) rather than to nuclear energy. Thus, as Fischhoff et al. (1981) and others have pointed out, the alternatives considered and the definition of "the problem" can significantly affect the outcome of efforts to assess the acceptability of a technology.

Table 6.7
Intercorrelations (t_B^2) *Between Acceptability Items for Nuclear Power*

Item	1	2	3	4	5	6	7
1. Regulation	—						
2. Deployment	.14	—					
3. Profit motive	−.10	−.09	—				
4. Government operate	−.04	−.06	.09	—			
5. Nuclear power research	.00	.00	.00	.03	—		
6. Nuclear power operation	−.00	−.01	.02	.13	.33	—	
7. Solar research	−.04	−.04	.04	.04	.07	.07	—
8. Solar operation	−.02	−.07	.04	.08	.06	.16	.29

Consistency of Views. Table 6.7 shows the intercorrelations (t_B^2) between the seven additional "regulation" items for nuclear power discussed above and the general index of "regulation" used in the analyses reported in Chapter 5. These values were calculated using data from all respondents (both samples in both regions). Generally speaking, the values are quite modest. This, of course, is what would be expected if, as we have argued, these items tap different policy issues concerning nuclear power which are not perfectly correlated in everyone's minds.

Further evidence of the multidimensionality of the acceptability of nuclear power regulation comes from multiple cross-tabulations of several "regulation" items. This analysis shows, for example, that of those respondents who favored building additional nuclear plants (419 respondents out of a total of 1,314), one-fifth (22 percent) also favored large increases in the strictness of nuclear power regulation (increases of three or more units out of a possible six on the response scale). In addition, 17 percent of those respondents who favored more nuclear power plants also thought that the government should operate them. A three-way cross-tabulation showed that, of those respondents who favored building more nuclear plants, 33 percent favored considerable increases in the strictness of regulation and/or government operation of such plants. Thus, many of the respondents who favored building more plants appear to have done so on the condition that the plants be more stringently regulated and/or operated by the government. Finally, even among those respondents who favored building more nuclear plants, half (49 percent) also favored a high degree of government support for research and development of solar energy (checking response scores 5 through 7 on a 1 to 7 scale).[2]

The "level of deployment" question in our survey is similar to a question concerning nuclear power often asked in national public opinion polls (e.g., Mitchell, 1980). Our analysis would indicate that responses to a single question of this type are likely to yield misleading answers. Opinions on an inherently multidimensional issue, like the regulation of nuclear power, cannot be properly assessed with a single unidimensional question. As Mitchell (1980: 7) has noted, the level of opposition or support for nuclear power indicated in public opinion polls "can be made to shift 40 percentage points, just by varying the assurance of safety [provided in question wording]." It would appear, then, that proper assessment of attitudes toward a technology and its "acceptability" requires the use of several questions that allow respondents to express both the complexity and the specificity of their opinions on the subject.

Salience of Technological Risk

Both the zero-order and multiple correlations reported in the preceding chapter are considerably lower than similar correlations reported by earlier expressed-preference researchers. Although this is due in part to the fact that several of these earlier studies reported correlations on aggregate, rather than individual-level, data, and to a lesser extent to the fact that t_B^2 values tend to be lower than r^2 values for comparable data, it may also be due to the fact that many members of the general public simply may not have thought through their positions on the subjects we asked as thoroughly as the more highly selected subjects in prior studies. As Fischhoff et al. (1981), among several others, have noted, many respondents in public opinion polls or expressed-preference research may have no opinion at all on a technology, or one that is only vague or poorly thought-out, but will respond to questions about it anyway, even though "don't know" responses alternatives are available to them and they are encouraged to use them if they are not sure of their answers.

Therefore, we included a measure of *salience* in our survey, that is, a measure of the degree to which respondents had well-thought-out opinions about the risks, benefits, and regulation of the six technologies in our study. This measure, which its developers, Yankelovich, Skelly, and White (Keene and Sackett, 1981), prefer to call "mushiness," was derived from answers to three questions: How often had the respondent discussed safety issues with friends and family (Question 39)?; How firm was their position on these issues (Question 40)?; and How personally involved were they in the issues (Question 41)? (Appendix C gives further details of the "mushiness" scale we used.)

To analyze the effects of salience on the results reported in Chapter 5, we computed the correlations between regulation and each risk and benefit factor for each technology, within three categories of respondents:

Table 6.8
*Correlations (t_B^2) Between Regulation of Nuclear Power and Risk
and Benefit Factors, Controlling for Salience
(New England Combined Sample)*

Dependent variable: Nuclear power regulation			
Salience	Low	Medium	High
Independent variables			
Overall risks	−.06	−.07	−.15
Risks understood	−.01	−.01	−.04
Catastrophic potential	−.00	−.01	−.10
Dread	−.02	−.05	−.22
Number of deaths	−.00	−.04	−.09
Overall benefits	−.00	−.00	.01
Economic benefits	−.00	.00	.00
Basic needs	−.01	.00	.02
Safety and security	−.00	.00	.02
Pleasure and satisfaction	−.00	.00	.01
Number of cases	219	266	200

those with high, medium, and low salience scores for that particular technology.[3] Table 6.8 shows the results of this analysis for the regulation of nuclear power for the Connecticut combined sample. (The results for the other five technologies and for the Sunbelt respondents were very similar to the results shown in Table 6.8 and thus are not included here.)

Table 6.8 shows that the strength of association between regulation and the various risk and benefit factors was a function of salience; in particular, as salience increased, so did the strength of the associations. This means that the low correlations reported in Chapter 5 may well have been due in part to respondents giving less than coherent answers to questions that they had thought little about. Indeed, Table 6.8 would suggest that most people's attitudes toward nuclear power regulation are, to the extent that they are a function of anything we measured, a function of their perceptions of overall risk and, to a very small extent, of dread. For those who have thought about nuclear power more carefully, overall risks and dread play a larger role and are augmented by the variables number of deaths, risks understood, and catastrophic potential.

Table 6.9 shows the degree of intercorrelation (t_B^2) between salience scores for the six different technologies. (The values are based on data from all respondents in the study.) The results indicate that respondents did not just range from the uninformed to the well-informed in general,

Table 6.9
Intercorrelations (t_B^2) *Between "Mushiness" Ratings for Six Technologies*
(All Samples Combined)

Technology	1	2	3	4	5	6
1. Nuclear power	—					
2. Nuclear weapons	.43	—				
3. Auto travel	.07	.08	—			
4. Handguns	.10	.17	.16	—		
5. Industrial chemicals	.37	.40	.09	.08	—	
6. Air travel	.12	.10	.28	.15	.08	—

but rather that they were better informed on some technologies than on others. Interestingly, what appear to be two salience clusters emerged, one involving air and auto travel, and the other nuclear power, nuclear weapons, and industrial chemicals.

It is reasonable to conclude, then, that salience is more of an issue in studies of randomly selected members of the general public, like the one we have reported, than it is in small, laboratory-type studies of small groups of well-informed and concerned respondents such as college students, members of the League of Women Voters, or members of chambers-of-commerce, like much of the early expressed-preference research. "Noise" added to the data by respondents who lack coherent opinions, however, is not just a price that must be paid for studying a representative sample of the general public but a recognition that results found in the laboratory seldom hold as strongly in the real world. Studying general population samples, in other words, may not produce correlations that are as impressive as those found in the laboratory, but they are nonetheless probably much more realistic.

Notes

1. The general rule for regression analysis is that there should be at least 30 cases for each independent variable in the equation. Not being able to compute multiple regressions may not be a great loss in this case, however, as the relative sizes of zero-order correlations for the general population samples, reported in Chapter 5, differed little from the relative sizes of the standardized regression coefficients and might, therefore, be expected to indicate the relative importance of each independent variable for the intervenor samples as well.

2. It might be argued that the apparent contradictions in these responses indicate nothing more than general ignorance or lack of interest on the part of our respondents. To test this possibility, we reanalyzed the data reported here (using the Connecticut combined sample), eliminating those respondents for whom nuclear power was of little salience. (Salience is discussed in the next section of this chapter.) The results were quite similar to those reported here. We conclude, therefore, that the cross-tabulation results reported here are not simply a matter of ignorance or lack of interest.

3. Since there was considerable statistical interaction between salience and the other variables in the study, as Table 6.8 shows, we could not include salience as an independent variable in the multiple regressions reported in Chapter 5.

7

Taking Action

People's views about the risks and benefits of technologies, and the safety standards that should apply to them, would be of little policy relevance unless they acted on these views at public meetings and in the voting booth. Indeed, Starr (1969, 1972) and other revealed-preference risk researchers presumed that it is just such actions that translate public sentiments about appropriate risk-benefit trade-offs into acceptable public policy.

Therefore, to assess the relationship between action and other aspects of our study, we asked respondents whether they had ever done any of ten specific things to express their "views on the restrictions and standards that apply to": the safety of automobile travel, handguns, nuclear power, commercial air travel, nuclear weapons, or transporting and disposing of industrial chemicals (Questions 9 through 14). The specific actions included: (1) writing a letter, telephoning, or sending a telegram to an editor, public official, or company; (2) signing a petition; (3) circulating a petition; (4) voting for or against a candidate for public office in part because of his or her position on the particular issue; (5) attending a public hearing or a meeting of a special interest organization; (6) speaking at a public hearing or forum; (7) boycotting a company; (8) joining or contributing money to an organization; (9) attending a public demonstration; (10) participating in a lawsuit.

Signing petitions, sending letters, and voting were the most common forms of action; circulating petitions, boycotting companies, and participating in lawsuits the least common. (Tables C.1 through C.6 in Appendix C provide details.) In Connecticut, actions pertaining to handguns were the most common (26 percent of the general public reported that they had engaged in at least one kind of action related to handguns), while in Arizona actions related to nuclear power were the most numerous (23 percent of the general public reported that they had taken at least one action concerning this technology). Air travel elicited the fewest intervenor-type actions in both regions. In general, Connecticut residents were somewhat more "active" with respect to technology safety than people living in Arizona, although the differences between regions were small and were statistically significant only for air travel ($p < .01$), industrial chemicals ($p < .01$), and handguns ($p < .05$).

But action can be directed at either the safety or the benefits of a technology, and our "action" questions did not distinguish which. To determine, therefore, whether the actions were likely to have been pro-safety or pro-benefits, we looked to Questions 30 to 35, which indicated whether the respondents' positions were pro-safety or pro-benefits with respect to each technology. Using this information we were able to score each respondent's action responses as being either pro-safety or pro-benefits, and to construct a pro-benefits/pro-safety action score for each respondent for each technology. These scores ranged between $+10$ (for those who indicated that they had taken all ten kinds of action and were pro-safety) and -10 (for those who indicated that they had taken all ten kinds of action and were pro-benefits). A score of 0 indicated that no action had been taken.

With but one exception, pro-safety actions outnumbered pro-benefits actions. The one exception was nuclear weapons action in Arizona, where a slightly higher percentage of the general public indicated that they had taken pro-benefits actions than indicated that they had taken pro-safety actions (Table 7.1). Overall, however, respondents' actions were overwhelmingly pro-safety, with 36 percent of the Connecticut, and 23 percent of the Arizona, general public samples reporting pro-safety actions, as opposed to 7 and 10 percent, respectively, reporting pro-benefits actions.

Analyzing Action

Action Scales. Since the incidence of all kinds of action was relatively low, it was crucial for our analysis that we be able to combine the

Table 7.1
**Mean Action Scores for Connecticut and Arizona
General Population Samples[a]**

Technology	Action	Connecticut General Public	Arizona General Public
Automobile travel	Pro-safety	15%	13%
	Pro-benefits	3	5
	No action	82	82
	Total	100%	100%
	Mean	.21	.11
	Variance	.79	1.26
	Number of cases	540	477
Handguns	Pro-safety	21%*	13%*
	Pro-benefits	5	7
	None	74*	80*
	Total	100%	100%
	Mean	.20	.09
	Variance	.98	1.15
	Number of cases	541	478
Nuclear power	Pro-safety	19%	17%
	Pro-benefits	5	6
	None	76	77
	Total	100%	100%
	Mean	.28	.25
	Variance	1.06	1.72
	Number of cases	541	478
Air travel	Pro-safety	6%*	2%*
	Pro-benefits	0	0
	None	94*	98*
	Total	100%	100%
	Mean	.08*	.02*
	Variance	.12	.08
	Number of cases	540	477
Nuclear weapons	Pro-safety	13%*	8%*
	Pro-benefits	10	11
	None	77	81
	Total	100%	100%
	Mean	.10*	− .04*
	Variance	1.15	1.29
	Number of cases	540	476

Table 7.1 (continued)

Technology	Action	Connecticut General Public	Arizona General Public
Industrial chemicals	Pro-safety	17%*	9%*
	Pro-benefits	2	1
	None	81*	90*
	Total	100%	100%
	Mean	.26	.17
	Variance	.84	.63
	Number of cases	540	476
Any technology	Pro-safety	36%*	23%*
	Pro-benefits	7	10
	Both	12	11
	None	45*	56*
	Total	100%	100%
	Number of cases	537	473

[a] The action score is the sum of all pro-safety (+) and pro-benefits (−) actions over items A–J. A positive score indicated that a respondent's actions, on average, were pro-safety, a negative score that they were, on average, pro-benefits, and a score of 0 either that they were, on average, neutral, or that there had been no action.
*Difference between Connecticut and Arizona general population samples significant at $p < 0.01$.

different kinds of action into a single action scale. Some kinds of action, however, did not correlate very highly with other kinds. Therefore, we analyzed all action intercorrelations to determine which types of action were correlated most strongly with which other types, and combined those that were most highly intercorrelated into a single "action" scale for each technology. Appendix C describes the details of these scales and lists the different action items included in the final scales for each technology. Although these scales excluded some action items, they were much more unidimensional than the total action scale described above. The scales were constructed so that a positive action score still indicates pro-safety actions, a negative score pro-benefits actions, and a score of 0 no action at all.

Augmented Samples. Although larger percentages than we expected of the general population samples in both regions indicated that they had engaged in some kind of action, a majority of those interviewed indicated that they had not engaged in any action and it was rare for anyone to report having engaged in more than one or two types of action.

Table 7.2
Variation in Action for Connecticut and Arizona Samples[a]

	Connecticut		Arizona	
Action Related to	General Population	Combined	General Population	Combined
Automobile travel	.159	.184	.155	.170
Handguns	.162	.192	.126	.160
Nuclear electric power	.203	.247	.198	.250
Air travel	.038	.046	.019	.023
Nuclear weapons	.199	.225	.172	.201
Industrial chemicals	.162	.237	.103	192

[a] The variations reported in this table, based on ordinal scales with ranges between 13 and 19 points, have upper bounds ranging between 0.462 (for air travel) and 0.474 (for nuclear power).

This meant that the variations in action scores for the two general population samples were quite low for all technologies and extremely low for some. Since analyzing the determinants of action, statistically, involves an analysis of the variation in action, there was little to analyze in most cases. Therefore, we "augmented" the variation in action by adding the two special samples of intervenors, who had already demonstrated that they had taken some action, to the two general population samples. As expected, the combined samples, which include the general public and the intervenors, showed more variation in action than did the general population samples alone (Table 7.2). All subsequent analyses in this chapter are based on these combined samples.

It is also noteworthy that there were marked differences in the variations in action by region (Table 7.2). Connecticut residents registered the most variation in action for all technologies except nuclear power, which was just slightly more variable in Arizona than in Connecticut. Nuclear electric power showed the most action variation, in both Connecticut and Arizona, and air travel the least. (Indeed, the variation in action with respect to the safety of air travel was so low in both states, even using the combined samples, that the regression analyses we report are probably of dubious validity.)

Combining the special intervenor samples with the general population samples is not standard research practice, and some might question the procedure. It seemed to us, however, that we had little choice in the matter if we were to do any kind of meaningful analysis of action. The remainder of this chapter would seem to prove us correct in this judgment, as the correlations between action and the other variables in our study, even using the augmented samples, are for the most part very low. Had we used only the general population samples, they would have been even lower. The conclusion, therefore, that we were able to account for very little of the variation in action is made with the full understanding that even those few modest correlations that we do report are inflated to some degree by our unusual sample design, and that a simple general population sample probably would produce no correlations with action worth mentioning at all.

Zero-Order Correlates of Action

Although all correlations (t_B^2), except one, between regulation (whether people thought that current standards and restrictions on each technology should be increased or decreased) and action were greater than 0.01, and thus substantively significant by the standards we adopted for the study, none were very strong. The highest was 0.09, for nuclear power; the lowest was 0.005, for air travel (Table 7.3). Our respondents' views on the "acceptability of current technology safety regulations," then, were not a good guide to whether or not they tried to do anything to get their views translated into public policy.

Therefore, we examined the correlations between each other variable in our study and action to determine whether any of these other risks, benefits, attitudinal, or sociodemographic variables might help explain the propensity of people to intervene directly in the technology risk-management process. Table 7.3 lists all these zero-order (t_B^2) correlations involving action with respect to each technology that were 0.01 or greater—that is, all variables in the study that accounted for at least 1 percent of the variation in action for a given technology. The list is not particularly long, and except, perhaps, for nuclear power, the correlations that are reported are not very strong.

As might have been expected, given the very low variation in air travel action, only two variables, political orientation (liberalism/conservatism) and reading technology magazines (Question 26), correlated at all with this variable in Connecticut, and only organization membership correlated with it in Arizona. But only a few variables correlate with auto travel action, as well, and this cannot be attributed to a lack of variation in this dependent variable, as the variation in auto travel action was reasonably high. Of all the variables in our study, only regulation, pastoralism, organization membership, and experts' judgment (Question 29-D) correlated with auto travel action in the Connecticut sample with a t_B^2

Table 7.3

Action Regressions for Six Technologies
(Connecticut and Arizona Combined Samples)

	Connecticut			Arizona		
Dependent Variable: **Auto Travel Action**						
Independent variables	t_B^2	B_o	Var.	t_B^2	B_o	Var.
Regulation	.02	.13	.43	.01	.10	.42
Environmental attitudes (pastoralism)	.01	.09	.46	a	a	a
Organization membership	−.02	−.12	.41	a	a	a
Experts' judgments (Question 29-D)[b]	.01	.08	.25	.02	.13	.25
Confidence in environmental groups	a	a	a	.01	.01	.37
Mobility (Question 64)	a	a	a	−.01	−.12	.16
T_B^2		.05			.05	
Number of cases		675			622	
Dependent Variable: **Air Travel Action**						
Independent variables	t_B^2	B_o	Var.	t_B^2	B_o	Var.
Regulation	.01	.07	.40	.01	.08	.38
Liberalism/conservatism	−.01	−.10	.40	a	a	a
Read technology magazines (Question 26)[b]	.01	.13	.25	a	a	a
Organization membership	a	a	a	.01	.12	.39
T_B^2		.03			.02	
Number of cases		665			620	
Dependent Variable: **Nuclear Power Action**						
Independent variables	t_B^2	B_o	Var.	t_B^2	B_o	Var.
Regulation	.09	.13	.42	.09	.11	.42
Overall risks	.08	.07	.41	.08	.09	.42
Number of deaths	.02	−.08	.38	.03	−.01	.38
Risks understood	a	a	a	.03	−.02	.43
Catastrophic potential	.03	.03	.42	.03	.05	.42
Dread	.08	.11	.43	.05	.02	.43
Basic needs	−.01	−.07	.30	−.01	−.06	.31
Confidence in established institutions[b]	−.02	−.07	.46	−.02	−.09	.46
Confidence in environmental groups[b]	.08	.15	.37	.04	.11	.37
Environmental attitudes (pastoralism)	.02	.04	.46	.02	.05	46

Table 7.3 (continued)

	Connecticut			Arizona		

Dependent Variable: Nuclear Power Action *(continued)*

Independent variables *(continued)*						
Attitude toward technology	−.07	−.11	.46	−.06	−.09	.46
Attitude toward government support	a	a	a	.03	.07	.45
Liberalism/conservatism[b]	a	a	a	−.06	−.12	.40
Military experience (Question 67)[b]	−.02	−.04	.16	a	a	a
Gender[c]	.02	.04	.25	a	a	a
Age	a	a	a	−.01	−.02	.26
Profit motive (Question 23B)	.08	.09	.36	a	a	a
Government operation (Question 23C)	.01	−.06	.39	.02	.02	.39
T_B^2		.23			.21	
Number of cases		633			565	

Dependent Variable: Nuclear Weapons Action

Independent variables	t_B^2	B_o	Var.	t_B^2	B_o	Var.
Regulation	.04	.10	.42	.04	.09	.41
Overall risks	.02	.01	.27	.03	.06	.35
Number of deaths	a	a	a	.01	.03	.37
Dread	.04	.10	.33	.01	−.05	.39
Overall benefits	a	a	a	−.06	−.11	.42
Economic benefits	−.02	−.03	.42	−.02	−.02	.42
Basic needs	−.05	−.11	.37	−.03	−.05	.39
Safety and security	−.06	−.13	.42	−.04	−.03	.42
Confidence in established institutions[b]	−.02	−.09	.46	−.02	−.08	.46
Confidence in environmental groups[b]	.02	.05	.37	.02	.07	.37
Attitude toward technology	−.03	−.06	.46	−.03	−.07	.46
Liberalism/conservatism[b]	.05	.11	.40	−.09	−.23	.40
Military experience (Question 67)[b]	−.01	−.05	.16	a	a	a
T_B^2		.16			.17	
Number of cases		632			570	

Dependent Variable: Handgun Action

Independent variables	t_B^2	B_o	Var.	t_B^2	B_o	Var.
Regulation	.03	.06	.42	.06	.15	.44
Number of deaths	.01	.01	.36	.02	.03	.40
Overall risks	.01	.01	.36	.04	.07	.40
Overall benefits	−.04	−.03	.39	−.04	−.03	.42
Economic benefits	−.01	.04	.40	−.02	−.02	.41

Table 7.3 (continued)

	Connecticut			Arizona		

Dependent Variable: Handgun Action (continued)

Independent variables (continued)

Basic needs	−.05	−.09	.32	−.02	−.03	.37
Safety and security	−.05	−.11	.41	−.03	−.05	.43
Pleasure	−.03	.02	.25	−.04	−.04	.36
Environmental attitudes (urbanism)	.02	.05	.47	.01	.06	.47
Organization membership	−.02	−.08	.41	a	a	a
Liberalism/conservatism	.02	.09	.40	a	a	a
Education	.03	.07	.40	a	a	a
Social class (Question 53)	.03	.05	.27	a	a	a
Burglarized (Question 19)[b]	.02	.09	.20	a	a	a
Gun ownership (Question 21)[b]	−.02	−.07	.23	−.03	−.06	.25
T_B^2		.12			.09	
Number of cases		591			599	

Dependent Variable: Industrial Chemicals Action

Independent variables	t_B^2	B_o	Var.	t_B^2	B_o	Var.
Regulation	.03	.06	.42	.02	.07	.38
Overall risks	.02	.01	.39	.02	.07	.40
Number of deaths	.02	.03	.41	.01	.04	.41
Catastrophic potential	.01	.00	.42	a	a	a
Dread	.05	.13	.42	a	a	a
Safety and security	−.01	−.05	.42	a	a	a
Environmental attitudes (pastoralism)	.02	.07	.46	.01	.03	.46
Confidence in environmental groups[b]	.04	.12	.37	.02	.10	.37
Attitudes toward technology	−.02	−.05	.46	−.01	−.09	.46
Liberalism/conservatism	.01	.04	.40	a	a	a
Read technology magazines (Question 26)[b]	a	a	a	.02	.06	.25
Talks with experts (Question 29-D)	a	a	a	.02	.08	.25
Organization membership	a	a	a	−.02	−.09	.39
Education	a	a	a	.01	.06	.40
T_B^2		.09			.09	
Number of cases		631			572	

[a] Not in the regression.
[b] Sign reversed.
[c] Male = 1; female = 2.

119

value greater than 0.01, and only regulation, confidence in consumer groups, experts' judgments, and mobility (Question 64) were this highly correlated with auto travel action in the Arizona sample.

Overall, nuclear power action was associated the most strongly with other variables in the study. In addition to regulation, nuclear power action was correlated significantly with overall risks, in both Connecticut and Arizona, and with three of the four qualitative risk factors in Connecticut and with all four risk factors in Arizona. Nuclear power action was not, however, correlated significantly with overall benefits in either sample, although it did correlate significantly with basic needs in both samples. Confidence in established institutions, confidence in environmental and consumer groups, pastoralism, technology orientation, military experience, and Question 23-C (whether the government should operate nuclear power plants) were correlated significantly with nuclear power action in both states. Government orientation, political orientation, and age were correlated with nuclear power action in Arizona, but not in Connecticut; gender and Question 23-B (whether the profit motive makes it difficult to operate nuclear power plants safely) were correlated with nuclear power action in Connecticut, but not in Arizona.

Unlike nuclear power action, which was more strongly correlated with risk than with benefit factors, nuclear weapons action was correlated more evenly with both types of factors, although the correlations tended to be stronger for benefit factors. Economic benefits, basic needs, and safety and security correlated significantly with nuclear weapons action in both states, and overall benefits correlated significantly with nuclear weapons action in Arizona. Potential deaths correlated significantly with nuclear weapons action in Arizona, and overall risks and dread correlated significantly with nuclear weapons action in Arizona and Connecticut. In addition to the various risk and benefits variables, confidence in established institutions and in environmental and consumer groups, technology orientation, and political orientation correlated significantly with nuclear weapons action in both states, and military experience correlated significantly in Connecticut.

As with nuclear power, action with respect to industrial chemicals correlated more strongly with risk than with benefits factors. In Connecticut, overall risks, number of deaths, catastrophic potential, and dread correlated with chemical action, at $t_B^2 \geq 0.01$, as did overall risks and number of deaths in Arizona. No benefit factor correlated significantly in the Arizona sample and only safety and security correlated significantly in the Connecticut sample. Pastoralism, confidence in environmental and consumer groups, and technology orientation in Connecticut, and education, organization membership, talks with experts, and reading technology magazines (Question 26) in Arizona, correlated significantly.

Regulation, overall risk, number of deaths, overall benefits, economic benefits, basic needs, safety and security, pleasure and satisfaction, urbanism, and gun ownership correlated significantly with handgun action in both states. In addition, organization membership, political orientation, education, social class (Question 53), and whether or not the respondent had been burglarized (Question 19) correlated significantly among Connecticut respondents. The sign of this last correlation, however, was negative, meaning that people who had been burglarized were more likely to have taken pro-safety than pro-benefits actions. This is opposite to what we hypothesized. (All other correlations reported so far, although small, are at least in the direction hypothesized.)

Action Regressions

Table 7.3 also reports regressions of action for the six technologies and two regions. (As with the regressions reported in Chapters 5 and 6, these regressions are based on ordinal, rather than product-moment, statistics.) The two regressions involving nuclear power and the two involving nuclear weapons account for reasonable proportions of the variation in nuclear power and nuclear weapons action in the two regions. The multiple correlations (T_B^2) for nuclear power action in the Connecticut and Arizona combined samples were 0.23 and 0.21, respectively; they were 0.16 and 0.17 for nuclear weapons. For the other four technologies, however, T_B^2 values were quite low, ranging from 0.12 for handgun action in Connecticut to 0.02 for air travel action in Arizona.

Except for nuclear power and nuclear weapons action, then, neither attitudes toward current technology safety regulations, risk and benefit factors, nor any other variable in our study accounted for very much of the variation in how much people intervened in the risk-benefit management process, and even in these two cases the proportion of variation explained is not great. For nuclear power action, regulation, overall risk, confidence in environmental and consumer groups, and attitudes toward technology played consistent roles in the regressions for both regions. For nuclear weapons action, only regulation, basic needs, and technology orientation had consistent zero-order correlations and regression coefficients with action in the two regions. The impact of all other variables, for both nuclear power action and nuclear weapons action was either very small, or inconsistent between regions.

Additional Analysis Using Activist Status

The analyses reported in Tables 7.1 and 7.3 treated intervention as a continuous variable, ranging from many pro-safety actions through no actions to many pro-benefits actions. It might be argued, however, that this conceptualization is inappropriate and that intervention should be treated as a nominal variable with the categories: pro-safety activists, pro-benefits activists, and non-activists. Intervention, in other words, might be not a quantitative behavioral dimension but rather a qualitative trait on which intervenors differ from non-intervenors, and pro-safety intervenors differ from pro-benefits intervenors.

Considering this possibility, we categorized each respondent as a pro-safety, pro-benefits, or non-intervenor for each technology. If the respondent had taken any pro-safety action at all, he or she was classified as a pro-safety activist; if the respondent had taken any pro-benefits action, she or he was classified as a pro-benefits activist; and the respondent was classified as non-activist if he or she had taken no action with respect to a given technology.

Since activist status, thus defined, is a nominal variable with more than two categories, t_B^2 is not an appropriate measure of association for measuring the correlation between this variable and other variables in the study. The most appropriate measure in this case is Goodman and Kruskal's t_b (1954), which measures association between two nominal variables (see Appendix D). We computed t_b correlations between activist status, for each technology, and all other variables in the study. As there were very few differences between regions, we combined all responses from both regions for presentation here. Table 7.4 summarizes the results of this analysis by listing all t_b correlations that were 0.01 or larger and were statistically significant, using a χ^2 test, at $p < .01$.

Although t_B^2 and t_b are different measures of association, and thus cannot be compared exactly, the patterns of results from the two types of analysis can be compared approximately. For auto and air travel, both forms of analysis yielded essentially the same results: Nothing much that we included in our survey correlated with either action or activist status, and what did correlate did not correlate very strongly. It is interesting to note, however, that the one variable that did correlate significantly with both activist status and action (in at least one region or the other) was organizational membership, a variable that correlated with the activist status of no other technology, and with action only in the cases of handguns in Connecticut and industrial chemicals in Arizona. This is somewhat surprising, as one might have expected activism on such controversial issues as nuclear power and nuclear weapons to be at least in part a

Table 7.4
Correlates (t_b) of Action Status[a] for Six Technologies

Technology	Auto Travel	Air Travel	Nuclear Power	Nuclear Weapons	Hand-guns	Industrial Chemicals
Independent Variables						
Regulation	.01	b	.03	b	.04	.02
Overall risk	b	b	.03	.02	.02	.02
Number of deaths	b	b	.02	.02	.02	.01
Risks understood	b	b	b	.02	.01	.01
Catastrophic potential	b	b	.02	.02	.02	b
Dread	b	b	.02	.03	.02	.01
Overall benefits	b	b	.03	.04	.02	.02
Economic benefits	b	b	b	.01	.01	.02
Basic needs	b	b	b	.03	.02	.01
Safety and security	b	b	b	.03	.03	b
Pleasure and satisfaction	b	b	b	—	.03	.01
Cognitive risk orientation	.01	b	b	b	b	b
Talks with experts	.02	b	b	b	b	b
Read technology magazines (Question 26)	b	.01	b	b	b	b
Organization membership	.04	.02	b	b	b	b
Education	.01	b	.06	.06	.05	.07
Income	.01	.02	.02	.03	.05	.03
SES (Question 53)	b	b	b	.01	b	.02
Age	b	b	.01	.01	.01	b
Gender[c]	b	b	b	b	.01	.01
Religion (Question 57)	b	b	.01	b	b	b
Employment (Question 47)	b	b	.02	.02	b	.02
Political party affiliation (Question 54)	b	b	.01	.01	b	b
Liberalism/conservatism (Question 55)	b	b	.05	b	b	b
Salience	.02	.03	.08	b	b	b

[a] Pro-safety, pro-benefits, or non-activist.
[b] Less then 0.01.
[c] Male = 1; female = 2.

function of people's involvement in social organizations in general. Our study found, however, that organizational membership is completely unrelated to activism in the nuclear arena, although it is related to activism in the areas of auto travel and air travel, probably the two least controversial technologies in our study.

The patterns of correlations for the remaining four technologies are noticeably different using the two analytic modes. Although both analyses indicated that activism was related to regulation and the perceptions of technological risks and benefits, the analysis involving activist status showed more qualitative risk and benefit factors to be related to activism than did the analysis involving the continuous action scale. In the case of attitudinal variables, however, just the opposite occurred; the analysis involving action showed several attitudinal variables to be related to intervention, while the analysis using the variable activist status found only one attitudinal variable, cognitive risk orientation, to be related to activism for only one technology (auto travel). In the case of sociodemographic variables, however, the t_b correlation analysis of activist status produced more significant correlations than did the t_B^2 analysis of action. In particular, education and income appeared to be important—important enough, in fact, to warrant a closer look at the relationships between these two variables and activist status.

Tables 7.5 through 7.8 show the relationships between years of education, median family income, and activist status for nuclear power, nuclear weapons, handguns, and industrial chemicals. (The correlations between education, income, and activist status for air and auto travel were so small that additional examination of these correlations would be pointless.) Several points emerge.

First, it may be noted that activist status, in general, was a function of education and income; that is, rates of activism increased as education and income increased. These increases, however, were not uniform for the four technologies. In the case of nuclear power (Table 7.5), the least well educated and the poorest respondents who took any action were five to one more likely to be pro-safety than pro-benefits activists. Among those activists who had more than a college education, however, the ratio was only about three to two, and for those who made more than $40,000, the ratio was approximately one to one. Three conclusions would seem in order: (1) our respondents were more likely to be pro-safety than pro-benefits nuclear power activists; (2) the greater our respondents' educations and incomes, the more likely they were to be activists, and (3) the greater our respondents' educations and incomes, the less likely they were to be pro-safety activists.

Table 7.5
Relationships (in Percents) Between Education, Income,
and Nuclear Power Activist Status (All Samples Combined)

	Education (in Years)			
	0–11	12	13–16	17+
Nuclear power activist status				
Pro-benefits	1%	4%	10%	19%
No action	94	79	63	50
Pro-safety	5	17	27	31
Total	100%	100%	100%	100%
Number of cases	233	357	457	279

	Family Income		
	Under $20,000	$20,000– $40,000	Over $40,000
Nuclear power activist status			
Pro-benefits	2%	8%	18%
No action	79	68	59
Pro-safety	19	24	22
Total	100%	100%	100%
Number of cases	394	458	371

In the case of nuclear weapons (Table 7.6), the better-educated and more affluent respondents were again more likely to be activists, but in this case education and income were essentially unrelated to whether respondents were pro-benefits or pro-safety activists. The numbers of pro-safety to pro-benefits activists in each education and income category, in other words, were approximately equal.

For handguns (Table 7.7), like nuclear power, respondents were more likely to be pro-safety than pro-benefits activists. In this case, however, increased education and income were associated with an increased likelihood of being a pro-safety activist. That is, the better-educated and more affluent a respondent was, the more likely he or she was to be a pro-safety activist in particular.

The relationships for industrial chemicals (Table 7.8) were similar to the relationships for nuclear power: people were more likely to be pro-

Table 7.6
Relationships (in Percents) Between Education, Income,
and Nuclear Weapons Activist Status (All Samples Combined)

	Education (in Years)			
	0–11	12	13–16	17+
Nuclear weapons activist status				
Pro-benefits	3%	9%	15%	20%
No action	96	83	68	59
Pro-safety	1	8	17	21
Total	100%	100%	100%	100%
Number of cases	222	357	455	280

	Family Income		
	Under $20,000	$20,000–$40,000	Over $40,000
Nuclear weapons activist status			
Pro-benefits	6%	13%	20%
No action	85	72	65
Pro-safety	9	15	15
Total	100%	100%	100%
Number of cases	394	459	370

safety than pro-benefits activists; the better-educated and more affluent people were, the more likely they were to be activists in general and the less likely they were to be pro-safety activists.

The relationships between education, income, and activist status, then, are complex and differed among the four technologies. Although education and income favored greater activism in every case, it favored pro-safety intervention more in some cases and pro-benefits intervention more in others. In all cases, however, the relationships were not only nonlinear, they were not even monotonic. Such relationships would not show up in ordinary least squares or t_B^2 analyses, as these two analytic forms are insensitive to relationships that are not, in the first case, linear, or, in the second case, monotonic. The fact, then, that education and income played essentially no role in the regressions reported in Table 7.3

Table 7.7
Relationships (in Percents) Between Education, Income,
and Handgun Activist Status (All Samples Combined)

	Education (in Years)			
	0–11	12	13–16	17+
Handgun activist status				
Pro-benefits	4%	6%	8%	10%
No action	92	80	68	57
Pro-safety	4	14	24	33
Total	100%	100%	100%	100%
Number of cases	223	357	457	281

	Family Income		
	Under $20,000	$20,000–$40,000	Over $40,000
Handgun activist status			
Pro-benefits	3%	9%	10%
No action	86	70	59
Pro-safety	11	21	31
Total	100%	100%	100%
Number of cases	394	459	372

is probably due to the fact that the relationships between these variables and activism are curvilinear.

Summary

It is often the case in social-psychological research that attitudes are found to be essentially uncorrelated with action. Our research is no exception; we found the correlation between attitudes and involvement in the technology risk-management process to be tenuous at best. Although we found small correlations between people's perceptions of technological risk and benefits, and their judgments about the acceptability of current technological safety standards, and activism for four technologies (nuclear power, nuclear weapons, handguns, and industrial chemicals), we found few correlations between activism and other attitudinal dimensions, in-

Table 7.8
Relationships (in Percents) Between Education, Income,
and Industrial Chemicals Activist Status (All Samples Combined)

	Education (in Years)			
	0–11	12	13–16	17+
Industrial chemicals activist status				
Pro-benefits	1%	2%	6%	14%
No action	94	83	69	53
Pro-safety	5	15	25	33
Total	100%	100%	100%	100%
Number of cases	222	356	455	280

	Family Income		
	Under $20,000	$20,000–$40,000	Over $40,000
Industrial chemicals activist status			
Pro-benefits	1%	4%	13%
No action	84	72	62
Pro-safety	15	24	25
Total	100%	100%	100%
Number of cases	393	456	372

cluding attitudes toward risk in general, attitudes toward technology, and attitudes toward the environment. In addition we found consistent, if small, relationships between activism and people's socioeconomic positions only for education and income. There was no consistent correlation between people's political persuasions and their inclination to take action in the technology risk-management arena, nor was activism associated with media exposure or any of the other variables included in our survey.

8

Conclusions

Activism

Measuring people's attitudes, and from these predicting their behavior, is an elusive business. Our attempt has been little more productive than those of many others. Although we were able to account for nearly a quarter of the variation in whether or not the members of our samples intervened in the nuclear power risk-management process, we could account for very little of the variation in auto or air travel activism and only modest amounts of the variation in activism directed at nuclear weapons, handguns, and industrial chemicals. The multiple correlations that we did compute, moreover, would have been even smaller had we not engaged in a little statistical hanky-panky (some would call it cheating) and "augmented" our general population samples with special samples of known activists. That is, had we not added the special samples of known activists to the general population samples in the two regions of our study, the correlations we would have obtained between activism and the various attitudinal and sociodemographic variables we measured would have been even smaller than they are.[1]

Although we would be less than candid if we did not admit that our measures of activism may have been flawed, we are forced nevertheless to the conclusion that activism in the technology risk-management arena may very well be explained to only a small extent by those variables that the literature has suggested might be determinants of this kind of behavior. Since these variables are all we investigated, however, they must constitute the main subject matter of the remainder of this chapter. It is presumed that factors we did not investigate will serve as the objects of future investigations.

Activism and Public Policy

Starr (1969 and 1972) and other revealed-preference technology risk researchers presumed, among other things, that there is a correlation between the public's attitude toward technological risks and benefits and prevailing technology safety regulations. Such a correlation is indispensable to their assertion that existing technology safety regulations reflect "socially acceptable" trade-offs between the risks and benefits of various technologies.

Although these researchers did not detail the mechanisms that translate public attitudes into acceptable regulation, they suggested that they are mediated by ongoing political and social processes. One mechanism, presumably, is state and federal government: since regulators are either directly or indirectly accountable to state legislatures or the U.S. Congress, one might presume that regulations in the long run will come to reflect the will of the people. A second mechanism is simple socialization: since regulators come, for the most part, from the main walks of American life, it would only be natural for their regulations to reflect dominant American values.

Our findings question these conclusions in four specific ways. First, we did not find a clear and consistent correlation between existing regulations and public attitudes toward regulation. Second, we did not find a clear and consistent correlation between people's attitudes toward technology risks and benefits and their involvement in those political processes that might translate these attitudes into public policy. Third, some people's views on technology safety regulation run counter to their views on government regulation in general. And fourth, it appears as though the values of the general public are different in certain important respects from the values of professional technology risk-managers.

The Acceptability of Current Regulations. We deliberately chose to study technologies that have been generating public debate. These technologies are neither obscure nor unimportant. Four—handguns, auto travel, air travel, and industrial chemicals—have long histories and have played, and continue to play, major roles in the U.S. economy. The two newer technologies—nuclear weapons and nuclear electric power—play important roles in our national defense and energy production. If any technologies should have generated sufficient debate for the political process to have revealed public sentiments accurately, these should have been among them.

Nevertheless, all four samples in our study—members of the general public in Connecticut and Arizona, as well as pro-safety *and* pro-benefits intervenors—judged, in some cases by rather large margins, that current safety regulations for each of these technologies are less stringent than they should be. Thus, our surveys suggest that existing technology safety regulations *do not* represent acceptable trade-offs between the risks and the benefits of technology in this country, at least if one interprets "acceptable" to mean "acceptable to the general public."

It should be pointed out, however, that the questions we asked our respondents did not specify the costs that would be incurred, or the benefits forgone, as a result of increased regulatory strictness. While these considerations might not have been salient to all respondents, responses might have been different if they had been. Even if question wordings had mentioned these issues, however, respondents might not have appreciated them fully, given only a simple written discussion. We are therefore limited in what we may conclude from the preferences our respondents expressed for greater regulatory strictness, even though these preferences were strong and consistent. This limitation is one to which all expressed-preference findings are, to some degree, subject, as Fischhoff et al. (1978) and others have pointed out.

Furthermore, our data on acceptability do not mean that the risk-benefit trade-offs now in place might not have been acceptable at one time. It might be, in other words, that the public was more accepting of technological risk during those years when current safety regulations for the technologies we studied evolved and only since then has become more risk-averse, and thus less accepting of these regulations. Given that the political process takes time, it might be argued that the current state of affairs represents not so much a lack of sensitivity to public preferences as simply a lag between changing public preferences and the realities of democratic politics.

If this argument is correct, however, we should have seen a trend toward increased regulatory strictness in recent years. We see no such trend. Although a few states have passed mandatory seat-belt laws, the Federal Department of Transportation has postponed earlier requirements for mandatory air bags (*New York Times,* 1986a). The federal government has also shown little inclination to improve airline safety (*New*

York Times, 1986b), and some argue that its conflicts with the air-traffic controllers' union and airline deregulation have degraded the overall safety of the airline industry. Although the nuclear accident at Chernobyl in the U.S.S.R. rekindled concern about the safety of nuclear reactors in this country (Echholm, 1986), no new safety programs have been initiated. Similarly, the chemical plant disaster at Bhopal, India, generated much talk but little regulatory action (Diamond, 1985). Although there was a national groundswell for a nuclear freeze (Shribman, 1983), the federal government only recently has engaged the Soviet Union in meaningful arms-control negotiations. And the U.S. Congress recently passed legislation reducing earlier restrictions on interstate sales of firearms (*New York Times,* 1986c).

Activism and the Political Process.   One of the more important points to emerge from our study, perhaps, is that people's attitudes toward technological risk and benefits and technological safety regulation seem to play only a small role in whether they try to make their attitudes known. Although our respondents' views concerning the acceptability of current regulations were correlated with activism in each of the six cases we studied, these correlations were generally quite small, ranging from 0.09, in the case of nuclear power action, to a mere 0.01, in the case of air travel action. Although a correlation of 0.09 is respectable by survey research standards (indicating that people's beliefs about the acceptability of nuclear power regulation account for 9 percent of their nuclear power activism), it nonetheless leaves a large, unexplained gap between people's beliefs and their actions.

It is altogether possible, of course, that this gap is due simply to our inability to measure action well. But if the gap represents a real discrepancy between people's beliefs and their actions and is not just a result of defects in our research instruments, then the finding that public sentiments regarding the acceptability of current regulations are not reflected very well in actual regulations could be explained rather easily: The public simply does not express its sentiments on the subject of technological safety regulation fully or accurately enough for the technology risk-management system to take heed.

This in no way demonstrates, of course, that taking heed of public sentiments ranks high on the list of technology risk-manager's priorities. It does suggest, however, that methods currently available to citizens for expressing their views on technological safety (public hearings, petitions, etc.) may not be very good vehicles for expressing these views, even when technology risk-managers are willing to listen.

Efficiency, however, is not an attribute often claimed of democratic government, nor, for that matter, is perfect representation. So long as those who wish to make their feelings known have mechanisms for so doing, and so long as these mechanisms are at least reasonably responsive to public sentiments, democracy, it might be said, is doing all that reasonably can be asked of it. If people do not choose to express their views, there is no way those views can become part of the democratic process.

Although most of the people in our general population samples indicated that they had made no effort to express their views on the safety of the six technologies we studied, surprisingly large minorities indicated that they had. This would seem to indicate that avenues of expression at least are available and are being used. To what effect, however, is another story, a story that we cannot tell since we did not study technology risk-management institutions themselves. All we can say from our surveys is that the majority of the people we surveyed, including those who have been expressing their views, think that current technology safety regulations are too lax. Presumably, then, current technology risk-management institutions are less than perfect instruments for turning public sentiments, even the sentiments of those who choose to speak, into public policy.

Regulation and Regulations. As we noted in Chapter 1, a large majority of Americans are opposed to government regulation even though they are in favor of specific regulations such as those we studied. This inconsistency could be responsible in part for the seeming reluctance of many people to engage the technology risk-management system at all and the relatively low correlations we found between attitudes about technology safety and activism. Many people who favor more stringent regulations, in other words, may at the same time oppose government regulation in general and thus be restrained from expressing their views on particular regulations. Although we could not test this hypothesis directly, as we did not ask our respondents about their views on government regulation in general, our findings on particular regulations and other researchers' findings on the views of Americans toward government regulation in general (Lipset and Schneider, 1983) are consistent with this hypothesis.

A more important consideration, however, is the possibility that these contradictions between regulation in general and regulations in particular might affect the decisions of technology risk-managers. Having been much more often the subject of opinion polls (Lipset and Schneider, 1983), the general attitude of Americans against regulation is probably much more widely known than attitudes toward specific regulations. Regulators, therefore, when making decisions about specific regulations, might easily assume that a majority of the public would be against more stringent regulations when, in fact, a majority would be in favor of them.

Speaking Different Languages.   The preceding example, however, is only one of several ways in which technology risk-managers might misread the public. As discussed in Chapters 1 and 3, there is ample evidence that technologists, by and large, focus on only one or two things—the probabilities of injury or of death—when considering the risks of a technology, and are inclined to think only in economic terms when considering a technology's benefits. As expressed-preference risk researchers have found, however, lay people include additional factors in their evaluations, including, in the case of risk, the catastrophic potential of a technology (its potential to cause many deaths at one time), the degree to which the risks of the technology are understood (and thus, presumably, capable of being controlled) by scientists and technicians, and certain intangible attitudes that lead people to particularly dread certain kinds of industrial accidents. We corroborated these earlier findings and found also that lay people define benefits in more than simple economic terms, including in their definitions such things as pleasure, safety and security, and the importance of the technology for satisfying basic human needs.

Although the discrepancy between lay and professional risk judgments has become common knowledge, being cited often in both the professional and lay literatures, it has nonetheless remained open to challenge, since it was derived almost exclusively either from surveys in other countries or from studies in this country of small, unrepresentative samples. One of the major contributions of our study is the corroboration of this finding, using representative samples of the American public. Thus, given this earlier work and our corroboration, it may be argued that scientists and technologists, who were once inclined to view the public as being irrational when it comes to the subject of technology, should appreciate that to some extent, at least, the issue is not irrationality but differences in the definitions of technological risks and benefits. Although it is true that many people give little thought to the risks and benefits of technology, or how the risks might best be ameliorated or the benefits realized, it is not true that all lay people's views are ill-informed or lacking in coherence. The fact is that a majority of the public, and the pro-safety intervenors who would seem to represent them, appear to evaluate risks differently than do scientists and technologists or those pro-benefits intervenors who appear to represent the more scientific and technological points of view in the media and at public hearings. As we noted in Chapter 3, how one defines "risk" and "benefit" is fundamentally a matter of values and philosophy and not of scientific fact, deduction, or logic.

Determinants of Acceptability

As part of their contention that the American public is irrational about technological risk, some technology risk-managers have lamented that those who oppose technology seem to do so on the basis of the technology's risks without paying any attention to the technology's many benefits. Our research would indicate that this attribution is, at best, only partly true. Although the perceptions of those we interviewed of the overall benefits of auto travel, air travel, and electricity were uncorrelated with their judgments about the acceptability of current safety regulations of these three industries, their perceptions of the overall benefits of nuclear weapons, handguns, and industrial chemicals did play a role in their judgments about appropriate levels of regulation for these industries. In addition, our respondents' perceptions of such individual elements as economic benefits, contribution to basic needs, contribution to people's pleasure, and contribution to people's safety and security played an additional role in many of their acceptability judgments. Therefore, while it is true that risk factors, by and large, played a larger role than benefit factors in our respondents' judgments about the acceptability of current technology safety regulations, it is not true that they ignored the benefits of technology altogether.

What is more important, however, is that most people rated the benefits of air and auto travel and electricity so highly that their ratings of benefits became essentially irrelevant when it came to making judgments about the appropriateness of various safety regulations. To make these ratings they had to rely on their perceptions of risk, which we found in our study to be much more variable than their perceptions of benefits. It was not uncommon, in fact, as noted in Chapter 6, for the people we surveyed to favor more extensive deployment of a technology, such as nuclear power, while at the same time favoring more stringent safety regulations or even outright government operation.

It does not appear to be true, then, as some technologists have implied, that Americans in general, or pro-safety intervenors in particular, are simply antitechnology. Those people we interviewed, both from the general public and from intervenor groups, by and large rated the benefits of technology quite highly (see in particular Chapter 2). Also, although we did find that our respondents' attitudes toward current technology safety standards correlated with their attitudes toward technology in general (those who were most favorable toward technology were most accepting of current technology safety standards), we also found these correlations to be rather weak. This suggests that people's attitudes toward technological safety are only in relatively small part a function of their overall attitudes toward technology, and that pro-safety intervention cannot be dismissed simply as antitechnology bias.

We also found respondents' views on technology safety standards to be only weakly, and inconsistently, correlated with their attitudes on the environment, their attitudes toward risk in general, and their attitudes toward government support for energy technology. They were also essentially uncorrelated with all sociodemographic variables except gender. (Women generally favored stricter safety regulations than did men.)

It is possible, of course, that in our effort to design a survey brief enough to use with members of the general public, we failed to include those attitudinal or demographic variables that in fact affect people's judgments of risk, benefit, and acceptability. Indeed, we did not include some of the variables that Renn (1981) used in his study, including certain variables that involve properties of technologies, such as the impact of technology on social justice, the environment, progress, quality of life, and democratic rights.

On the other hand, the results of all relevant studies of which we are aware, including that of Renn, concur on the relatively small role played by attitudinal and demographic variables. Although it is possible that future research may change this picture, we must conclude for now that people's stances toward technology safety regulation cut across traditional sociodemographic and attitudinal lines.

The one thing we did find to correlate consistently with judgments about technology safety regulations was perceptions of risk, both overall risk and various specific components of risk. In many cases, perceptions of overall benefits and various specific benefit factors also correlated with these judgments. Although these factors, along with gender and people's attitudes toward technology in general, did not account for all of the variation in acceptability we encountered, they accounted for a reasonable amount of it and remain, until additional correlates can be discovered, the best predictors of it.

From the Laboratory to the Field

The National Science Foundation grant that in part supported the study we have reported in this volume is subtitled "methodological investigation." This reflects the fact that one of the objectives of the study was to develop techniques for translating the laboratory-style investigations of earlier expressed-preference research into full field surveys. We close this volume, then, with a few comments on some of the methodological aspects of our study.

Correlations and Regressions. It is uncommon for research-ers to use multiple regression to analyze survey data. There are several reasons for this. Standard multiple regression, based as it is on product-moment statistics, is designed specifically for continuous, interval data. Surveys, however, usually contain many discontinuous variables, such as gender, religious preference, or political party affiliation, and numerous ordinal variables, such as social class, income, or attitudes. Although it is possible, and not altogether uncommon, to include both nominal and ordinal variables in standard regression analyses, the interpretation of such regressions becomes somewhat difficult, particularly for polytomous nominal classifications that must be divided into several "dummy" vari-ables. (Dichotomies, such as gender, are much easier to handle in stan-dard regression analyses.) In the case of ordinal variables, regression coefficients do not have the usual meaning of "slope" that is so useful when interpreting relationships between equal-interval variables.

More important, however, product-moment statistics make demands on the normality of univariate distributions and the linearity of bivariate and multivariate distributions that are often hard for survey data to meet. Although there is a fair amount of debate in the literature over just how limiting these demands are, most statisticians suggest that skewed and nonlinear data be transformed so that their distributions are approxi-mately normal at the univariate level and linear at the bivariate and mul-tivariate levels. Once data have been transformed, however, ordinary-least-squares regression coefficients become hard to interpret (this is especially true for such things as attitude scale scores) and the generalizability of findings becomes difficult.

Nevertheless, we felt it was important to use regression analysis for the data we had gathered. We wanted to find out, first of all, if any of the zero-order correlations reported previously in the literature were spuri-ous, and then we wanted to know just how much of the variation in acceptability and action these variables, combined, could account for. Since ordinary-least-squares regressions presented such momentous ana-lytic problems, however, we adopted a relatively new, nonparametric, ordinally based regression procedure that avoids many of the more de-manding assumptions of the product-moment system. So far as we know, this is the largest study to have used these statistics yet reported in the literature. Our impressions of the new statistics are that they are useful, particularly for survey data.

First of all, the new statistics make it possible to compute zero-order (t_B^2) and multiple (T_B^2) correlations without worrying about such things as skewness and kurtosis at the univariate level or linearity at the bivariate level. (Linearity at the multivariate level is almost impossible to check using any kind of regression analysis.) This second advantage is particularly important when dealing with low correlations involving variables with only a few categories (such as are common in surveys), where linearity is almost impossible to judge from scatter plots.

Given that we were trodding uncharted statistical paths, however, we checked our analyses against ordinary product-moment correlations and regressions, comparing the results of the new system with those we would have derived using more conventional procedures. In general, we would have drawn similar conclusions had we used ordinary-least-squares regression. This is consistent with the claim of "robustness" often made for product-moment statistics. In some cases, however, the results using the two systems were noticeably different. In particular, product-moment correlations (both zero-order correlations and regression coefficients) were sometimes larger (relative to other correlations) than the comparable nonparametric correlations. Close examination of the data in these cases indicated that the data were skewed and that the magnitudes of the product-moment correlations were due in part to this aberration in the data. Although data transformations would have eliminated these errors, it would have been necessary in many cases to use different transformations for different samples. Not only would this have made it difficult to compare the results from different samples in our study, it would also have made it hard to generalize the results of our study to other populations. All things considered, it was easier just to report the nonparametric statistics.[2]

In doing this, however, we lost the ability to report the statistical significance of our multiple regressions; the sampling distributions of multiple tau-B and the nonparametric regression coefficient are not known. This, however, is a trivial loss when dealing with samples of 600 or more cases, as any correlation that is even remotely significant, substantively, with such large samples will be highly significant statistically.

Variation Accounted For.　The nonparametric correlations that we have reported, like the product-moment correlations they replace, have a "variation accounted for" interpretation. This makes the discussion of both kinds of statistics particularly easy. Unfortunately, this interpretation also highlights the fact that we accounted for less of the variation in action and acceptability than we might have liked. To some extent the anemic quality of the correlations we have reported is due to factors that are trivial; in other respects, however, it is likely due to factors that are substantively rather important.

As mentioned in Chapter 4, neither zero-order nor multiple tau-B correlations are as powerful as their product-moment counterparts, and, even when based on the same data, will tend to be somewhat lower (on the order of 10 percent lower for samples of the size we analyzed). Some of the "smallness" in the correlations we reported, then, is due to the fact that we chose to report nonparametric, rather than product-moment, correlation coefficients.

At the zero-order level, we also reported tau-B squared rather than tau-B correlations. This is equivalent to reporting the coefficient of determination (r^2) rather than Pearson's coefficient of correlation (r). Although it has become reasonably common practice to report the variation accounted for measure, r^2, rather than the more traditional r, such practice does make correlations look rather small, particularly to those who have become accustomed to the more traditional measures. This is an especially serious problem when correlations are small. A tau-B of 0.90, for example, still looks large when it is squared to become 0.81. A tau-B of 0.30, however, which may strike some as a relatively strong correlation, does not look nearly as strong when reported as a tau-B squared of 0.09. In both cases, of course, the measures are arithmetically identical.

These matters, however, are stylistic and trivial. A more substantively important reason why the correlations we have reported have tended to be lower than similar correlations reported in earlier expressed-preference literature has to do with differences in the designs of these studies and the design of ours. As we discussed in Chapters 3 and 4, several of these studies used "technology," rather than "respondent," as the unit of analysis. The effect of this practice, as noted earlier, is to magnify correlations between such things as perceptions of risk and the acceptability of technology safety regulations over what they would have been had they been computed at the individual level. One of the more important contributions of our research to the expressed-preference literature, therefore, may be the fact that we computed correlations across individuals, rather than technologies, and thus more accurately reflect the true sizes of these individual-level correlations. The fact that the correlations were smaller in our study does not detract from their validity; indeed, the lower values we found are surely the more accurate.

Salience. Another, very important, reason for the relatively low correlations we found involves salience. Had we analyzed only those data provided by respondents who indicated that technological risks, benefits, and regulations were important issues to them, the correlations between these and other variables would have been considerably higher. The salience of the issues, in other words, was correlated with the strength of other correlations. This is a classic example of statistical "interaction," and explains why we did not introduce the variable "salience" in our various regression equations (the logic of regression specifically excludes variables that interact in this way). It also, however, helps to explain why the findings of many earlier expressed-preference studies were so much more robust than ours; the earlier studies were conducted on special samples (community leaders, students, members of the League of Women Voters, technologists) for whom the risks, benefits, and regulation of technology were no doubt more salient than they were for the public at large. The findings from our surveys, then, are probably much more realistic estimates of the American public than the findings from these earlier studies.

Nevertheless, one may question whether surveys are appropriate vehicles for measuring regulatory preferences. While surveys surely measure current sentiments about technological risks, benefits, and regulations more accurately than the techniques used by revealed-preference researchers, they have the disadvantage of weighting all respondents' preferences equally. That is, they give just as much weight to the opinions of those who have never even thought about the subject as they do to those who have thought through the issues carefully and may even have taken steps to make their conclusions known to policy makers.

Asking students, technologists, or similar specialized groups what they think is no solution, however, even though these groups might be better informed. Who is to say, after all, that these or any other group should get preferential treatment when it comes to determining something as important to everyone's well-being as technological safety? Including a measure of salience in a general population survey, as we did, helps, although it still leaves it to the researcher to make the value judgment of just how salient a topic has to be before people's opinions on it should be counted. We chose not to make such a judgment, and simply reported everyone's opinions along with the caveat that these opinions in many cases do not correlate with other opinions, probably because many respondents simply had not had time or reason to organize their thoughts on the subject prior to the time we interviewed them.

This does suggest one answer, however, to a question we asked earlier: If all the variables we included in our surveys could account for so little of the variation in our respondents' judgments about the acceptability of current safety regulations or their propensity to take action to change them, what variables did we miss? The answer could be, simply, none. That is, we may have accounted for most of the variation that was to be accounted for, the rest being "noise," or "random variation," introduced by the fact that we were asking people to make snap judgments on issues that may have been of little importance to them and about which they had thought little.

Research Strategies. For all these reasons, we must conclude that the population survey may not be the best vehicle for studying the relationship between public sentiments on technology safety and existing safety regulations. Although we would be among the first to admit that there is much to be learned on this subject with carefully designed surveys, we would be among the last to deny that many things that need to be learned cannot be learned efficiently in this manner. We would note, for example, that although our surveys provided the information that our respondents were less than satisfied with current technology safety regulations, they did not tell us nearly all that we might have liked to know about why this dissatisfaction existed and told us essentially nothing about what might be done about it. The causes of the dissatisfaction, in fact, may be only in part personal, and thus accessible by survey methods. Other causal factors, less readily tapped by interviews, might include such things as interest group politics, bureaucratic inertia, and poor media presentations. The next round of research on technological safety, then, might profitably focus on these arenas even though they are not areas of research that lend themselves readily to survey techniques.

Technological risk is an important, and unavoidable, aspect of modern life; it is one of the prices we pay for the goods and services that play such an important role in advanced technological society. Although stringent technological safety regulations can reduce these risks, they exact an economic penalty that the business community is not inclined to pay unless required to do so. The public at large, therefore, must determine how strict the safety regulations on technology should be—that is, the price that is to be paid for desired levels of safety.

Theoretically the public makes its wishes known on these matters through political institutions that oversee the special technology risk-management agencies that have been established to measure risks and to set appropriate safety standards. Our surveys, as well as other expressed-preference research, have found evidence, however, that these agencies are not setting standards that are completely acceptable to the public. Whether this is a new phenomenon, reflecting changing public sentiments on technological risk, or is a matter of long standing we cannot say for sure, although it does appear to us that the gaps between technology safety regulation and public opinion that we measured probably are not abating. While this may be due in part to the tendency we spoke of earlier for technologists to use a more restricted definition of "risk" than would the general public, other reasons probably exist also, including inadequate communication of current regulations to the public by responsible agencies. Since technology risk-management institutions are so important to our technological lives, these and related issues deserve much more study than they have received to date.

Notes

1. As we discussed in Chapter 4, however, the correlations and regressions we reported for overall risks, overall benefits, and acceptability of current technology safety regulations were essentially unaffected by these procedures. While it might have been technically more appropriate to have reported the results from the general population samples only, in Chapters 5 and 6, we reported the results from the combined samples so that the results in these two chapters would be more comparable to the action regressions we reported in Chapter 7.

2. Computing nonparametric correlations and comparing them with product-moment correlations is an efficient way of examining any continuous-data set to see if it meets many of the assumptions of product-moment statistics. When the relative sizes of the two types of correlations do not agree, one is alerted to the fact that some kind of transformation is in order before computing additional parametric statistics. This technique is particularly useful for survey data involving variables with only a few categories that are almost impossible to screen for linearity with traditional scatter plots.

Survey Questions

THE ROPER CENTER

Office for Teaching and Research
Institution for Social and Policy Studies

YALE UNIVERSITY

Public Perceptions of Technological Risks:
A Methodological Study

CASE #

SAMPLE ....

REGION ....

CODES FOR TIME	
Before 10 a.m.	0
10 a.m.-12 p.m.	1
12:01-2 p.m.	2
2:01-4 p.m.	3
4:01-5 p.m.	4
5:01-6 p.m.	5
6:01-7 p.m.	6
7:01-8 p.m.	7
8:01-9 p.m.	8
After 9 p.m.	9

TIME   AM
INTERVIEW
BEGAN _____ PM

CODE TIME ....

1. In general, would you say that recently you have been taking a **good deal of interest** in current events and what's happening in the world today, **some interest** or **not very much interest?**

Good deal 3
Some 2
Not very much 1
Don't know 8

2. I am going to name some institutions in this country. As far as the **people running** these institutions are concerned, would you say you have a great deal of confidence, only some confidence, or hardly any confidence at all in them?

READ EACH ITEM. CODE ONE FOR EACH. REPEAT THE QUESTION, OR CATEGORIES, IF NECESSARY.

	A great deal of confidence	Only some confidence	Hardly any confidence at all	Don't know
A. Organized religion	1	2	3	8
B. Education	1	2	3	8
C. Medicine	1	2	3	8
D. The Press	1	2	3	8
E. TV	1	2	3	8
F. Organized labor	1	2	3	8
G. Major companies	1	2	3	8
H. Banks and financial institutions	1	2	3	8
I. Executive branch of the federal government	1	2	3	8
J. U.S. Supreme Court	1	2	3	8
K. Congress	1	2	3	8
L. U.S. Environmental Protection Agency	1	2	3	8
M. U.S. Consumer Product Safety Commission	1	2	3	8
N. Military	1	2	3	8
O. Scientific community	1	2	3	8
P. Consumer interest groups	1	2	3	8
Q. Environmental groups	1	2	3	8

3. Now, I am going to ask you two questions about several technologies or industries. The first asks your opinion about current conditions—as they are **NOW**. The second question asks for your opinion on what the conditions **SHOULD BE**.

Some people believe that the current restrictions and standards that deal with **the safety of automobile travel** are not very strict—point number 1 on this scale.

```
   1          2          3          4          5          6          7
NOT VERY                                                      EXTREMELY
STRICT                                                          STRICT
```

Others feel that the current restrictions and standards that deal with **the safety of automobile travel** are extremely strict—point number 7 on this scale. Other people, of course, fall somewhere in between.

A. How strict do you think restrictions and standards are **NOW** on the safety of automobile travel, or haven't you thought much about this?

ENTER CODE . . . . ▢

Haven't thought much 8

B. How strict do you think the restrictions and standards on the safety of automobile travel **SHOULD BE**, or haven't you thought much about this?

```
   1          2          3          4          5          6          7
NOT VERY                                                      EXTREMELY
STRICT                                                          STRICT
```

ENTER CODE . . . . ▢

Haven't thought much 8

4. Some people believe that the current restrictions and standards that deal with **transporting and disposing of industrial chemicals** are not very strict—point number 1.

```
 1            2          3          4          5          6          7
 ┌─────────────────────────────────────────────────────────────────┐
NOT VERY                                                   EXTREMELY
STRICT                                                      STRICT
```

Others feel that the current restrictions and standards that deal with **transporting and disposing of industrial chemicals** are extremely strict—point number 7. Others fall somewhere in between.

A. How strict do you think restrictions and standards are **NOW** on transporting and disposing of industrial chemicals, or haven't you thought much about this?

ENTER CODE . . . .

Haven't thought much 8

B. How strict do you think the restrictions and standards on transporting and disposing of industrial chemicals **SHOULD BE**, or haven't you thought much about this?

```
 1            2          3          4          5          6          7
 ┌─────────────────────────────────────────────────────────────────┐
NOT VERY                                                   EXTREMELY
STRICT                                                      STRICT
```

ENTER CODE . . . .

Haven't thought much 8

5. Next, think about the safeguards associated with maintaining **nuclear weapons** as a part of our national defense.

   A. How strict do you think safeguards are **NOW** on maintaining nuclear weapons as part of our national defense, or haven't you thought much about this?

1	2	3	4	5	6	7
NOT VERY STRICT						EXTREMELY STRICT

   ENTER CODE . . . .

   Haven't thought much 8

   B. How strict do you think the safeguards on maintaining nuclear weapons as part of our national defense **SHOULD BE**, or haven't you thought much about this?

1	2	3	4	5	6	7
NOT VERY STRICT						EXTREMELY STRICT

   ENTER CODE . . . .

   Haven't thought much 8

6. Next, think about the restrictions that deal with buying, selling, and owning **handguns**.

A. How strict do you think restrictions are **NOW** on buying, selling, and owning handguns, or haven't you thought much about this?

1	2	3	4	5	6	7
NOT VERY STRICT						EXTREMELY STRICT

ENTER CODE ....

Haven't thought much 8

B. How strict do you think the restrictions on buying, selling, and owning handguns **SHOULD BE**, or haven't you thought much about this?

1	2	3	4	5	6	7
NOT VERY STRICT						EXTREMELY STRICT

ENTER CODE ....

Haven't thought much 8

7. Next, consider the restrictions and standards that deal with the safety of **nuclear electric power**.

    A. How strict do you think the restrictions and standards are **NOW** on nuclear electric power, or haven't you thought much about this?

        ENTER CODE ....

        Haven't thought much 8

    B. How strict do you think the restrictions and standards on nuclear electric power **SHOULD BE**, or haven't you thought much about this?

        ENTER CODE ....

        Haven't thought much 8

8. Finally on this question, think about the restrictions and standards that deal with the **safety of commercial air travel**.

    A. How strict do you think restrictions and standards are **NOW** on commercial air travel, or haven't you thought much about this?

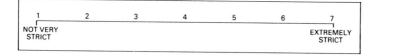

1	2	3	4	5	6	7
NOT VERY STRICT						EXTREMELY STRICT

ENTER CODE ....

Haven't thought much   8

    B. How strict do you think the restrictions and standards on commercial air travel **SHOULD BE**, or haven't you thought much about this?

1	2	3	4	5	6	7
NOT VERY STRICT						EXTREMELY STRICT

ENTER CODE ....

Haven't thought much   8

9. Some people do different things to make their feelings known on issues that concern them.

Here is a list of actions people have taken in order to express their views.

READ EACH ITEM.

Have you done any of these things to express your views on the restrictions and standards that apply to **the safety of automobile travel?**

```
Yes ........................................... 1
No .............. (GO to Q. 10) .............. 2
Don't know or can't remember ................. 8
```

ASK ONLY IF "YES" TO QUESTION 9.

Which ones have you done?

CODE FOR EACH. REPEAT THE QUESTION OR ANSWER CATEGORIES, IF NECESSARY.

	YES	NO	DON'T KNOW
A. Written a **letter, telephoned**, or sent a **telegram** to an editor, public official or company.	1	2	8
B. **Signed** a petition.	1	2	8
C. **Circulated** a petition.	1	2	8
D. **Voted** for or against a candidate for public office in part because of his or her position on this issue.	1	2	8
E. Attended a **public hearing** or a meeting of a **special interest organization.**	1	2	8
F. **Spoken** at a public hearing or forum.	1	2	8
G. **Boycotted** a company.	1	2	8
H. **Joined** or **contributed** money to an organization.	1	2	8
I. Attended a **public demonstration.**	1	2	8
J. Participated in a **lawsuit.**	1	2	8

K. Other:
    Specify: _____

10. Have you done any of these things to express your views on the restrictions that apply to **handguns**.

$$
\begin{aligned}
&\text{Yes} \ \dots\dots\dots\dots\dots\dots\dots\dots\dots\dots\dots\dots\dots\dots\dots \ 1 \\
&\text{No} \ \dots\dots\dots\dots \ \text{(GO to Q. 11)} \ \dots\dots\dots\dots \ 2 \\
&\text{Don't know or can't remember} \ \dots\dots\dots\dots\dots \ 8
\end{aligned}
$$

ASK ONLY IF "YES" TO QUESTION 10.

Which ones have you done?

CODE FOR EACH. REPEAT THE QUESTION OR ANSWER CATEGORIES, IF NECESSARY.

	YES	NO	DON'T KNOW
A. Written a **letter, telephoned**, or sent a **telegram** to an editor, public official or company.	1	2	8
B. **Signed** a petition.	1	2	8
C. **Circulated** a petition.	1	2	8
D. **Voted** for or against a candidate for public office in part because of his or her position on this issue.	1	2	8
E. Attended a **public hearing** or a meeting of a **special interest organization**.	1	2	8
F. **Spoken** at a public hearing or forum.	1	2	8
G. **Boycotted** a company.	1	2	8
H. **Joined** or **contributed** money to an organization.	1	2	8
I. Attended a **public demonstration**.	1	2	8
J. Participated in a **lawsuit**.	1	2	8

K. Other:
   Specify: _____

11. Have you done any of these things to express your views on the restrictions and standards that apply to **the safety of nuclear electric power?**

Yes 1
No .... (GO to Q. 12) 2
Don't know or can't remember 8

ASK ONLY IF "YES" TO QUESTION 11.

Which ones have you done?

CODE FOR EACH. REPEAT THE QUESTION OR ANSWER CATEGORIES, IF NECESSARY.

	YES	NO	DON'T KNOW
A. Written a **letter, telephoned,** or sent a **telegram** to an editor, public official or company.	1	2	8
B. **Signed** a petition.	1	2	8
C. **Circulated** a petition.	1	2	8
D. **Voted** for or against a candidate for public office in part because of his or her position on this issue.	1	2	8
E. Attended a **public hearing** or a meeting of a **special interest organization.**	1	2	8
F. **Spoken** at a public hearing or forum.	1	2	8
G. **Boycotted** a company.	1	2	8
H. **Joined** or **contributed** money to an organization.	1	2	8
I. Attended a **public demonstration.**	1	2	8
J. Participated in a **lawsuit.**	1	2	8

K. Other:
   Specify: _____

12. Have you done any of these things to express your views on the restrictions and standards that apply to **the safety of commercial air travel?**

Yes 1
No .... (GO to Q. 13) 2
Don't know or can't remember 8

ASK ONLY IF "YES" TO QUESTION 12.

Which ones have you done?

CODE FOR EACH. REPEAT THE QUESTION OR ANSWER CATEGORIES, IF NECESSARY.

	YES	NO	DON'T KNOW
A. Written a **letter, telephoned**, or sent a **telegram** to an editor, public official or company.	1	2	8
B. **Signed** a petition.	1	2	8
C. **Circulated** a petition.	1	2	8
D. **Voted** for or against a candidate for public office in part because of his or her position on this issue.	1	2	8
E. Attended a **public hearing** or a meeting of a **special interest organization.**	1	2	8
F. **Spoken** at a public hearing or forum.	1	2	8
G. **Boycotted** a company.	1	2	8
H. **Joined** or **contributed** money to an organization.	1	2	8
I. Attended a **public demonstration.**	1	2	8
J. Participated in a **lawsuit.**	1	2	8

K. Other:
   Specify: _____

13. Have you done any of these things to express your views on the safeguards associated with maintaining **nuclear weapons** as part of our national defense?

Yes 1
No .... (GO to Q. 14) 2
Don't know or can't remember 8

ASK ONLY IF "YES" TO QUESTION 13.

Which ones have you done?

CODE FOR EACH. REPEAT THE QUESTION OR ANSWER CATEGORIES, IF NECESSARY.

	YES	NO	DON'T KNOW
A. Written a **letter, telephoned**, or sent a **telegram** to an editor, public official or company.	1	2	8
B. **Signed** a petition.	1	2	8
C. **Circulated** a petition.	1	2	8
D. **Voted** for or against a candidate for public office in part because of his or her position on this issue.	1	2	8
E. Attended a **public hearing** or a meeting of a **special interest organization.**	1	2	8
F. **Spoken** at a public hearing or forum.	1	2	8
G. **Boycotted** a company.	1	2	8
H. **Joined** or **contributed** money to an organization.	1	2	8
I. Attended a **public demonstration.**	1	2	8
J. Participated in a **lawsuit.**	1	2	8

K. Other:
   Specify: _____

14. Have you done any of these things to express your views on the restrictions and standards that apply to **transporting and disposing of industrial chemicals?**

> Yes 1
> No .... (GO to Q. 15) 2
> Don't know or can't remember 8

ASK ONLY IF "YES" TO QUESTION 14.

Which ones have you done?

CODE FOR EACH. REPEAT THE QUESTION OR ANSWER CATEGORIES, IF NECESSARY.

	YES	NO	DON'T KNOW
A. Written a **letter, telephoned**, or sent a **telegram** to an editor, public official or company.	1	2	8
B. **Signed** a petition.	1	2	8
C. **Circulated** a petition.	1	2	8
D. **Voted** for or against a candidate for public office in part because of his or her position on this issue.	1	2	8
E. Attended a **public hearing** or a meeting of a **special interest organization**.	1	2	8
F. **Spoken** at a public hearing or forum.	1	2	8
G. **Boycotted** a company.	1	2	8
H. **Joined** or **contributed** money to an organization.	1	2	8
I. Attended a **public demonstration**.	1	2	8
J. Participated in a **lawsuit**.	1	2	8

K. Other:
   Specify: _____

15. How often do you usually drive a car or truck?

```
Every day  .............. (ASK A) .............. 1
A few times a week  .......... (ASK A) ......... 2
Once a week  ............. (ASK A) ............ 3
Less than once a week  ........ (ASK A) ........ 4
Never  ............. (GO TO Q. 16) ............ 5
```

ASK ONLY IF R DRIVES

A. Have you ever received a ticket, or been charged by the police, for a traffic violation—other than for illegal parking in the last 5 years (since 1977)?

```
Yes  ......................................... 1
No  .......................................... 2
Don't know  .................................. 8
```

16. How often do you use seat belts when you travel in an automobile—always, almost always, usually, sometimes, seldom, or never?

```
Always  ...................................... 1
Almost always  ............................... 2
Usually  ..................................... 3
Sometimes  ................................... 4
Seldom  ...................................... 5
Never  ....................................... 6
Never ride in automobiles  ................... 8
```

17. Have you ever been shot at or threatened with a handgun?

    Yes 1
    No 2
    Can't remember 8

18. Is there any area right around here—that is within a mile—where you would be afraid to walk alone at night?

    Yes 1
    No 2
    Not sure 8

19. Has anyone ever broken into, or somehow illegally entered your (apartment or home)?

    Yes 1
    No 2
    Can't remember 8

20. Has anyone ever taken something directly from you by using force—such as a stickup, mugging or threat?

    Yes 1
    No 2
    Can't remember 8

21. Do you happen to have any firearms in your (apartment/home, garage, or out buildings)?

```
Yes  ................. (ASK A) ................ 1
No   ............................................ 2
Not sure  ..................................... 8
```

IF "YES"

A. Which of the following are these?

	YES	NO	DON'T KNOW
Handgun(s)	1	2	8
Shotgun(s)	1	2	8
Rifle(s)	1	2	8
Other	1	2	8
(Specify) _____			

22. Have you ever traveled by airplane on a scheduled commercial flight?

```
Yes  ................. (ASK A) ................ 1
No   ............. (GO TO Q. 23) ............. 2
```

IF "YES" TO QUESTION 22.

A. In the **last year**, how many times have you flown on a commercial airplane?

```
None  ......................................... 0
One trip  ..................................... 1
Two-five trips  ............................... 2
Six or more trips  ........................... 3
Don't know  .................................. 8
```

23. Now I am going to read you three statements that will help us understand how you feel about several issues. For each, please tell me how much you agree or disagree with it. There are no right or wrong answers. Try to answer each question, even if you must guess how you feel, using one of the five categories on this card.

READ EACH ITEM. CODE ONE FOR EACH. REPEAT QUESTIONS OR CATEGORIES, IF NECESSARY.

	Strongly Agree	Agree	Neutral	Disagree	Strongly Disagree	Don't Know
A. The risks associated with advanced technology have been exaggerated by events such as Three Mile Island and the Love Canal.	5	4	3	2	1	8
B. The profit motive of private companies makes it difficult for the safe operation of nuclear electric power plants.	5	4	3	2	1	8
C. Nuclear electric power plants should be operated by the government, rather than by private industry.	5	4	3	2	1	8

24. In general, which of the following do you rely on **most** for information you trust on public issues such as the topics we have been discussing—television, newspapers, books and magazines, or radio?

> Television 1
> Newspapers 2
> Books and magazines 3
> Radio 4
> None 5
> Don't Know 8

25. How often do you watch television news or documentary programs—every evening, 3 or 4 times a week, once or twice a week, or less often?

> Every evening .... (Ask A) 1
> Three or four times a week .... (Ask A) 2
> Once or twice a week .... (Ask A) 3
> Less often .... (Ask A) 4
> Never (VOLUNTEERED ONLY) ... (Go to Q. 26) .. 5
> Don't know 8

ASK ONLY IF WATCH TV NEWS OR DOCUMENTARIES

A. When you watch TV news and documentary shows do you pay a **great deal of attention** to issues such as the ones on technology we have been discussing; do you **pay some attention**; or **don't you pay much attention** to these issues?

> Don't pay much attention 1
> Pay some attention 2
> Pay a great deal of attention 3
> Don't know 8

26. Do you regularly read magazines such as **Time, Consumer Reports, Newsweek, Science,** or **Scientific American** that report on issues dealing with technology industry or products?

Yes .... (ASK A) 1
No .... (GO To Q. 27) 2

ASK ONLY IF YES

A. When you read these magazines, how much attention do you pay to issues on technology, industry, or products: A **great deal of attention; some attention;** or **not much attention?**

Not much attention 1
Some attention 2
A great deal of attention 3
Don't know ....: 8

27. Do you read a **daily** newspaper regularly?

Yes .... (ASK A) 1
No .... (GO TO Q. 28) 2

ASK ONLY IF YES

A. When you read newspapers how much attention do you pay to issues about technology, industry, or products: A **great deal of attention; some attention; not much attention?**

Not much attention 1
Some attention 2
A great deal of attention 3
Don't know 8

28. Do you regularly listen to radio news and public information programs?

Yes .... (ASK A) 1
No .... (GO TO Q. 29) 2

ASK ONLY IF YES

A. When you listen to radio news and public information programs how much attention do you pay to issues dealing with technology, industry or products: A **great deal of attention; some attention;** or **not much attention?**

Not much attention 1
Some attention 2
A great deal of attention 3
Don't know 8

29. In general, do you rely much on each of the following to provide information you trust on issues related to technology, industry or products? (Answer Yes or No).

READ EACH ITEM.

	YES	NO	DON'T KNOW
A. Family members	1	2	8
B. Friends or neighbors	1	2	8
C. Co-workers	1	2	8
D. Talks with experts	1	2	8

30. Do you **favor** further increasing the safety of auto travel through such things as improved auto design and added safety features **or** do you **oppose** such measures because they would be too expensive?

Favor 1
Oppose 2
Not sure 8

31. Which **one** of the following positions comes closest to expressing your views on industrial chemicals?

READ TWO POSITIONS.

Position (1)   Industrial chemicals have contributed so much to our standard of living that we should do all we can to encourage the development and distribution of new industrial chemicals.

Position (2)   Industrial chemicals have been such a mixed blessing for our society (country) that we should be much more careful before allowing new industrial chemicals to be developed and distributed.

INDICATE POSITION TAKEN.

Favors Position (1) 1
Favors Position (2) 2
Not sure 8

32. Do you **favor** further increasing the safety of commercial air travel through improved airplane design and added safety features at airports **or** do you **oppose** such measures because they would be too expensive?

Favor 1
Oppose 2
Not sure 8

33. I am going to read to you three statements, each of which represents how some people feel about nuclear electric power generation. Please listen carefully and tell me which **one** view you favor the most.

READ THE THREE POSITIONS.

Position (1)   All currently operating nuclear electric power plants should continue operating, with careful safety monitoring. If more electricity is needed, more nuclear power plants should be built.

Position (2)   All currently operating nuclear electric power plants should continue operating, with careful safety monitoring, but **no more** new nuclear power plants should be built until more is known about the safety risks involved. If more electricity is need, some other form of power generation should be used.

Position (3)   All nuclear electric power plants should be shut down permanently and no more should be allowed to be built. If more electricity is needed, some other form of power generation should be used.

INDICATE POSITION TAKEN.

Favor Position (1) "continue operating" 1
Favor Position (2) "continued, but no new ones" .. 2
Favor Position (3) "shut down permanently" 3
Not sure 8

34. Which **one** of the following three positions comes closest to expressing your views on handgun restrictions?

    READ THREE POSITIONS.

    Position (1)   The use, sale, and ownership of handguns should be banned.

    Position (2)   The use, sale, and ownership of handguns should be allowed, but should be restricted by licensing handgun dealers and owners.

    Position (3)   The use, sale, and ownership of handguns for lawful purposes should not be restricted by government.

    INDICATE POSITION TAKEN.

    Favors Position (1) "ban" 1
    Favors Position (2) "licensing" 2
    Favors Position (3) "no restrictions" 3
    Not sure 8

35. In order to maintain our national defense, which **one** of these three views do you favor most?

    READ THREE POSITIONS.

    Position (1)   We should strive to maintain nuclear superiority over the Soviet Union by continuing to manufacture nuclear weapons.

    Position (2)   We should increase our arsenal of nuclear weapons to achieve equality with the Soviet Union.

    Position (3)   Our current nuclear arsenal is more than sufficient to deter any potential aggressor; we need manufacture no more nuclear weapons.

    INDICATE POSITION TAKEN.

    Favors Position (1) 1
    Favors Position (2) 2
    Favors Position (3) 3
    Not sure 8

36. The next question concerns the costs of energy development and production. On this scale, rate how much, if any, "**the government**" should pay for each of the following:

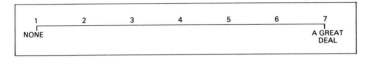

1	2	3	4	5	6	7
NONE						A GREAT DEAL

READ AND ENTER CODE IN BOXES FOR EACH ITEM.

A. Research and development costs for nuclear electric power ....

Don't know   8

B. The costs of operating and maintaining nuclear electric power plants ....

Don't know   8

C. Research and development costs for solar energy ....

Don't know   8

D. The costs of installing and operating solar energy devices ....

Don't know   8

E. The costs of installing energy conservation measures in private residences ...

Don't know   8

37. Suppose two friends were having a discussion about how to deal with industrial chemical waste disposal. Both agree that there is the need to regulate the transportation and disposal of industrial chemical wastes and that current dumps should be cleaned up. However, each has a different opinion on paying victims who have been harmed:

Person (1): feels the matter of compensating (paying) victims who have been harmed **should be settled on a case by case basis in the courts.** This means the victims would have to sue the company involved. Payment would result if the court found the company responsible for the harm.

Person (2): feels the compensating (paying) of victims who have been harmed **should be regulated and paid for by the government**. This means the victims would file a claim with a government agency which, on finding harm done, could award payment from a fund contributed to by all the companies in the business. No single company would have to be proven responsible.

With which person do you most agree?

Person (1) .... "courts" 1
Person (2) .... "government fund" 2
Don't know 8

38. In your opinion, over the next 20 years will the **benefits** to society resulting from continued technological and scientific innovation outweigh the related risks to society, or not?

Yes, benefits will outweigh risks 1
No, benefits will **not** outweigh risks 2
It depends (VOLUNTEERED ONLY) 3
Don't know 8

39. On a scale of 1 to 6, where "1" means that you and your friends and family **rarely, if ever,** discuss the following issues and "6" means that you and your friends and family discuss it relatively **often,** where would you place yourself?

1	2	3	4	5	6
RARELY IF EVER DISCUSSED					OFTEN DISCUSSED

READ AND ENTER CODE IN BOXES FOR EACH TECHNOLOGY.

A. The safety of automobile travel .... ☐

        Don't know 8

B. The safety of industrial chemicals .... ☐

        Don't know 8

C. Nuclear weapons .... ☐

        Don't know 8

D. Handguns .... ☐

        Don't know 8

E. The safety of nuclear electric power .... ☐

        Don't know 8

F. The safety of commercial air travel .... ☐

        Don't know 8

40. On a scale of 1 to 6, where "1" means you could change your mind **very easily** on the following issues, and "6" means that you are likely to **stick with your position** no matter what, where would you place yourself?

```
         1           2           3           4           5           6
      CHANGE MIND                                              STICK WITH
      VERY EASILY                                              YOUR POSITION
```

READ AND ENTER CODE IN BOXES FOR EACH TECHNOLOGY.

A. The safety of automobile travel ....
            Don't know 8

B. The safety of industrial chemicals ....
            Don't know 8

C. Nuclear weapons ....
            Don't know 8

D. Handguns ....
            Don't know 8

E. The safety of nuclear electric power ....
            Don't know 8

F. The safety of commercial air travel ....
            Don't know 8

41. On a scale of 1 to 6, where "1" means that the following issues affect you personally **very little** and "6" means that you really feel **deeply involved** in these issues, where would you place yourself?

```
   1          2          3          4          5          6
PERSONALLY                                          PERSONALLY
INVOLVED                                            INVOLVED
VERY LITTLE                                         DEEPLY
```

READ AND ENTER CODE IN BOXES FOR EACH TECHNOLOGY.

A. The safety of automobile travel .... ☐

                Don't know 8

B. The safety of industrial chemicals .... ☐

                Don't know 8

C. Nuclear weapons .... ☐

                Don't know 8

D. Handguns .... ☐

                Don't know 8

E. The safety of nuclear electric power .... ☐

                Don't know 8

F. The safety of commercial air travel .... ☐

                Don't know 8

42. On a scale of 1 to 6, where "1" means that you feel you **definitely need** more information on the following issues and "6" means that you **do not** feel you need to have any more information on them, where would you place yourself?

READ AND ENTER CODE IN BOXES FOR EACH TECHNOLOGY.

A. The safety of automobile travel ....

        Don't know 8

B. The safety of industrial chemicals ....

        Don't know 8

C. Nuclear weapons ....

        Don't know 8

D. Handguns ....

        Don't know 8

E. The safety of nuclear electric power ....

        Don't know 8

F. The safety of commercial air travel ....

        Don't know 8

43. Now I am going to read you a series of statements that will help us understand how you feel about a number of things. For each, please tell me how much you agree or disagree with it. There are no right or wrong answers. Try to answer each question, even if you must guess how you feel, using one of the five categories on this card.

    READ EACH ITEM. CODE ONE FOR EACH. REPEAT QUESTIONS OR CATEGORIES, IF NECESSARY.

		Strongly Agree	Agree	Neutral	Disagree	Strongly Disagree	Don't Know
A.	People should budget their personal expenses and then always live within their budgets.	5	4	3	2	1	8
B.	Life is too short; I shall never be able to do everything I would like to.	5	4	3	2	1	8
C.	It is great to be living in these exciting times.	5	4	3	2	1	8
D.	I think I worry too much.	5	4	3	2	1	8
E.	People should be self-controlled and self-disciplined.	5	4	3	2	1	8
F.	The less one owns, the fewer troubles one has.	5	4	3	2	1	8
G.	Success is more dependent on luck than on ability.	5	4	3	2	1	8
H.	Most people can be trusted.	5	4	3	2	1	8
I.	In general, I like to take risks.	5	4	3	2	1	8

	Strongly Agree	Agree	Neutral	Disagree	Strongly Disagree	Don't Know
J. Feelings are just as important for decisions as figures and facts.	5	4	3	2	1	8
K. The government should pay for promising projects which, however, may possibly fail.	5	4	3	2	1	8
L. It is better to have life go along smoothly than to be surprised, even when the surprises are pleasant.	5	4	3	2	1	8
M. It is more important to have a rich emotional life than success in life.	5	4	3	2	1	8
N. I am like those people who enjoy hang-gliding, mountain climbing, downhill skiing, or some other exciting and risky sport.	5	4	3	2	1	8
O. I like to bet on long shots.	5	4	3	2	1	8
P. Usually reason is a better guide to action than feelings.	5	4	3	2	1	8
Q. Sometimes I feel I don't have enough control over the direction my life is taking.	5	4	3	2	1	8
R. I hope for new experiences almost every day.	5	4	3	2	1	8
S. People should strive to attain their important goals even when uncertain of success.	5	4	3	2	1	8
T. It is important for me to have an exciting life.	5	4	3	2	1	8

44. Next, I would like you to think about the benefits people get from some industries and their products. One way to think about these benefits is to imagine what it would be like if the products, or services these technologies provide, were not easily available, or even did not exist at all. When making your ratings think **only** of benefits; we will deal with hazards or risks later. Think of benefits to you and your family, as well as benefits to the rest of the people of the country.

    A. Using a scale, where "1" means **no benefits** and "7" means **very great benefits,** how would you rate the **overall** benefits for each of the following:

1	2	3	4	5	6	7
NO BENEFITS						VERY GREAT BENEFITS

READ AND ENTER CODE IN BOXES FOR EACH TECHNOLOGY.

(1) Automobile travel .... ☐

           Don't know 8

(2) Industrial chemicals .... ☐

           Don't know 8

(3) Nuclear weapons .... ☐

           Don't know 8

(4) Handguns .... ☐

           Don't know 8

(5) Electricity .... ☐

           Don't know 8

(6) Commercial air travel .... ☐

           Don't know 8

B. Now consider just the **economic** benefits, such as, jobs, income, and increased productivity for each of the following.

READ EACH ITEM.

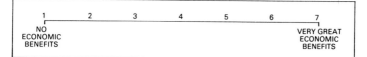

ENTER CODE IN BOXES FOR EACH TECHNOLOGY.

(1) Automobile travel ....

        Don't know 8

(2) Industrial chemicals ....

        Don't know 8

(3) Nuclear weapons ....

        Don't know 8

(4) Handguns ....

        Don't know 8

(5) Electricity ....

        Don't know 8

(6) Commercial air travel ....

        Don't know 8

C. Next consider benefits related to **basic human needs**, such as, health, food, shelter, and clothing.

READ EACH ITEM.

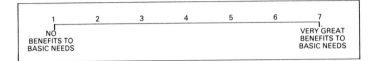

| 1 | 2 | 3 | 4 | 5 | 6 | 7 |

NO BENEFITS TO BASIC NEEDS

VERY GREAT BENEFITS TO BASIC NEEDS

ENTER CODE IN BOXES FOR EACH TECHNOLOGY.

(1) Automobile travel ....

Don't know 8

(2) Industrial chemicals ....

Don't know 8

(3) Nuclear weapons ....

Don't know 8

(4) Handguns ....

Don't know 8

(5) Electricity ....

Don't know 8

(6) Commercial air travel ....

Don't know 8

D. Now think about **safety** and **security** benefits, such as, protection from enemies, criminals, fire, natural hazards, insect and animal pests and so on.

1	2	3	4	5	6	7
NO SAFETY AND SECURITY BENEFITS						VERY GREAT SAFETY AND SECURITY BENEFITS

READ AND ENTER CODE IN BOXES FOR EACH TECHNOLOGY.

(1) Automobile travel ....

 Don't know 8

(2) Industrial chemicals ....

 Don't know 8

(3) Nuclear weapons ....

 Don't know 8

(4) Handguns ....

 Don't know 8

(5) Electricity ....

 Don't know 8

(6) Commercial air travel ....

 Don't know 8

E. Now think about your **personal pleasure** or **satisfaction**. On this scale "1" means **no personal pleasure or satisfaction** and "7" means **very great personal pleasure or satisfaction**. Where would you place yourself on this scale for each of the following?

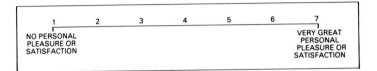

READ AND ENTER CODE IN BOXES FOR EACH TECHNOLOGY.

(1) Automobile travel ....

Don't know 8

(2) Industrial chemicals ....

Don't know 8

(3) Handguns ....

Don't know 8

(4) Electricity ....

Don't know 8

(5) Commercial air travel ....

Don't know 8

45. The next section is designed to help us understand your attitudes toward the environment. It contains a series of statements on various subjects. As I read each statement, tell me how much you agree or disagree with it. Again, there are no right or wrong answers. Try to answer each question, even if you must guess using one of the five categories on this card.

READ EACH ITEM. CODE ONE FOR EACH. REPEAT QUESTIONS OR CATEGORIES, IF NECESSARY.

	Strongly Agree	Agree	Neutral	Disagree	Strongly Disagree	Don't Know
A. I like amusement parks.	5	4	3	2	1	8
B. Machines increase people's freedom.	5	4	3	2	1	8
C. The idea of walking into the forest and "living off the land" for a week appeals to me.	5	4	3	2	1	8
D. Life in the city is more interesting than life on a farm.	5	4	3	2	1	8
E. It is exciting to go shopping in a large city.	5	4	3	2	1	8
F. When buying clothes, I usually look more for comfort than for style.	5	4	3	2	1	8
G. Suburbs should replace the city as the center of cultural life.	5	4	3	2	1	8
H. Cities are too noisy and crowded for me.	5	4	3	2	1	8
I. I often feel uneasy in a large crowd of people.	5	4	3	2	1	8
J. I can identify many of the local flowers and trees.	5	4	3	2	1	8

	Strongly Agree	Agree	Neutral	Disagree	Strongly Disagree	Don't Know
K. Our **national forests** should be preserved in their natural state, with roads and buildings prohibited.	5	4	3	2	1	8
L. Small town life is too boring for me.	5	4	3	2	1	8
M. I enjoy a change in the weather, even when it turns bad.	5	4	3	2	1	8
N. Hiking is boring.	5	4	3	2	1	8
O. Jet air travel is one of the great advances of our society.	5	4	3	2	1	8
P. The wilderness is cruel and harsh.	5	4	3	2	1	8
Q. I often wish for the seclusion of a weekend retreat.	5	4	3	2	1	8
R. Modern communities are plastic and ugly.	5	4	3	2	1	8
S. Science does as much harm as good.	5	4	3	2	1	8
T. The cultural life of a big city is very important to me.	5	4	3	2	1	8
U. It's fun to walk in the rain even if you get wet.	5	4	3	2	1	8
V. Mental problems are more common in the city than in the country.	5	4	3	2	1	8
W. Given enough time, science will solve most human problems.	5	4	3	2	1	8

46. All activities involve some risks. Accidents can occur no matter what measures are taken to avoid them. Think about the hazards and risks related to industries and their products: for example, risks of illness, injury or death to those who use the products, as well as those who make them; air, water, land pollution or other environmental damage; community disorder; national disaster. Consider **only** risks, not benefits. Think of hazards or risks to you and your family, as well as risks to the rest of the people in the country.

A. Here is a scale, where "1" means **no risks overall** and "7" means **very great risks overall**, how would you rate each industry or product?

1	2	3	4	5	6	7
NO RISKS						VERY GREAT RISKS

READ AND ENTER CODE IN BOXES FOR EACH INDUSTRY.

(1) Automobile travel . . . .

              Don't know 8

(2) Industrial chemicals . . . .

              Don't know 8

(3) Nuclear weapons . . . .

              Don't know 8

(4) Handguns . . . .

              Don't know 8

(5) Nuclear electric power . . . .

              Don't know 8

(6) Commercial air travel . . . .

              Don't know 8

B. The risks of some industries and their products are **well** known and understood by scientists and technical people. The risks of other industries and products are **not** well known and understood by scientists and technical people. How would you rate each industry or product on this scale?

```
   1        2        3        4        5        6        7
   |
  RISKS                                              RISKS
WELL KNOWN                                        NOT WELL
   AND                                           KNOWN AND
UNDERSTOOD                                       UNDERSTOOD
```

READ AND ENTER CODE IN BOXES FOR EACH INDUSTRY.

(1) Automobile travel ....

              Don't know 8

(2) Industrial chemicals ....

              Don't know 8

(3) Nuclear weapons ....

              Don't know 8

(4) Handguns ....

              Don't know 8

(5) Nuclear electric power ....

              Don't know 8

(6) Commercial air travel ....

              Don't know 8

C. One of the risks of industries and their products is the risk of death. On this scale where "1" means **few** and "7" means **many**, how many deaths are likely to occur in this country in the next year, as a result of each of the following?

1	2	3	4	5	6	7

FEW
DEATHS

MANY
DEATHS

READ AND ENTER CODE IN BOXES FOR EACH INDUSTRY.

(1) Automobile travel ....

  Don't know 8

(2) Industrial chemicals ....

  Don't know 8

(3) Nuclear weapons ....

  Don't know 8

(4) Handguns ....

  Don't know 8

(5) Nuclear electric power ....

  Don't know 8

(6) Commercial air travel ....

  Don't know 8

D. The risks of death from some industries and their products affect people only one at a time. The risks of death from other industries and their products can affect large numbers of people in a single event. How would you rate the risk of death from each industry or product on this scale?

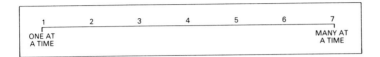

READ AND ENTER CODE IN BOXES FOR EACH INDUSTRY.

(1) Automobile travel ....

Don't know 8

(2) Industrial chemicals ....

Don't know 8

(3) Nuclear weapons ....

Don't know 8

(4) Handguns ....

Don't know 8

(5) Nuclear electric power ....

Don't know 8

(6) Commercial air travel ....

Don't know 8

E. Some industries and their products produce risks that people have learned to live with and can think about reasonably calmly. Other industries and products produce risks for which people have very great dread. How do you feel about each industry or product on this scale?

```
1        2        3        4        5        6        7
COMMON,                                            VERY GREAT
NO DREAD                                             DREAD
```

READ AND ENTER CODE IN BOXES FOR EACH INDUSTRY.

(1) Automobile travel . . . . ☐

               Don't know 8

(2) Industrial chemicals . . . . ☐

               Don't know 8

(3) Nuclear weapons . . . . ☐

               Don't know 8

(4) Handguns . . . . ☐

               Don't know 8

(5) Nuclear electric power . . . . ☐

               Don't know 8

(6) Commercial air travel . . . . ☐

               Don't know 8

47. Last week were you working full time, part time; going to school; keeping house; or what?

CIRCLE ONE CODE ONLY. IF MORE THAN ONE RESPONSE, GIVE PREFERENCE TO SMALLEST CODE NUMBER THAT APPLIES.

```
Working full time  .......... (ASK A) .......... 1
Working part time  .......... (ASK A) .......... 2
With a job, but not at work because of temporary
   illness, vacation, strike  ....... (ASK B) ....... 3
Unemployed, laid off, looking for work
   ................ (GO TO Q. 48) ............... 4
Retired  .............. (ASK C) ............... 5
In school  ............. (ASK C) ............. 6
Keeping house  ........... (ASK C) .......... 7
Other  ........ (SPECIFY AND ASK C) ........ 8
```

A. **IF WORKING, FULL OR PART TIME**: How many hours did you work last week, at all jobs?

Hours: ☐☐

```
┌─────────────────┐
│  NOW GO TO Q. 48 │
└─────────────────┘
```

B. **IF WITH A JOB, BUT NOT AT WORK**: How many hours a week do you usually work, at all jobs?

Hours: ☐☐

```
┌─────────────────┐
│  NOW GO TO Q. 48 │
└─────────────────┘
```

C. **IF RETIRED, IN SCHOOL, KEEPING HOUSE, OR OTHER**: Did you ever work for as long as one year?

```
Yes  .............. (ASK Q. 48) ............... 1
No  .............. (GO TO Q. 49) .............. 2
```

ASK ONLY IF R. IS WORKING NOW OR HAS EVER WORKED.

48. What kind of work do (do/did you normally) do? That is, what (is/was) your job called?

    OCCUPATION: _____

    A. **IF NOT ALREADY ANSWERED, ASK:**
    What (do/did) you actually do in that job? Tell me, what (are/were) some of your main duties?

    B. What kind of place (do/did) you work for?

       INDUSTRY: _____

    C. **IF NOT ALREADY ANSWERED, ASK:**
    What (do/did) they (make/do)?

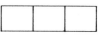

    D. **IF ALREADY ANSWERED, CODE WITHOUT ASKING:** (Are/Were) you self-employed or (do/did) you work for someone else?

                Self-employed 1
                    Someone else 2

49. Are you currently—married, widowed, divorced, separated, or have you never been married?

                    Married 1
                    Widowed 2
                    Divorced 3
                    Separated 4
                    Never married 5

50. How many children have you had?

                   ENTER NUMBER:

51. From what countries or part of the world did your ancestors come?

IF SINGLE COUNTRY IS NAMED, REFER TO NATIONAL CODES
BELOW, AND ENTER CODE NUMBER IN BOXES:

IF MORE THAN ONE COUNTRY IS NAMED, ENTER CODE 88
AND ASK A.

A. **IF MORE THAN ONE COUNTRY NAMED:** Which of these
countries do you feel closer to?

IF ONE COUNTRY NAMED, REFER TO CODES BELOW,
AND ENTER CODE NUMBER IN BOXES:

IF CAN'T DECIDE ON ONE COUNTRY, ENTER CODE 88.

NATIONAL CODES

American Indian	30	Mexico	17
Africa	01	Netherland (Dutch/Holland)	18
Austria	02	Norway	19
Belgium	36	Philippines	20
Canada (French)	03	Poland	21
Canada (Other)	04	Portugal	32
China	05	Puerto Rico	22
Czechoslovakia	06	Rumania	35
Denmark	07	Russia (USSR)	23
England and Wales	08	Scotland	24
Finland	09	Spain	25
France	10	Sweden	26
Germany	11	Switzerland	27
Greece	12	Yugoslavia	34
Hungary	13	Other (SPECIFY)	29
India	31		
Ireland	14	More than one country/can't decide	
Italy	15	on one	88
Japan	16	Don't know	98
Lithuania	33		

52. Would you say your own health, in general, is excellent, good, fair, or poor?

                    Excellent 1
                    Good 2
                    Fair 3
                    Poor 4
                    Don't know 8

53. If you were asked to use one of four names for your social class, which would you say you belong in: the lower class, the working class, the middle class, or the upper class?

                    Lower class 1
                    Working class 2
                    Middle class 3
                    Upper class 4

54. Generally speaking, do you usually think of yourself as a Republican, Democrat, Independent, or what?

                    Republican .... (ASK A) 1
                    Democrat .... (ASK A) 2
                    Independent .... (ASK B) 3
                    Other party affiliation (SPECIFY AND ASK B)
                    ————————————————— 4
                    No preference .... (ASK B) 5

   A. **IF REPUBLICAN OR DEMOCRAT**: Would you call yourself a strong (Republican/Democrat) or not a very strong (Republican/Democrat)?

                    Strong 1
                    Not very strong 2

   NOW GO TO Q. 55

   B. **IF INDEPENDENT, "NO PREFERENCE," OR "OTHER"**: Do you think of yourself as closer to the Republican or Democratic Party?

                    Republican 3
                    Democratic 4
                    Neither 5

55. We hear a lot of talk these days about liberals and conservatives. I'm going to show you a seven-point scale on which the **political** views that people might hold are arranged from extremely liberal—point 1—to extremely conservative—point 7. Where would you place yourself on this scale?

1) Extremely liberal 1
2) Liberal 2
3) Slightly liberal 3
4) Moderate, middle of the road 4
5) Slightly conservative 5
6) Conservative 6
7) Extremely conservative 7

56. In 1980, you remember that Carter ran for President on the Democratic ticket against Reagan for the Republicans. Do you remember for sure whether or not you voted in that election?

Voted .... (ASK A) 1
Did not vote .... (ASK B) 2
Ineligible .... (ASK B) 3
Refused .... (GO TO Q. 57) 7
Don't know/don't remember
.... (GO TO Q. 57) 8

A. **IF VOTED:** Did you vote for Carter or Reagan?

Carter .... (GO TO Q. 57) 1
Reagan .... (GO TO Q. 57) 2
Other candidate (SPECIFY AND GO TO Q. 57)

_____ 3
Didn't vote for President .... (ASK B) 4
Don't know/don't remember .. (GO TO Q. 57) .. 8

B. **IF DID NOT VOTE OR INELIGIBLE:** Who would you have voted for, for President, if you had voted?

Carter 1
Reagan 2
Other 3
Don't know/don't remember 8

57. What is your religious preference? Is it Protestant, Catholic, Jewish, some other religion, or no religion?

```
Protestant  ............. (ASK A) ............. 1
Catholic  ..................................... 2
Jewish  ....................................... 3
None ............ (SKIP TO Q. 58) ............ 4
Other (SPECIFY RELIGION AND/OR CHURCH
    AND DENOMINATION)
_____  5
```

A. **IF PROTESTANT**: What specific denomination is that, if any?

```
Baptist  ...................................... 1
Methodist  ................................... 2
Lutheran  .................................... 3
Presbyterian  ................................ 4
Episcopalian  ................................ 5
Other (SPECIFY)
_____  6
No denomination given or non-denominational
    church  .................................. 7
```

(OTHER)

ASK EVERYONE WITH ANY RELIGIOUS PREFERENCE NAMED IN Q. 57.

Would you call yourself a strong (RELIGIOUS PREFERENCE) or a not very strong (RELIGIOUS PREFERENCE)?

```
Strong ....................................... 1
Not very strong .............................. 2
Somewhat strong (VOLUNTEERED) ............ 3
Don't know  .................................. 8
```

58. In what religion were you raised?

```
Protestant  ................................... 1
Catholic  ..................................... 2
Jewish  ....................................... 3
None  ......................................... 4
Other (SPECIFY RELIGION AND/OR CHURCH
    AND DENOMINATION)
_____  5
```

59. What is the highest grade in elementary school or high school that you finished and got credit for? CODE EXACT GRADE.

No formal school 00
1st grade 01
2nd grade 02
3rd grade 03
4th grade 04   GO TO Q. 60   9th grade 09
5th grade 05   10th grade 10
6th grade 06   11th grade 11   ASK A & B
7th grade 07   12th grade 12
8th grade 08   Don't know 98

IF FINISHED 9TH-12TH GRADE OR DK:

A. Did you ever get a high school diploma or a GED certificate?

Yes .... (ASK B) 1
No .... (ASK B) 2
Don't know .... (ASK B) 8

B. Did you ever complete one or more years of college for credit—not including schooling such as business college, technical, or vocational school?

Yes .... ASK (1) & (2) 1
No .... (GO TO Q. 60) 2
Don't know 8

IF YES TO B:

(1) How many years did you complete?

1 year 0
2 years 1
3 years 2
4 years 3
5 years 4
6 years 5
7 years 6
8+ years 7
Don't know 8

(2) Do you have any college degrees?

Yes .... [ASK (3)] 1
No 2
Don't know 8

(3) **IF YES TO (2):** What degree or degrees? CODE HIGHEST DEGREE EARNED.

Associate/Junior College 2
Bachelor's 3
Graduate 4
Don't know 8

(4) **IF YES TO (2):** What is your degree in? _____

IF ONE PERSON HOUSEHOLD, GO TO Q. 61

60. Now I would like you to think about the people who live in this household. Please include any persons who usually live here but are away temporarily—on business, on vacation, or in a general hospital—and include all babies and small children. Do not include college students who are living away at college, persons stationed away from here in the Armed Forces, or persons away in institutions.

Is everyone in this household related to you in some way?

Yes 1
No . . . . (ASK A) 2

A. **IF NO:** How many persons in this household are **not** related to you in any way?

PERSONS:

61. (Just thinking about your family now—those people in the household who **are** related to you . . .) How many persons in the family, including yourself, received any money last year—1981— from any job or employment, or any other source?

PERSONS:

62. In which of these groups did your total **family** income, from **all** sources, fall last year—1981— before taxes, that is. Just tell me the letter.

Total income includes interest or dividends, rent, social security, other pensions, alimony or child support, unemployment compensation, public aid (welfare), armed forces or veterans allotment.	A. Under $1,000 . . . . 01 B. $1,000 to 2,999 . . . . 02 C. $3,000 to 3,999 . . . . 03 D. $4,000 to 4,999 . . . . 04 E. $5,000 to 5,999 . . . . 05 F. $6,000 to 6,999 . . . . 06 G. $7,000 to 7,999 . . . . 07 H. $8,000 to 9,999 . . . . 08 I. $10,000 to 12,499 . . . . 09 J. $12,500 to 14,999 . . . . 10 K. $15,000 to 17,499 . . . . 11 L. $17,500 to 19,999 . . . . 12 M. $20,000 to 22,499 . . . . 13 N. $22,500 to 24,999 . . . . 14 O. $25,000 to 29,999 . . . . 15 P. $30,000 to 39,999 . . . . 16 Q. $40,000 to 74,999 . . . . 17 R. $75,000 or over . . . . 18 Refused . . . . 97 Don't know 98

63. Now we would like to know something about the groups and organizations to which you currently belong. Here is a list of various kinds of organizations. Could you tell me whether or not you are a member of each type?

READ EACH ITEM. CODE ONE FOR EACH.

	YES	NO	DON'T KNOW
A. Fraternal groups	1	2	8
B. Service clubs	1	2	8
C. Veterans' groups	1	2	8
D. Political clubs	1	2	8
E. Labor unions	1	2	8
F. Sports groups	1	2	8
G. Youth groups	1	2	8
H. School service groups	1	2	8
I. Hobby or garden clubs	1	2	8
J. School fraternities or sororities	1	2	8
K. Nationality groups	1	2	8
L. Farm organizations	1	2	8
M. Literary, art, or music groups	1	2	8
N. Professional or academic societies	1	2	8
O. Church-affiliated groups	1	2	8
P. Discussion or study groups	1	2	8
Q. Any other groups?	1	2	8

Specify: _____

64. Did you live in this same **house** five years ago, that is, since the summer of 1977?

```
Yes  . . . . . . . . . . . . . (GO TO Q. 65) . . . . . . . . . . . . 1
No  . . . . . . . . . . . . . . . . (ASK A) . . . . . . . . . . . . . . 2
Don't know  . . . . . . . . . . . . . . . . . . . . . . . . . . . . . . . 8
```

ASK ONLY IF NO ON Q. 64:

A. Did you live in the same **state** five years ago?

```
Yes  . . . . . . . . . . . . . (GO TO Q. 65) . . . . . . . . . . . . 1
No  . . . . . . . . . . . . . . . . [ASK (1)] . . . . . . . . . . . . . . 2
Don't know  . . . . . . . . . . . . . . . . . . . . . . . . . . . . . . . 8
```

IF NO TO A:

(1) In which **state** did you live five years ago? _____

STATE CODES

Alabama 63	Louisiana 73	Oklahoma 72
Alaska 94	Maine 11	Oregon 92
Arizona 87	Maryland 52	Pennsylvania 23
Arkansas 71	Massachusetts 14	Rhode Island 16
California 93	Michigan 34	South Carolina 57
Colorado 86	Minnesota 41	South Dakota 45
Connecticut 15	Mississippi 64	Tennessee 62
Delaware 51	Missouri 43	Texas 74
Washington, D.C. 55	Montana 81	Utah 85
Florida 59	Nebraska 46	Vermont 12
Georgia 58	Nevada 84	Virginia 54
Hawaii 95	New Hampshire 13	Washington State . . . 91
Idaho 82	New Jersey 22	West Virginia 53
Illinois 32	New Mexico 88	Wisconsin 31
Indiana 33	New York 21	Wyoming 83
Iowa 42	North Carolina 56	Foreign country 01
Kansas 47	North Dakota 44	
Kentucky 61	Ohio 35	_____

65. Do you (or your [SPOUSE]) belong to a labor union? CIRCLE ONLY **ONE** CODE.

Yes, respondent belongs 1
Yes, spouse belongs 2
Yes, both belong 3
No, neither R. nor spouse belongs 4
Don't know 8

66. Were you born in this country?

Yes 1
No 2
Don't know 8

67. Have you ever been on active duty for military training or service?

Yes .... (ASK A) 1
No .... (GO TO Q. 68) 2

IF YES TO Q. 67 ASK:

A. Have you ever served on active duty in the military overseas?

Yes .... (ASK B) 1
No .... (GO TO Q. 68) 2

B. Was this during a war or military conflict?

Yes .... (ASK C) 1
No .... (GO TO Q. 68) 2

C. Which war?

World War I 1
World War II 2
Korean 3
Vietnam 4
Other _____ ... 5

68. What is the year of your birth?

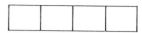

69. CODE RESPONDENT'S GENDER:

Male 1
Female 2

70. CODE WITHOUT ASKING ONLY IF THERE IS **NO** DOUBT IN YOUR MIND.

What race do you consider yourself?

RECORD VERBATIM **AND** CODE.

White 1
Black 2
Other (SPECIFY) 3

NOTE: IF YOU **ASKED** R'S RACE, CHECK BOX ....

Thank you very much for your time and help.

May I have your name and telephone number just in case my office wants to verify this interview?

ENTER NAME AND PHONE NUMBER.
IF NO PHONE OR REFUSED, CIRCLE APPROPRIATE CODE.

RESPONDENT'S NAME: _____

TELEPHONE NUMBER: _____ / _____
AREA CODE   NUMBER

No phone number 1
Refused phone number 2

IF TELEPHONE NUMBER IS GIVEN, ASK A:

A. Is this phone located in your own home?

Yes 3
No (SPECIFY WHERE PHONE IS LOCATED) 4

_____

THANK YOU.

TIME	
INTERVIEW	AM
ENDED: _____	PM

INTERVIEWER COMMENTS

INTERVIEWER COMMENTS

INTERVIEWER REMARKS
(TO BE FILLED OUT **AS SOON AS POSSIBLE** AFTER LEAVING RESPONDENT)

A. Length of interview:

Minutes

B. Date of interview:

Month

Day

Year

C. In general, what was the respondent's attitude toward the interview? CODE ONE.

Friendly and interested 1
Cooperative but not particularly interested 2
Impatient and restless 3
Hostile 4

D. Was respondent's understanding of the questions . . . CODE ONE.

Good? 1
Fair? 2
Poor? 3

E. INTERVIEWER'S SIGNATURE: _____

F.

  INTERVIEWER'S NUMBER:

ENTER CASE # IN BOX ON BACK COVER

B

Data Collection

Sample Design

One of the study's original goals was to test the extent to which findings from prior risk-perceptions research in the United States could be replicated with a different research design: the sample survey. The quasi-laboratory research designs used in previous risk-perception studies conducted in this country involved only small, specially selected, nonprobability, convenience samples of people such as students, interest group members, and experts. The results of these studies cannot be generalized to the population as a whole. Therefore, we originally proposed to interview a full-probability sample of eligible adults from the general population (somewhere in the Northeast). Reviewers from the National Science Foundation recommended, however, that the study be extended to include a full-probability sample of adults from the Sunbelt region of the United States, and that additional special samples of advocates from the two regions be included.

The Northeast-Sunbelt contrast was deemed necessary because perceptions about technology might be influenced by regional growth factors existing at the time: a decline in population and economic growth in the Northeast, and extraordinarily high levels of growth in the Sunbelt. The samples of advocates were added to assure adequate numbers of respon-

Table B.1
Sample Design by Region

Samples	New England	Southwest	Total
General population[a]			
Compiled interviews	542	479	1,021
Response rate	77.3%	62.5%	70.4%
Advocates sampled	150	149	299
Total completed interviews	692	628	1,320

[a]Both general population samples are full-probability samples.

dents who had taken direct action to try to influence the risk-management process (it was assumed that samples from the general population would yield too few such respondents). Table B.1 shows the sample design by region.

Sample Selection

Northeast. We chose Connecticut as the area for sample selection in the Northeast. Its proximity to Yale University allowed us maximum control over data collection, including sample selection; interviewer hiring, training, and supervision; and coding.

After considering several alternatives, including a multistage area probability sample, we selected a sample frame based on a list drawn from an electric utility company's residential household customers. This list consisted of the names and addresses of customers at the household level where the service was received (i.e., the address where the meter was located and where repair calls were made), not the billing addresses. This avoided post office box addresses and third-party billing names and addresses.

The utility company's service area encompasses all of the state of Connecticut except the townships of New Haven, Bridgeport, and Wallingford, which are serviced by other utility companies. It includes a major metropolitan area (Hartford), suburban Fairfield County, and rural northern Connecticut, as well as a number of small- and medium-sized communities (e.g., Danbury, New London, Waterbury). In 1980, Connecticut had 3,107,576 residents in 1,093,678 households. Approximately 2,300,000 residents and 810,000 households were included in the sample frame. Using an up-to-date computerized list provided by the utility company, we randomly selected 800 households. No stratification was used since the study region was geographically small enough to be easily reached from the base of operation. Therefore, the selection process, at the household level, was totally random.

Vacation homes and some buildings receiving residential electric rates that were not residences (e.g., commercial establishments, churches, government buildings) were designated out of frame. No provision was made for selecting a particular household when the address on the sampled list turned out to be a master-metered, multifamily dwelling unit. There are very few master-metered buildings in Connecticut, as most were converted to single-metered apartments when energy prices rose in the 1970s. Out of 800 addresses selected, 11 were found to be master-metered multifamily units (only 1.4 percent of the selected households.)

Since names were available, a personalized letter was mailed to each household a few days before the arrival of the interviewer, and gave members of the household an opportunity to call the study director for more information. It is important to note, however, that although names appeared on the sample list, it was the household (i.e., the address) that was randomly selected at this stage. If the resident named on the list had moved, the current residents at the address were included in the study.

At the household level, one eligible adult was selected randomly for interviewing using a "Kish table" (Kish, 1965: 398–404). A short "screening interview" conducted with the first resident of the household contacted provided the information necessary for this selection. The operational definition of an eligible respondent was an English-speaking adult, 18 years of age or older, who was a permanent resident in the selected household. College students who normally lived outside the household during the academic year were not considered eligible.

The advocate samples in Connecticut were drawn from lists of individuals who had testified at state or federal hearings held on matters related to technological safety. Since the testimony of these persons was itself available at the state capital (Hartford), we were able to classify intervenors as being either pro-safety or pro-benefits. We therefore randomly selected respondents from each group until we completed 75 interviews from each. Intervenors were initially contacted by telephone, at which time an appointment was made for conducting the interview. Even though we chose intervenors at random from the lists we were able to compile, no claim can be made that we identified all possible intervenors. Therefore, the samples of intervenors should be considered as nonprobability and purposive.

The Sunbelt.   In searching for an appropriate Sunbelt location we investigated the social, economic, and demographic characteristics of six areas: Arizona, Florida, New Mexico, North Carolina, southern California, and Texas. We sought an area that would provide maximum similarity to the Connecticut study region on demographic factors (e.g., population size; urban, rural, suburban mix; socioeconomic characteristics of the residents) as well as maximum contrast on regional growth and attitudes toward technology. The practical consideration of being able to identify a good sample frame and the logistical factor of being able to complete the data collection also played an important role in the final choice of Sunbelt area.

We chose Arizona as the state that most closely met these criteria. Since the state is so large, however, we designated Maricopa County as the area for the survey. In 1980 Arizona had 2,718,425 residents of which 1,509,262 (56 percent) lived in Maricopa County. Maricopa County encompasses a large city (Phoenix), which is the state capital, several small cities (e.g., Wickenberg, Buckeye), several medium-sized cities (e.g., Glendale, Tempe), and a rural hinterland. Table B.2 compares the social and eco-

Table B.2
Social and Demographic Characteristics

Demographic Characteristics	Connecticut General Population ($n = 542$)	Arizona General Population ($n = 479$)	Advocate Samples Both Regions ($n = 299$)
Mean age	45	44	46
Gender			
Male	45%	48%	83%
Female	55	52	17
Race			
White	94%	94%	96%
Nonwhite	6	6	4
Gross family income			
Under $15,000	22%	35%	5%
$15,000—$29,999	36	36	17
$30,00–$74,999	36	24	66
Over $75,000	6	5	12
Median income[a]	$24,750	$19,025	$36,210
Education			
Mean years of school	13	13	17
High school diploma	82%	77%	98%
College degree	31%	24%	83%

Table B.2 (continued)

Demographic Characteristics	Connecticut General Population (*n* = 542)	Arizona General Population (*n* = 479)	Advocate Samples Both Regions (*n* = 299)
Religious preference			
Protestant	37%	45%	48%
Catholic	44	32	25
Jewish	3	2	6
Other	5	10	5
None	11	11	16
Married	68%	62%	81%
Lived in a different state 5 years ago (1977)	12%	21%	12%
Self-designated liberal/ conservative views			
Liberal	30%	25%	34%
Moderate	35	35	18
Conservative	35	40	48
Political party affiliation			
Democrat	29%	34%	29%
Republican	26	30	39
Independent	38	26	30
No preference/other	7	10	2
Voted in 1980 presidential election	74%	60%	95%

Data are percentages (adjusted for missing values), except where otherwise indicated (e.g., mean).
[a]Median income is approximate since it was interpolated from grouped income categories ordered on a scale from 1 to 18.

nomic characteristics of the respondents for all of the samples in both study regions.

After an unsuccessful search for a list sample frame (e.g., utility company list, automobile registration list), it became obvious that the only sampling technique available for producing a full-probability sample of the general population would be a multistaged area probability sample. The National Opinion Research Center (NORC) at the University of Chicago was contracted to design the Arizona sample; hire, train, and supervise the interviewers; and complete the data collection. NORC utilized its standard procedures for area probability sample surveys except that the processes of listing households and interviewing the selected respondent were combined. The following description of the area probability sample is based on a report prepared by Roger Tourangeau of the Sampling Department of the National Opinion Research Center.

A sample of 100 geographical segments was selected within the Phoenix Standard Metropolitan Statistical Area (including the city of Phoenix and the remainder of Maricopa County). This area had been selected in part because it had a high growth rate, on the order of 10 percent every three years. Next, individual housing units were drawn within each sampled segment. Finally, an eligible respondent was selected at each sampled housing unit. Selections at each stage were made with fixed selection probabilities.

The initial geographic segments consisted of blocks, or, within less developed areas, blocklike units. Each segment's probability of selection depended on the 1980 Census count of occupied housing units:

$$\text{Prob (Segment } i) = (100 \times \text{MOS}_i)/\text{MOS}, \tag{1}$$

in which

MOS_i = the measure of size for segment i (that is, the number of occupied housing units, based on 1980 Census data); and

MOS = the total measure of size for the Phoenix SMSA (total number of occupied housing units).

One hundred corresponds to the number of segments selected.

Two of the segments fell within Indian reservations. After some discussion, it was decided to drop these two segments. In effect, the eligible population was redefined to include the population of the Phoenix SMSA living outside reservations.

Segments were selected with unequal probabilities; larger segments had larger probabilities of selection. Therefore, within-segment sampling rates were set to compensate for these inequalities. Within any segment, the sampling rate was inversely proportional to the measure of size:

$$\text{Prob (Within)} = \frac{b}{\text{MOS}_i}. \tag{2}$$

The constant b was set at seven, which represents the targeted number of selections per segment.

The overall probability of selecting an individual housing unit is the product of (1) and (2):

$$\text{Prob (HU)} = \frac{100 \times \text{MOS}_i}{\text{MOS}} \times \frac{b}{\text{MOS}_i} = \frac{100 \times b}{\text{MOS}}. \qquad (3)$$

As Equation (3) reveals, the probability is a constant; any eligible housing unit has the same chance of selection.

Because of growth (that is, new construction) the actual number of housing units in each segment differed from the 1980 Census count (MOS_i). For this reason, the actual number of selections in each segment varied somewhat, depending on the amount of growth:

$$n_i = \frac{b}{\text{MOS}_i} \times B_i, \qquad (4)$$

in which

n_i = the expected number of selected housing units in segment i,

b/MOS_i = the sampling rate for segment i, and

B_i = the actual number of housing units in segment i.

The expected number of selections (n) would equal the targeted number (b) only if the measure of size (MOS_i) were perfectly accurate. Since it was assumed that growth had been approximately 10 percent since the 1980 Census was taken, however, it was assumed that B_i would be about 10 percent larger, on average, than MOS_i. It was therefore expected that about 770 addresses (or households) would be selected.

Early field results suggested, however, that 10 percent was too low an estimate and that the growth was unevenly distributed across segments. Therefore, NORC altered the within-segment sampling rates to assure that the final sample size would be close to the original goal.

Interviewing had not yet begun in 45 of the segments, so their sampling rates were changed. In 43 of these segments, b (equation 2) was reduced from 7.0 to 6.29; in 2 other segments that had special problems, b was reduced to 3.7. The listing below presents the final, within-segment sampling rate for each segment in terms of the factor b. Overall, housing units were sampled with one of three probabilities:

$$\text{Probability} = \frac{100 \times \text{MOS}_i}{\text{MOS}} \times \frac{b_i}{\text{MOS}_i} = \frac{100 \times b_i}{\text{MOS}}. \qquad (5)$$

The values of b_i for each segment were:

FINAL RATE	SEGMENTS
7.0 (*b*)	7, 8, 9, 10, 12, 13, 14, 16, 17, 20, 23, 24, 29, 31, 32, 33, 34, 35, 37, 40, 41, 42, 43, 44, 45, 46, 47, 48, 49, 50, 51, 52, 54, 55, 56, 58, 60, 62, 64, 65, 66, 68, 73, 74, 75, 76, 79, 84, 86, 87, 90, 97

	SEGMENTS
3.7 (*b*)	18, 99

	SEGMENTS
6.29 (*b*)	1, 2, 3, 4, 5, 6, 11, 15, 19, 21, 22, 25, 26, 27, 28, 30, 36, 38, 39, 53, 57, 59, 61, 67, 69, 70, 71, 72, 77, 78, 80, 81, 82, 83, 85, 88, 89, 91, 93, 94, 95, 96

Segments 98 and 100 were dropped from the sample, as they were located on Indian reservations. Segment 63 included no selections because of demolition.

Once a housing unit was selected, interviewers contacted the residents and randomly selected one respondent. Taking into account this final stage of selection, the overall selection probability for any given respondent was the product of the probability of selecting the housing unit times the probability of selecting one respondent from among those eligible in the household:

$$\text{Prob (Respondent}_{ij}) = \frac{100 \times b_i}{\text{MOS}} \times \frac{1}{g_{ij}}, \tag{6}$$

in which

Prob (Respondent$_{ij}$) = the selection probability for a respondent in segment i who lives in housing unit j, and

g_{ij} = the number of eligible persons in housing unit j.

Table B.3 shows the details of the random selection with response rates for both probability samples.

Table B.3

Response and Nonresponse Rates for the Full-Probability Samples

Disposition of Cases	Connecticut (Roper Center)	Arizona (NORC)
A. Original sample	800	877
B. Out-of-sample frame	98	110
1. No English spoken	16	13
2. Vacant dwelling	17	47
3. Address not a dwelling unit	65	48
4. Field staff listing errors	0	2
C. Net sample (A–B)	702	767
D. Completed cases	542	479
E. Refusals	113	184
1. Refused screener	48	77
2. Selected respondent refused interview	65	107
F. Final noninterview, other	47	104
1. Wrong respondent selected	0	5
2. Unable to gain access (security)	0	5
3. No one ever home	18	37
4. Selected respondent never available	19	40
5. Selected respondent too ill or senile	10	17
. . .		
H. Eligibility rate (C/A)	.878	.875
I. Response rate (D/C)	.772	.625
J. Refusal rate (E/C)	.161	.240

The intervenor samples from Arizona were drawn from lists compiled in a similar manner to the list compiled in Connecticut; however, there were fewer relevant public hearings and record keeping was less systematic in Arizona. Also, the personal testimony of most intervenors was unaccessible, thus preventing the designation of pro-safety or pro-benefits in most cases. The final sample of intervenors from Arizona, therefore, includes all people who gave identifiable pro-safety or pro-benefits testimony plus additional people who gave testimony that could not be classified (indeed, some of these additional persons may have attended only the relevant hearings). NORC conducted the interviews with the individuals on the advocate list after making an appointment by telephone.

Weighting

Two of the terms in equation (6), b_i and g_{ij}, are variables. This means that the probability of selecting each respondent was not exactly equal. To compensate for these unequal selection probabilities, it is necessary to take these two variables into account according to the formula:

$$\text{Prob (Respondent}_{ij}) = (K) \times \frac{b_i}{g_{ij}}. \qquad (7)$$

That is, it is necessary to weight the answers given by each respondent according to each respondent's probability of being selected and interviewed.

The simplest approach is to weight the data for each case by the inverse of b_i/g_{ij}. A slightly more complicated method, which gives the same results, is to calculate a preliminary weight (i.e., g_{ij}/b_i) and then multiply all the preliminary weights by a constant so that the sum of the final weights is equal to the number of completed cases. The appropriate constant is the number of completed cases divided by the sum of the preliminary weights. The advantage of this latter approach, which we employed, is that weighted and unweighted n's remain approximately the same.

Table B.4

Comparison of Summary Statistics for Weighted and Unweighted Data Connecticut Sample Only (n = 542)

Questionnaire Item	Mean	Standard Error	Variance
Desired Restrictions and Standards			
Automobiles	5.819	0.057	1.577
Weighted	5.788	0.058	1.608
Industrial chemicals	6.629	0.033	0.549
Weighted	6.617	0.034	0.602
Nuclear weapons	6.695	0.031	0.492
Weighted	6.691	0.032	0.510
Handguns	6.146	0.062	2.011
Weighted	6.095	0.062	2.058
Nuclear electric power	6.575	0.038	0.736
Weighted	6.548	0.040	0.761
Air travel	6.473	0.038	0.736
Weighted	6.445	0.040	0.804

Table B.4 (continued)

Questionnaire Item	Mean	Standard Error	Variance
Overall Benefits			
Automobiles	6.112	0.052	1.452
Weighted	6.100	0.052	1.454
Industrial chemicals	4.744	0.074	2.855
Weighted	4.720	0.075	2.922
Nuclear weapons	3.637	0.087	3.956
Weighted	3.634	0.086	3.885
Handguns	2.712	0.078	3.250
Weighted	2.796	0.078	3.245
Electricity	6.546	0.039	0.814
Weighted	6.522	0.040	0.860
Air travel	6.062	0.052	1.457
Weighted	6.039	0.052	1.421
Overall Risks			
Automobiles	4.955	0.059	1.890
Weighted	4.951	0.059	1.839
Industrial chemicals	5.603	0.056	1.685
Weighted	5.595	0.056	1.638
Nuclear weapons	6.350	0.049	1.296
Weighted	6.357	0.049	1.278
Handguns	5.845	0.063	2.105
Weighted	5.795	0.063	2.126
Nuclear electric power	5.030	0.067	2.372
Weighted	5.028	0.066	2.296
Air travel	4.137	0.070	2.645
Weighted	4.092	0.070	2.601
Sociodemographics			
Education	13.161	0.132	9.430
Weighted	13.089	0.133	9.565
Income	13.663	0.167	13.958
Weighted	14.073	0.158	12.489
Gender	1.548	0.021	0.248
Weighted	1.520	0.021	0.250
Age	44.689	0.723	282.756
Weighted	43.375	0.711	273.727

Table B.5
Comparison of Summary Statistics for Weighted and Unweighted Data
Arizona Sample Only (n = 479)

Questionnaire Item	Mean	Standard Error	Variance
Desired Restrictions and Standards			
Automobiles	5.697	0.056	1.461
Weighted	5.677	0.055	1.391
Industrial chemicals	6.651	0.032	0.492
Weighted	6.636	0.033	0.518
Nuclear weapons	6.718	0.032	0.474
Weighted	6.697	0.033	0.513
Handguns	5.408	0.081	3.076
Weighted	5.439	0.079	2.966
Nuclear electric power	6.624	0.034	0.510
Weighted	6.625	0.033	0.504
Air travel	6.395	0.044	0.877
Weighted	6.410	0.041	0.787
Overall Benefits			
Automobiles	6.088	0.055	1.429
Weighted	6.085	0.053	1.356
Industrial chemicals	4.469	0.076	2.700
Weighted	4.417	0.075	2.641
Nuclear weapons	3.849	0.090	3.813
Weighted	3.859	0.089	3.712
Handguns	3.403	0.087	3.632
Weighted	3.431	0.087	3.632
Electricity	6.506	0.045	0.972
Weighted	6.487	0.045	0.988
Air travel	5.914	0.064	1.978
Weighted	5.856	0.067	2.119
Overall Risks			
Automobiles	4.711	0.066	2.096
Weighted	4.682	0.067	2.120
Industrial chemicals	5.328	0.062	1.799
Weighted	5.320	0.062	1.807
Nuclear weapons	5.855	0.068	2.197
Weighted	5.848	0.068	2.144

Table B.5 (continued)

Questionnaire Item	Mean	Standard Error	Variance
Overall Risks (*continued*)			
Handguns	5.308	0.077	2.822
Weighted	5.319	0.077	2.805
Nuclear electric power	4.879	0.076	2.711
Weighted	4.880	0.076	2.701
Air travel	3.720	0.073	2.512
Weighted	3.720	0.072	2.428
Sociodemographics			
Education	12.781	0.146	10.112
Weighted	12.710	0.144	9.900
Income	12.052	0.206	18.780
Weighted	12.420	0.202	18.032
Gender	1.522	0.023	0.250
Weighted	1.518	0.023	0.250
Age	43.543	0.779	288.445
Weighted	42.956	0.766	278.584

Table B.5 reports the mean, standard error, and variance of 22 key variables for the Arizona general population sample computed with weighted and unweighted data. The differences in each case are very small—so small, in fact, that we used unweighted data for all the analyses reported in the text.

The Connecticut general population sample was a simple random sample to the household level. This eliminated any bias for unequal segment probabilities. There was, however, a potential bias resulting from the selection of a single adult within each household. This selection bias can be corrected by weighting each respondent's data by the number of eligible adults in the household. Following Kish (1965: 400) we made these adjustments so that we could compare weighted with unweighted results. Differences, as shown in Table B.4, are negligible. Therefore, as with the Arizona general population sample, we used unweighted data for our subsequent analyses of the Connecticut general population sample.

C

Scales

We used more than one survey item to measure many of the variables in our study. Our first analytic task, therefore, was to combine many of these single items into scales. Following is a list of the types of scales we needed:

ACTION	Continuous and discrete action scales for six technologies.
ACCEPTABILITY	Acceptability of current restrictions and standards for six technologies.
ENVIRONMENT	Environmental attitudes ("pastoralism" and "urbanism").
TECHNOLOGY	Attitudes toward technology.
RISK ORIENTATION	Cognitive orientation toward risk.
CONFIDENCE	Confidence in "establishment" organizations and in environmental and consumer groups.
GOVERNMENT SUPPORT	Attitudes concerning government support of (energy) technologies.

SALIENCE
: Salience of technological issues, with subscales for six technologies.

MEMBERSHIP
: Membership in voluntary organizations.

SES
: Socioeconomic class.

These scales were needed for analyses involving four separate sample configurations: the Connecticut general public, the Connecticut general public plus testifiers, the Arizona general public, and the Arizona general public plus testifiers. Therefore, each scale had to be examined four times to make sure it included only items that would measure each variable reliably in each sample.

We began the scale construction process by factor analyzing the set of items we had included in the survey to measure each variable, using the Connecticut general public plus testifiers sample. We started with this sample for two reasons: (1) we finished surveying in Connecticut first, and (2) this sample was likely to maximize the variance on individual items, particularly the "action" items. (Testifiers not only took more action than members of the general public, but, it might be assumed, probably also had more strongly felt opinions about the safety and benefits of technology.)

Because the Connecticut combined sample is not random, however, and because most of the items used to construct scales are ordinal, rather than interval, product-moment-based statistical procedures (ordinary factor analyses and ordinary reliability analyses) are subject to misinterpretation. Therefore, we employed factor and reliability analysis models based on the nonparametric statistic tau-B, rather than the parametric, product-moment correlation coefficient. Although this is the first time, to the best of our knowledge, that anyone has reported a nonparametric procedure for computing item-total correlations and alpha reliability coefficients, Ploch (1974) suggests the nonparametric factor analysis procedure we used, which consists simply of factor analyzing a matrix of tau-B item intercorrelations. The nonparametric item-total correlation we used is simply the tau-B correlation between each item and the total scale. We devised a nonparametric reliability coefficient, standardized-item alpha, computed according to the formula:

$$\text{alpha} = \frac{K(\bar{t}_B)}{1 + (K - 1)(\bar{t}_B)},$$

where K = number of items in the scale, and $\bar{t}_B$ = the average tau-B between items. This is the same formula used to compute standardized-item alpha with product-moment correlations (Hull and Nie, 1981: 256), except that the average tau-B is substituted for $\bar{r}$.

Although tau-B-based factor and reliability analyses are preferable for our data, they are also very expensive in terms of computer time, and necessitate some hand calculations (for computing standardized-item alpha). We therefore conducted factor analyses only on the Connecticut general public plus testifiers sample, and computed more than one alpha coefficient only when an examination of the tau-B intercorrelation matrix indicated that deleting an item might raise the alpha coefficient. Once final scales were established on the Connecticut combined sample, however, we conducted additional reliability analyses on the other samples using the scales derived from the Connecticut combined sample. Only in a few cases, where item-total correlations were particularly low, did we delete additional items and recompute item-total correlations and standardized-item alpha coefficients for all four samples.

Despite the fact that some of the scales we used had been developed earlier by other researchers, and other scales had been pretested by us in earlier research, coefficients of reliability for many scales turned out to be rather lower than we might have hoped. It must be remembered, however, that tau-B is a somewhat less powerful statistic than r (Ploch, 1974, estimates about 10 percent less powerful), and thus alpha coefficients computed with tau-B correlations will generally be lower than alpha coefficients computed with Pearson's r. Tau-B is also, however, a more accurate statistic than r for computing correlations that are monotonic, but not linear. Since many item-total relationships are probably not linear, item-total correlations might be expected in many cases to be higher using tau-B than they would be using r. In our study, standardized-item alpha coefficients of reliability, computed by ordinary methods, tended to be about 10 percent higher than those we report here, while part-whole correlations, using product-moment correlations, were on average considerably lower, reflecting the nonmonotonicity of the relationships.

The scales that we constructed, although not possessed of high alpha coefficients, do appear to be quite consistent across two very different geographical regions—Connecticut and Arizona. We feel reasonably confident in using them, therefore, even when their reliability coefficients are in some cases lower than we might have liked. (Test-retest consistency, after all, is surely a better measure of reliability than the alpha coefficient.) In any event, these are the best scales we could devise and, rather than abandon important variables, we have used them as they are in our analysis. The remainder of this appendix is a description of each scale.

Action

For each of the six technologies, we asked repondents (Questions 9 through 14) whether they had ever:

A. Written a letter, telephoned, or sent a telegram to an editor, public official, or company.
B. Signed a petition.
C. Circulated a petition.
D. Voted for or against a candidate for public office in part because of his or her position on this issue.
E. Attended a public hearing or a meeting of a special interest organization.
F. Spoken at a public hearing or forum.
G. Boycotted a company.
H. Joined or contributed money to an organization.
I. Attended a public demonstration.
J. Participated in a lawsuit.
K. Other.

The response categories were: "yes," "no," and "don't know." Tables C.1 through C.6 show the percentages of each sample that took each kind of action, as well as the percentages that took at least one kind of action and thereby, at least at some minimal level, can be classified as activists.

Although these items classify respondents as either activists or nonactivists, they do not indicate whether the action taken was on the side of safety or of benefits. For this, we used Questions 30 through 35, which asked respondents whether they favored or opposed increased safety or further development of each of the six technologies; that is, whether the action could be presumed to have been pro-safety or pro-benefits. Question 30, for example, asked:

> Do you favor further increasing the safety of auto travel through such things as improved auto design and added safety features or do you oppose such measures because they would be too expensive?

If a person indicated that he or she had taken action with respect to the safety of automobile travel (Question 9) and that he or she favored increasing the safety of auto travel (Question 30), we scored the action response as being pro-safety. If, however, the person opposed increasing the safety of automobile travel because such measures would be too expensive (Question 30), we scored the action as being pro-benefits. For Question

Table C.1
Percentages of Respondents Who Took Action with Respect to the Safety or Benefits of Automobile Travel

Action	Connecticut		Arizona	
	General	Combined	General	Combined
Written a letter	8.1**	11.4	3.8**	5.7
Signed a petition	5.9*	6.8	10.0*	9.4
Circulated a petition	0.7	1.6	1.0	1.1
Voted	6.5	8.0	9.8	10.7
Attended a public hearing	3.1	5.4	4.6	6.5
Spoken at a public hearing	0.9	3.6	1.5	3.8
Boycotted a company	3.5	3.8	4.0	4.0
Joined or contributed money to an organization	2.8	4.6	3.5	3.8
Attended a demonstration	0.7	1.2	1.5	1.6
Participated in a lawsuit	1.3	1.7	1.3	1.1
Other	0.2	0.7	0.0	0.5
Any action	19.6	23.0	18.4	20.4
Number of cases	541	691	479	628

Difference in proportions between Connecticut and Arizona general population samples statistically significant (two-tailed test) at:
*$p < .05$.
**$p < .01$.

Table C.2
Percentages of Respondents Who Took Action with Respect to the Safety or Benefits of Handguns

Action	Connecticut		Arizona	
	General	Combined	General	Combined
Written a letter	4.4	7.4	4.0	5.9
Signed a petition	12.6	14.2	8.8	10.8
Circulated a petition	0.9	2.3	1.9	1.6
Voted	13.5	14.5	11.7	16.1
Attended a public hearing	2.0	3.6	3.3	4.3
Spoken at a public hearing	0.6	2.6	0.4	1.0
Boycotted a company	0.9	0.9	0.4	1.0
Joined or contributed money to an organization	5.4	7.4	5.2	7.3
Attended a demonstration	1.1	1.6	1.0	1.1
Participated in a lawsuit	0.4	0.7	0.2	0.2
Other	0.6	1.2	0.2	0.2
Any action	25.9*	29.2	19.5*	25.2
Number of cases	541	691	478	627

*Difference in proportions between Connecticut and Arizona general population samples statistically significant at $p < .05$.

Table C.3
Percentages of Respondents Who Took Action with Respect to the Safety or Benefits of Nuclear Power

Action	Connecticut		Arizona	
	General	Combined	General	Combined
Written a letter	3.1	8.7	4.0	7.2
Signed a petition	14.6	17.7	15.7	18.8
Circulated a petition	0.9	2.2	1.7	2.4
Voted	8.5	12.2	11.9	16.2
Attended a public hearing	5.9	11.4	7.1	13.7
Spoken at a public hearing	0.6	3.6	1.0	4.0
Boycotted a company	0.6	1.2	0.6	1.1
Joined or contributed money to an organization	5.4	9.0	3.3	5.6
Attended a demonstration	2.6	4.8	3.8	5.4
Participated in a lawsuit	0.2	0.6	0.2	0.5
Other	0.2	1.7	0.0	1.0
Any action	23.7	30.2	22.8	29.9
Number of cases	541	691	479	628

No difference in proportions between Connecticut and Arizona general population samples statistically significant at $p < .05$.

Table C.4
Percentages of Respondents Who Took Action with Respect to the Safety or Benefits of Air Travel

Action	Connecticut		Arizona	
	General	Combined	General	Combined
Written a letter	3.3	3.9	1.9	2.2
Signed a petition	0.7	1.2	0.2	0.3
Circulated a petition	0.0	0.1	0.0	0.0
Voted	0.4	0.6	0.2	1.1
Attended a public hearing	1.1	1.3	0.8	1.3
Spoken at a public hearing	0.4	0.9	0.4	0.8
Boycotted a company	2.0	2.2	0.4	0.3
Joined or contributed money to an organization	0.6	1.3	0.2	0.6
Attended a demonstration	0.0	0.6	0.2	0.3
Participated in a lawsuit	0.2	0.3	0.0	0.0
Other	0.7	0.9	0.4	0.3
Any action	6.8*	8.0	2.9*	4.3
Number of cases	541	691	479	628

*Difference in proportions between Connecticut and Arizona general population samples statistically significant at $p < .01$.

Table C.5

Percentages of Respondents Who Took Action with Respect to the Safety or Benefits of Nuclear Weapons

Action	Connecticut		Arizona	
	General	Combined	General	Combined
Written a letter	3.0	7.1	3.8	6.1
Signed a petition	9.2	11.3	9.0	11.2
Circulated a petition	0.7	1.6	1.9	2.2
Voted	13.7	14.5	13.4	17.1
Attended a public hearing	6.7	9.0	4.4	7.0
Spoken at a public hearing	0.7	2.9	0.6	1.1
Boycotted a company	0.2	0.3	1.0	1.3
Joined or contributed money to an organization	3.9	6.1	2.7	4.5
Attended a demonstration	3.5	4.3	2.7	2.9
Participated in a lawsuit	0.4	0.3	0.0	0.0
Other	0.2	1.2	0.0	0.8
Any action	23.1	27.4	19.9	24.4
Number of cases	541	691	477	626

No difference in proportions between Connecticut and Arizona general population samples statistically significant at $p < .05$.

31, dealing with industrial chemicals, favoring position 2 was the pro-safety response; for Question 33, on nuclear power, positions 2 and 3 were scored as pro-safety; for Question 34, concerning handguns, positions 1 and 2 were taken to indicate a pro-safety response; and for Question 35, about nuclear weapons, position 3 was considered the pro-safety response.

Continuous Scales

Knowing the number of kinds of actions a person has taken, as well as whether these actions could be presumed to be pro-safety or pro-benefits, it is possible to construct "continuous" action scales ranging from strongly pro-safety, through no action, to strongly pro-benefits. One must decide, however, what weight to assign each kind of action. Are signing and circulating petitions, for example, equally significant, or should circulating a petition be assigned a greater value than signing a petition, and if so, how much greater value?

We used factor analysis (using principal components with oblique rotation of a matrix of tau-B intercorrelations) to try to answer these

Table C.6
Percentages of Respondents Who Took Action with Respect to the Safety or Benefits of Industrial Chemicals

Action	Connecticut		Arizona	
	General	Combined	General	Combined
Written a letter	2.8	10.7	2.7	9.2
Signed a petition	9.4	12.2	6.9	7.5
Circulated a petition	0.9	2.3	1.0	1.4
Voted	5.0	8.4	5.4	8.8
Attended a public hearing	5.2*	14.8	2.3*	13.2
Spoken at a public hearing	1.1	9.0	0.2	6.4
Boycotted a company	0.4	1.3	1.3	2.1
Joined or contributed money to an organization	3.5**	8.7	0.4**	3.0
Attended a demonstration	1.7	3.5	1.5	3.2
Participated in a lawsuit	0.2	1.4	0.0	1.3
Other	0.9	3.2	0.0	1.8
Any action	19.2	30.2	10.4	22.3
Number of cases	541	691	479	628

Difference in proportions between Connecticut and Arizona general population samples statistically significant (two-tailed test) at:
*$p < .05$.
**$p < .01$.

questions. The purpose of the analysis was to generate factor scores that could serve as weights for each type of action. Unfortunately, the factor analysis did not generate weights that made much sense, and scales constructed using these weights proved to correlate no more highly with the independent variables of our study than simpler additive scales; that is, scales that assigned each action a weight of 1. Therefore, we used the simpler additive model for our continuous action scales. Each pro-safety action is scored $+1$; each pro-benefits action, -1. Action is the sum of these scores (omitting the category "other"). Table C.7 shows the average action score for the four samples.

Reliability analyses of the six action scales (one for each technology) revealed, however, that some action items did not correlate very highly with other items and that item-total correlations between some individual items and the total scale scores were quite low. For these reasons we removed some items from some scales. Tables C.8 through C.13 show item-total correlations (tau-B) and standardized-item alpha reliability coefficients (computed with tau-B correlations) for the six final continuous

Table C.7
Action Scores for Connecticut and Arizona Samples[a]

| | Connecticut | | Arizona | |
	General	Combined	General	Combined
Automobile				
Mean	.21	.33	.11	.14
Variance	.79	1.61	1.26	1.58
Handguns				
Mean	.20	.26	.09	.05
Variance	.98	1.65	1.15	1.40
Nuclear power				
Mean	.28	.40	.25	.27
Variance	1.06	2.87	1.72	2.67
Air travel				
Mean	.08*	.11	.02*	.03
Variance	.12	.30	.08	.12
Nuclear weapons				
Mean	.10*	.20	−.04*	−.04
Variance	1.15	1.91	1.29	1.77
Industrial chemicals				
Mean	.26	.43	.17	.24
Variance	.84	2.85	.63	1.79
Number of cases	539	685	472	614

[a]The action score is the sum of all pro-safety (+) and pro-benefits (−) actions over items A–J. A positive mean indicates that, on average, the sample was pro-safety; a negative mean that the sample was, on average, pro-benefits.
*Difference in means between the Connecticut and Arizona general population samples significant at $p < .01$.

action scales for Connecticut and Arizona general population and combined samples.

Discrete Action Scales

The action scales just discussed assume that the number of kinds of actions a person has taken, and whether these actions are directed at greater safety or at greater benefits, can be described by a continuous scale. This might not be a reasonable assumption. People who take action, whether pro-safety or pro-benefits, may be qualitatively different from people who take no action; and pro-safety activists may be qualitatively different from pro-benefits activists. Therefore, we constructed a second type of action scale; one that makes no assumptions about the continuity of

Table C.8
Reliability Analysis of Automobile Travel Continuous Action Scale

| | Item-Total Correlations[a] | | | |
| | Connecticut | | Arizona | |
Action	General	Combined	General	Combined
Written a letter	.64	.70	.46	.55
Signed a petition	.56	.56	.75	.69
Circulated a petition	.22	.30	.26	.25
Voted	.59	.60	.74	.73
Attended a public hearing	.43	.51	.52	.59
Spoken at a public hearing	.23	.40	.30	.45
Joined or contributed money to an organization	.39	.47	.45	.44
Attended a demonstration	.18	.23	.30	.29
Participated in a lawsuit	.25	.28	.26	.24
Standardized-item alpha[b]	.65	.82	.73	.75
Number of cases	540	686	477	625

[a] tau-B.
[b] Computed with tau-B correlations.

Table C.9
Reliability Analysis of Handgun Continuous Action Scale

| | Item-Total Correlations[a] | | | |
| | Connecticut | | Arizona | |
Action	General	Combined	General	Combined
Written a letter	.50	.57	.54	.58
Signed a petition	.81	.77	.80	.77
Circulated a petition	.24	.33	.39	.31
Attended a public hearing	.33	.40	.51	.50
Spoken at a public hearing	.18	.36	.17	.23
Joined or contributed money to an organization	.54	.57	.63	.64
Attended a demonstration	.25	.27	.29	.26
Standardized-item alpha[b]	.65	.78	.76	.74
Number of cases	540	690	477	626

[a] tau-B.
[b] Computed with tau-B correlations.

Table C.10
Reliability Analysis of Nuclear Power Continuous Action Scale

| Action | Item-Total Correlations[a] | | | |
| | Connecticut | | Arizona | |
	General	Combined	General	Combined
Written a letter	.36	.55	.42	.51
Signed a petition	.76	.73	.81	.77
Circulated a petition	.21	.29	.29	.30
Voted	.58	.63	.72	.73
Attended a public hearing	.50	.63	.57	.69
Spoken at a public hearing	.16	.45	.22	.37
Boycotted a company	.16	.21	.18	.21
Joined or contributed money to an organization	.48	.56	.40	.45
Attended a demonstration	.34	.41	.41	.44
Standardized-item alpha[b]	.71	.84	.81	.83
Number of cases	539	688	478	625

[a] tau-B.
[b] Computed with tau-B correlations.

Table C.11
Reliability Analysis of Air Travel Continuous Action Scale

| Action | Item-Total Correlations[a] | | | |
| | Connecticut | | Arizona | |
	General	Combined	General	Combined
Signed a petition	.39	.49	.38	.39
Attended a public hearing	.56	.56	.65	.73
Boycotted a company	.72	.69	.53	.39
Joined or contributed money to an organization	.32	.52	.38	.48
Attended a demonstration	[b]	.37	.38	.27
Participated in a lawsuit	.23	.27	[b]	[b]
Standardized-item alpha[c]	.32	.73	.20	.14
Number of cases	540	688	477	626

[a] tau-B.
[b] Action not taken.
[c] Computed using tau-B correlations.

Table C.12
Reliability Analysis of Nuclear Weapons Continuous Action Scale

| | Item-Total Correlations[a] | | | |
| | Connecticut | | Arizona | |
Action	General	Combined	General	Combined
Written a letter	.36	.52	.44	.51
Signed a petition	.64	.65	.67	.68
Circulated a petition	.19	.26	.33	.33
Voted	.76	.72	.81	.83
Attended a public hearing	.55	.59	.48	.54
Spoken at a public hearing	.18	.33	.18	.23
Joined or contributed money to an organization	.42	.49	.40	.45
Attended a demonstration	.40	.42	.39	.36
Standardized-item alpha[b]	.69	.82	.78	.81
Number of cases	540	689	476	624

[a] tau-B.
[b] Computed with tau-B correlations.

Table C.13
Reliability Analysis of Industrial Chemicals Continuous Action Scale

| | Item-Total Correlations[a] | | | |
| | Connecticut | | Arizona | |
Action	General	Combined	General	Combined
Written a letter	.40	.62	.51	.65
Signed a petition	.69	.62	.80	.56
Circulated a petition	.24	.31	.32	.27
Voted	.51	.53	.71	.62
Attended a public hearing	.51	.71	.47	.76
Spoken at a public hearing	.21	.57	.13	.54
Joined or contributed money to an organization	.44	.56	.20	.38
Attended a demonstration	.29	.35	.38	.38
Standardized-item alpha[b]	.67	.84	.72	.78
Number of cases	539	687	476	624

[a] tau-B.
[b] Computed with tau-B correlations.

action. The scale consists simply of three classifications: people who have taken no action, people who have taken one or more pro-benefits types of action, and people who have taken one or more pro-safety types of action. Table C.14 shows the percentages of each sample that can be classified as pro-safety, pro-benefits, or nonactivist for each technology, as well as the percentages that can be classified as pro-safety, pro-benefits, both (i.e., who took pro-safety actions with regard to one technology and pro-benefits actions with regard to another), or nonactivist with respect to all six technologies.

Table C.14
Percentages of Respondents Who Took Pro-Safety, Pro-Benefits,
or No Action

Technology	Action	Connecticut		Arizona	
		General	Combined	General	Combined
Automobile	Pro-safety	15%	19%	3%	14%
travel	Pro-benefits	3	3	5	6
	None	82	78	82	80
	Total	100%	100%	100%	100%
	Number of cases	540	687	477	625
Handguns	Pro-safety	21%*	24%	13%*	16%
	Pro-benefits	5	5	7	10
	None	74*	71	80*	74
	Total	100%	100%	100%	100%
	Number of cases	541	691	478	627
Nuclear	Pro-safety	19%	23%	17%	20%
power	Pro-benefits	5	7	6	10
	None	76	70	77	70
	Total	100%	100%	100%	100%
	Number of cases	541	690	478	626
Air travel	Pro-safety	6%*	7%	2%*	3%
	Pro-benefits	0	0	0	1
	None	94*	93	98*	96
	Total	100%	100%	100%	100%
	Number of cases	540	688	477	626

Table C.14 (continued)

Technology	Action	Connecticut		Arizona	
		General	Combined	General	Combined
Nuclear	Pro-safety	13%*	15%	8%*	10%
weapons	Pro-benefits	10	12	11	14
	None	77	73	81	76
	Total	100%	100%	100%	100%
	Number of cases	540	689	476	624
Industrial	Pro-safety	17%*	24%	9%*	17%
chemicals	Pro-benefits	2	6	1	5
	None	81*	70	90*	78
	Total	100%	100%	100%	100%
	Number of cases	540	689	476	625
Any	Pro-safety	36%*	38%	23%*	24%
technology	Pro-benefits	7	8	10	12
	Both	12	15	11	17
	None	45*	39	56*	47
	Total	100%	100%	100%	100%
	Number of cases	537	682	473	619

Difference in proportions between Connecticut and Arizona general population samples statistically significant (two-tailed test) at:
*$p < .01$.

Acceptability of Technology

Questions 3 through 8 asked respondents to judge how strict they "think restrictions and standards are NOW . . . " on each of the six technologies included in the survey, as well as, "how strict do you think the restrictions and standards on . . . SHOULD BE." For both questions, respondents were asked to respond on the following seven-point scale:

1	2	3	4	5	6	7

NOT VERY   EXTREMELY
STRICT   STRICT

We calculated the acceptability of current restrictions and standards by subtracting respondents' answers to the first question ("are *now*") from their answers to the second question ("*should be*"). This resulted in a 12-point scale on which a positive score indicates a judgment that standards and restrictions should be increased, a negative score a judgment that restrictions and standards should be relaxed, and a score of zero a judgment that current restrictions and standards should not be changed.

This method of computing the acceptability of current restrictions and standards of technologies departs from procedures used earlier by Fischhoff et al. (1978) and by us (Gardner et al., 1982). In these earlier studies, acceptability was measured directly by asking respondents to rate how strict the restrictions and standards on technologies "should be" on a scale such as the following:

1	2	3	4	5	6	7
MUCH MORE LENIENT			SAME AS NOW		MUCH MORE STRICT	

The disadvantage of the earlier procedure was that it left ambiguous just how strict people felt restrictions and standards should be; that is, it measured what people thought things should be in reference to what they thought they were at the time. To avoid this ambiguity in our survey, we used a response scale that measured peoples' judgments about what restrictions and standards should be on an absolute, rather than a relative, scale. That is, we used the same kind of response scale that we used to measure people's perceptions of how strict standards "are *now*." Even though this procedure had the advantage of measuring directly peoples' opinions about how strict the restrictions and standards on each technology should be, it had the disadvantage of measuring acceptability only indirectly; that is, as the difference between respondents' answers to the "are now" and "should be" questions.

As we began to tally the survey results, it appeared as if this alternative procedure might have been a mistake. In particular, we became concerned by the fact that very high proportions of respondents in all samples had positive acceptability scores (see Table C.15), indicating that very high proportions of the people in the surveyed areas of Connecticut and Arizona favored stricter standards and restrictions. This appeared unusual, as the judgment often expressed at the time by politicians and the press was that the mood Americans were in was to "get government off their backs." Since restrictions and standards on technologies involve government regulations, we were surprised to find so few people favoring fewer restrictions and standards and so many favoring more.

We were further made suspicious of our findings by the fact that the percentages favoring stricter standards and regulations in our survey were in many cases higher than the percentages we had found two years earlier in our survey of selected groups from Connecticut and New York (Gard-

Table C.15
Acceptability of Current Restrictions and Standards of Six Technologies

Standards with Respect to	Should Be	Connecticut		Arizona	
		General	Combined	General	Combined
Automobile travel	Stricter	75%*	75%	68%*	66%
	No change	15**	15	22**	22
	Less strict	10	10	10	12
	Total	100%	100%	100%	100%
	Number of cases	541	691	478	627
Industrial chemicals	Stricter	92%	88%	92%	89%
	No change	7	10	7	8
	Less strict	4**	2	1**	3
	Total	100%	100%	100%	100%
	Number of cases	438	687	479	627
Nuclear weapons	Stricter	79%	78%	81%	79%
	No change	20	21	18	20
	Less strict	1	1	1	1
	Total	100%	100%	100%	100%
	Number of cases	438	688	479	628
Handguns	Stricter	85%**	85%	74%**	71%
	No change	9**	10	17**	18
	Less strict	6	5	9	11
	Total	100%	100%	100%	100%
	Number of cases	539	688	479	628
Nuclear power	Stricter	77%	76%	81%	76%
	No change	20	29	18	21
	Less strict	3*	4	1*	3
	Total	100%	100%	100%	100%
	Number of cases	540	689	479	628
Air travel	Stricter	70%	68%	68%	65%
	No change	29	31	31	34
	Less strict	1	1	1	1
	Total	100%	100%	100%	100%
	Number of cases	539	689	479	628

Difference in proportions between Connecticut and Arizona general population samples statistically significant (two-tailed test) at:
*$p < .05$.
**$p < .01$.

ner et al., 1982). Although these earlier groups were not random samples of the general public, they were samples of reasonably diverse groups and should not, it would seem, produce results so dissimilar from the results we found in our later surveys of the general public.

There are, however, three equally plausible explanations for these differences. The first is that the samples selected for our earlier study, although diverse, were not representative of the general public. The second is that the samples were representative, but that the mood of the public had changed during the intervening time between our pretest study and our main survey. The third is that the differences have something to do with the fact that we asked the "acceptability" questions differently in the two studies.

A Special Experiment. Since it was important for us to know whether our new procedures obtained an accurate measure of people's opinions about whether the standards and restrictions on technologies should be stricter, less strict, or left as they are, we conducted a special experiment to compare the two methods of asking the "acceptability" question. Using two questionnaire forms, one asking the acceptability questions as we had in our pretest and the other as we had asked the questions in our main survey, Gardner and Gould conducted a short survey of undergraduate students, 99 from Florida State University and 100 from the University of Michigan–Dearborn. On both campuses, students were assigned, at random (using a table of random numbers), one or the other version of the questionnaire. Table C.16 compares the percentages of students (both samples combined) who received each version of the questionnaire in terms of whether they thought that standards and restrictions should be made stricter, less strict, or left as they are.

Evidently, how the question is asked does make a difference. In all cases, higher proportions of those students who were asked to rate directly the acceptability of current restrictions and standards favored stricter standards than did students who indirectly rated the acceptability of current restrictions and standards now and how strict they should be. (These differences are statistically significant, however, with respect to only three of the six technologies.) These differences indicate that the way we measured acceptability on our survey *does not* artifactually inflate estimates of the proportions of respondents desiring stricter restrictions and standards; if anything, our survey estimates are low.

The only explanations for the differences between our pretest and survey results, then, is that the pretest samples were very unrepresentative of the population as a whole or that the mood of the public had changed considerably in the intervening years. We suspect that the former explana-

Table C.16
Percentages of Students Using Two Questionnaire Forms Who Indicated That Restrictions and Standards Should Be Made Stricter, Less Strict, or Left Unchanged

Standards with Respect to	Should Be	Pretest Form	Survey Form
Automobile travel	Stricter	82%	72%
	No change	10	24*
	Less strict	8	4
	Total	100%	100%
	Number of cases	101	83
Industrial chemicals	Stricter	100%	90%**
	No change	0	9**
	Less strict	0	1
	Total	100%	100%
	Number of cases	99	89
Nuclear weapons	Stricter	86%	51%**
	No change	12	43**
	Less strict	2	6
	Total	100%	100%
	Number of cases	94	79
Handguns	Stricter	79%	83%
	No change	15	13
	Less strict	6	4
	Total	100%	100%
	Number of cases	105	91
Nuclear power	Stricter	89%	62%
	No change	11	35
	Less strict	0	3
	Total	100%	100%
	Number of cases	85	66
Air travel	Stricter	78%	45%
	No change	22	55
	Less strict	0	0
	Total	100%	100%
	Number of cases	99	85

Differences in proportions between Connecticut and Arizona general population samples statistically significant (two-tailed test) at:
*$p < .05$.
**$p < .01$.

Table C.17

*Relationship Between Acceptability of Standards and Perceived Risks
and Benefits of Six Technologies—Special Student Sample*

| | Relationship (tau-B) Between Acceptability of Technology and: | | | |
| | Perceived Risks | | Perceived Benefits | |
Technology	Pretest Form	Survey Form	Pretest Form	Survey Form
Automobile travel	.17*	.08	.02	−.15*
Number of cases	101	82	101	83
Industrial chemicals	.13	.09	−.10	−.11
Number of cases	95	87	90	81
Nuclear weapons	.09	.13*	−.10	−.08
Number of cases	91	78	90	77
Handguns	.40**	.20**	−.33**	−.36**
Number of cases	104	90	104	91
Nuclear power	.24**	.21*	−.02	.06
Number of cases	83	64	83	66
Air travel	.14*	.08	.14*	−.06
Number of cases	98	84	99	85

*Statistically significant at $p < .05$.
**Statistically significant at $p < .01$.

tion is likely to be the correct one, but in either case, we can be reasonably certain that our survey estimates of the proportions of persons desiring stricter standards on the safety of technology are not inflated by any artifact of the way we asked the question; indeed, had we asked the question differently, the proportions would probably have been even higher.

Nevertheless, the question remains of whether the way we asked the acceptability question on the survey might have affected other results of our study. Of particular importance is whether this might have affected the relationships between the acceptability of technology and people's perceptions of the risks and benefits of technology.

To help answer this question, we asked the students in our special experiment to rate not only the acceptability of each technology but also the risks and benefits of each technology. Table C.17 shows the relationships between acceptability and perceived risks and perceived benefits for each technology for students who received the pretest questionnaire form and for those who used the survey form.

The results are not altogether conclusive. In general, as we also found in our survey, the perceived risks and benefits of technology are only weakly correlated with the acceptability of current restrictions and standards on technology (with the correlations involving perceived risk being the stronger). For five of the six technologies, however, the correlations with perceived risk were stronger using the direct, pretest form of measuring acceptability. This would suggest that the indirect, survey form of measuring acceptability is a conservative estimate not only of the proportion of persons favoring stricter standards and restrictions on technologies but also of the relationship of this variable to people's perceptions of the risks and benefits of technology.

If, then, one has no need to know the absolute value of people's judgments about how strict standards and restrictions should be on technologies, it would seem best to measure the acceptability of current restrictions and standards directly. If, however, one wants to know both people's judgments about how strict standards should be, in absolute terms, as well as their judgments about the acceptability of current restrictions and standards, then the indirect method of measuring acceptability that we adopted for our survey would seem to be an adequate, if slightly conservative, measure of this variable.

Attitudes Toward the Environment

In response to the burgeoning growth of environmental psychology in the 1960s and 1970s, George McKechnie developed an "environmental response inventory," consisting of 184 carefully selected "statements tapping attitudes toward a wide array of environmental themes, including conservation, recreation and leisure activities, architecture and geography, science and technology, urban life and culture, aesthetic preferences, privacy, and adaptation" (1974: 1). Three of the subscales from this inventory are particularly relevant to our study: Pastoralism (PA), Urbanism (UR), and Environmental Adaptation (EA). The Pastoralism scale, according to McKechnie (1974: 2), taps the following themes:

> Opposition to land development; concern about population growth; preservation of natural resources, including open space; acceptance of natural forces as shapers of human life; sensitivity to pure environmental experiences; self-sufficiency in the natural environment.

The Urbanism scale includes the themes:

> Enjoyment of high-density living; appreciation of unusual and varied stimulus patterns of the city; interest in cultural life; enjoyment of interpersonal richness and diversity.

Environmental Adaptation involves:

> Modification of the environment to satisfy needs and desires, and to provide comfort and leisure; opposition to government control over private land use; preference for highly designed or adapted environments; use of technology to solve environmental problems; preference for stylized environmental details.

The Pastoralism and Environmental Adaptation scales, as developed by McKechnie, contain 22 items each; the Urbanism scale contains 20 items. These were far too many items to include in our survey, which had many other equally, or more, important areas to cover in an approximately one-hour interview. Therefore, we selected only eight items each from the Pastoralism and Urbanism scales, and seven items from the Environmental Adaptation scale. The items we chose are as follows:

Pastoralism

45-C The idea of walking into the forest and "living off the land" for a week appeals to me.

45-J I can identify many of the local flowers and trees.

45-K Our national forests should be preserved in their natural state, with roads and buildings prohibited.

45-M I enjoy a change in the weather, even when it turns bad.

45-N Hiking is boring. (Reverse scoring.)

45-P The wilderness is cruel and harsh. (Reverse scoring.)

45-Q I often wish for the seclusion of a weekend retreat.

45-U It's fun to walk in the rain even if you get wet.

Urbanism

45-D Life in the city is more interesting than life on a farm.

45-E It is exciting to go shopping in a large city.

45-G Suburbs should replace the city as the center of cultural life. (Reverse scoring.)

45-H Cities are too noisy and crowded for me. (Reverse scoring.)

45-I I often feel uneasy in a large crowd of people. (Reverse scoring.)

45-L Small-town life is too boring for me.

45-T The cultural life of a big city is very important to me.

45-V Mental problems are more common in the city than in the country. (Reverse scoring.)

Environmental Adaptation

45-A I like amusement parks.

45-B Machines increase people's freedom.

45-F	When buying clothes, I usually look more for comfort than for style. (Reverse scoring.)
45-O	Jet air travel is one of the great advances of our society.
45-R	Modern communities are plastic and ugly. (Reverse scoring.)
45-S	Science does as much harm as good. (Reverse scoring.)
45-W	Given enough time, science will solve most human problems.

We had no *a priori* reason to choose these particular items; we simply chose those items that appeared to us to capture best the major themes of the scale while preserving, as much as possible, a balance between positively and negatively worded statements.

Factor analyses (with principal components and oblique rotation, of a matrix of tau-B intercorrelations) indicated, however, that some of the items, despite the careful selection by McKechnie, did not fit well into their respective scales. It appeared as if three items would have to be dropped from the Pastoralism scale, one from the Urbanism scale, and three from the Environmental Adaptation scale.

With so few items left in each scale, we checked to see whether a more acceptable single scale of environmental attitudes could be constructed from all 23 items. It could not. Although factor analysis of these 23 items (again using principal components, oblique rotation, and a matrix of tau-B correlations) for the Connecticut combined sample revealed a sub-scale structure not unlike that suggested by McKechnie, several items did not load on their appropriate factors; only seven of the eight UR scale items loaded highly on factor 1; only five of the seven PA items loaded highly on factor 2; and only four of the EA items loaded highly on factor 3 (see Table C.18).

Because of these findings, it would not be proper to include all the items in each subscale proposed by McKechnie. Therefore, the three environmentalism subscales we chose are defined as follows: Pastoralism—items C, K, N, R, and Q; Urban–Rural Orientation—items D, E, G, H, I, and T; and Environmental Adaptation—items B, O, S, and W. Reliability analyses of the three scales indicate that while item-total correlations (tau-B) are reasonably high, standardized-item alpha coefficients of reliability are quite low, especially for the Environmental Adaptation subscale. (See Table C.19.)

Attitudes Toward Technology

McKechnie's Environmental Adaptation scale refers not to the environment *per se* but to science and technology. Indeed, it was our plan to

Table C.18
Factor Structure of McKechnie Environmentalism Items[a]

Item	Subscale	Factor 1	Factor 2	Factor 3
45-A	EA	.00	.07	−.08
45-B	EA	−.22	−.02	−.66
45-C	PA	.13	.71	.06
45-D	UR	−.68	−.33	−.09
45-E	UR	−.41	−.13	−.28
45-F	EA	.14	.06	.22
45-G	UR	.58	−.04	.03
45-H	UR	.74	.13	−.02
45-I	UR	.33	−.06	.21
45-J	PA	.16	.22	−.11
45-K	PA	.14	.36	−.10
45-L	UR	−.56	−.19	−.08
45-M	PA	.07	.19	−.04
45-N	PA	−.12	−.62	−.07
45-O	EA	.03	.01	−.74
45-P	PA	−.12	−.60	.04
45-Q	PA	.03	.68	−.04
45-R	EA	.12	.17	.16
45-S	EA	.12	−.10	.32
45-T	UR	−.70	.04	−.14
45-U	PA	.02	.32	−.06
45-V	UR	.15	.11	−.03
45-W	EA	.07	−.03	−.42

[a]Principal components, oblique rotation, tau-B matrix, Connecticut combined sample ($n = 681$).

use the EA scale to measure respondents' attitudes toward these subjects. Unfortunately, as discussed in the previous section, the items from this scale did not constitute what would appear to be a reliable whole. Therefore, in an attempt to construct a more reliable attitudes-toward-technology scale, we took the four items from McKechnie's EA scale that correlated most highly with one another and added two items not on McKechnie's original list:

23-A The risks associated with advanced technology have been exaggerated by events such as Three Mile Island and the Love Canal.

38 In your opinion, over the next 20 years will the benefits to society resulting from continued technological and scientific

Table C.19
Reliability Analysis of Environmentalism Scales

Scale	Item-Total Correlations[a]			
	Connecticut		Arizona	
	General	Combined	General	Combined
Pastoralism (PA)				
Items: 45-C	.63	.62	.69	.67
45-K	.43	.44	.43	.41
45-N	.52	.51	.55	.55
45-P	.51	.50	.52	.52
45-Q	.54	.53	.54	.53
Standardized-item alpha[b]	.62	.61	.61	.60
Number of cases	539	688	474	622
Urbanism (UR)				
Items: 45-D	.56	.56	.56	.56
45-E	.50	.46	.47	.49
45-G	.40	.43	.30	.33
45-H	.63	.64	.57	.57
45-I	.42	.40	.45	.42
45-L	.49	.44	.44	.46
45-T	.56	.57	.51	.52
Standardized-item alpha[b]	.75	.69	.70	.70
Number of cases	535	685	473	622
Environmental Adaptation (EA)				
Items: 45-B	.51	.50	.53	.53
45-O	.43	.43	.46	.46
45-S	.53	.52	.58	.57
45-W	.51	.51	.56	.55
Standardized-item alpha[b]	.39	.38	.38	.37
Number of cases	538	688	477	626

[a] tau-B.
[b] Based on tau-B item intercorrelations.

innovation outweigh the related risks to society, or not? (Reverse scoring.)

Since these two items were scored on a three-point scale, while the EA scale items were scored on a five-point scale, we changed the response categories for these two items to 1, 3, and 5.

Table C.20
Reliability Analysis of Technology Attitude Scale

| | Item-Total Correlations[a] | | | |
| | Connecticut | | Arizona | |
Scale Items	General	Combined	General	Combined
23-A	.44	.49	.37	.45
38	.60	.60	.58	.57
45-B	.40	.41	.40	.42
45-O	.29	.28	.32	.33
45-S	.43	.45	.51	.53
45-W	.36	.36	.40	.39
Standardized-item alpha[b]	.14	.13	.22	.23
Number of cases	537	686	477	626

[a] tau-B.
[b] Computed with tau-B item correlations.

The scale that includes the two additional items is more accurate (as measured by the standardized-item alpha coefficient) than the original EA scale, although the reliability coefficient is still quite low. Table C.20 gives the item-total correlations (tau-B) and standardized-item alpha reliability coefficients (computed with tau-B item correlations) for Connecticut and Arizona samples.

Cognitive Risk Orientation

Within the past decade or so, there have been several attempts to relate people's cognitive orientations to other predispositions or behaviors (cf. Schwartz, 1968; Fishbein and Ajzen, 1975). Among other things, such attempts have had in common the fact that they obtained measures not of a single predisposition but of several. The work of Kreitler and Kreitler (1976) and Lobel (1982) looks especially promising for predicting people's behavior.

Kreitler and Kreitler's conceptual scheme divides beliefs into four components: beliefs about (1) the nature of self, (2) the self's goals, (3) people, situations, and events, and (4) norms, rules, standards, and values. Specific beliefs within each cognitive component pertain to specific behaviors. In order to develop a scale of cognitive orientations toward risk, therefore, we devised (and borrowed) survey items about risk that fit into each of the four categories. The following are the items we selected:

Beliefs about the self

1. The nature of the self.

43-D   I think I worry too much.

43-I   In general, I like to take risks.

43-N   I am like those people who enjoy hang gliding, mountain climbing, downhill skiing, or some other exciting and risky sport.

43-O   I like to bet on long shots.

43-Q   Sometimes I feel I don't have enough control over the direction my life is taking.

2. The self's goals.

43-B   Life is too short; I shall never be able to do everything I would like to.

43-F   The less one owns, the fewer troubles one has.

43-M   It is more important to have a rich emotional life than success in life.

43-R   I hope for new experiences almost every day.

43-T   It is important for me to have an exciting life.

Beliefs about non-self

3. People, situations, and events.

43-A   People should budget their personal expenses and then always live within their budgets.

43-E   People should be self-controlled and self-disciplined.

43-H   Most people can be trusted.

43-L   It is better to have life go along smoothly than to be surprised, even when the surprises are pleasant.

43-S   People should strive to attain their important goals even when uncertain of success.

4. Norms, rules, standards, and values.

43-C   It is great to be living in these exciting times.

43-G   Success is more dependent on luck than on ability.

43-J   Feelings are just as important for decisions as figures and facts.

43-K   The government should pay for promising projects which, however, may possibly fail.

43-P   Usually reason is a better guide to action than feelings.

Our first analytic task was to assess whether the items in the four separate cognitive areas formed separate scales. Factor analyses (using

Table C.21
Factor Structure of Cognitive Risk Orientation Items[a]

Item	Subscale	Factor 1	Factor 2
43-A	(3) People, situations, and events	−.17	.62
43-B	(2) Self's goals	.02	.13
43-C	(4) Norms, rules, standards, and values	.08	.23
43-D	(1) Nature of self	−.12	.19
43-E	(3) People, situations, and events	−.04	.71
43-F	(2) Self's goals	−.05	.15
43-G	(4) Norms, rules, standards, and values	−.01	−.27
43-H	(3) People, situations, and events	−.14	−.27
43-I	(1) Nature of self	.72	−.06
43-J	(4) Norms, rules, standards, and values	−.05	.01
43-K	(4) Norms, rules, standards, and values	.09	.00
43-L	(3) People, situations, and events	−.13	.29
43-M	(2) Self's goals	−.04	.07
43-N	(1) Nature of self	.67	−.04
43-O	(1) Nature of self	.60	−.21
43-P	(4) Norms, rules, standards, and values	.05	.48
43-Q	(1) Nature of self	.00	−.03
43-R	(2) Self's goals	.48	.19
43-S	(3) People, situations, and events	.24	.39
43-T	(2) Self's goals	.58	.18

[a]Principal components, oblique rotation, tau-B matrix, Connecticut combined sample ($n = 678$).

principle components, oblique rotation, and matrices of tau-B intercorrelations) of the Connecticut combined sample data indicated that they did not.

Since Kreitler and Kreitler (1976: 390) argued that equal weights should be assigned to each of the four belief areas, we combined all 20 items into a single factor analysis (again using principal components, oblique rotation, and a tau-B correlation matrix). Five beliefs about "self" items, three "nature of self," and two "self's goals" items loaded highly on factor 1 (see Table C.21); and four beliefs about "non-self" items, three "people, situations, and events" items, and one "norms, rules, standards, and values" item loaded highly on factor 2.

Table C.22 shows the reliability analysis of the five items that loaded highly on factor 1. Although the coefficients of reliability for this scale are not very high, the item-total correlations are fairly high and are consistent across samples.

Table C.22
Reliability Analysis of Cognitive Risk Orientation Scale

| | Item-Total Correlations[a] | | | |
| | Connecticut | | Arizona | |
Scale Items	General	Combined	General	Combined
43-I	.59	.60	.62	.62
43-N	.58	.57	.62	.62
43-O	.47	.47	.55	.53
43-R	.50	.49	.55	.53
43-T	.54	.53	.61	.60
Standardized-item alpha[b]	.62	.62	.71	.69
Number of cases	540	687	475	622

[a] tau-B.
[b] Computed with tau-B item correlations.

Reliability analysis of the four items that loaded most highly on factor 2 indicates that these items do not form an acceptable additive scale: the coefficient of reliability for the Connecticut combined sample was only 0.47, and item-total correlations were not very high. Therefore, we used only the one scale, constructed from items representing beliefs about the self, in the final analysis.

Confidence in Organizations

Question 2 asked respondents how much confidence they had in the people running various organizations: (A) organized religion, (B) education, (C) medicine, (D) the press, (E) TV, (F) organized labor, (G) major companies, (H) banks and financial institutions, (I) executive branch of the federal government, (J) U.S. Supreme Court, (K) Congress, (L) U.S. Environmental Protection Agency, (M) U.S. Consumer Product Safety Commission, (N) military, (O) scientific community, (P) consumer interest groups, and (Q) environmental groups. This is a standard question, often included in public opinion polls (Davis, 1983). Table C.23 shows the percentages of respondents who had a "great deal of confidence" in those running each kind of organization.

This list of organizations is quite varied, and we had no *a priori* reason to believe that confidence in any one organization would necessarily be correlated with confidence in any other. Therefore, we factor analyzed the 17 items (using principal components, oblique rotation, and a matrix of tau-B correlations). Five relatively distinct factors emerged (see

Table C.23
Percentages of Respondents Indicating That They Had a Great Deal of
Confidence in Those Running Various Organizations

Organization	Connecticut		Arizona	
	General	Combined	General	Combined
Organized religion	26	25	25	23
Education	33	30	29	28
Medicine	58*	56	46*	45
The press	15	15	16	15
TV	11	9	13	11
Organized labor	10	10	9	7
Major companies	22	20	19	20
Banks and financial institutions	32	29	33	31
Executive branch of federal government	20	20	22	22
U.S. Supreme Court	39	41	38	42
Congress	13	13	13	12
E.P.A.	25*	22	13*	12
Consumer Product Safety Commission	36	32	32	27
Military	36	32	41	39
Scientific community	51	53	49	52
Consumer interest groups	33*	32	21*	22
Environmental groups	33*	33	20*	20
Sample size	542	692	479	628

Differences in proportions between Connecticut and Arizona general population samples statistically significant (two-tailed test) at:
*$p < .01$.

Table C.24). Items loading the highest on Factor 1 are what might be called "establishment"; those loading the highest on factor 2 are, in the same sense, "non-establishment," except for the executive branch of the federal government which loaded negatively on this factor.

Reliability analysis of the items loading highly on each factor indicates, however, that all factors do not form good additive scales. Therefore, we combined the organizations that loaded most highly on factors 1, 4, and 5, which appeared in many respects to be similar, into a single scale of what might be called "confidence in established organizations." (See Table C.25.) The two items that load the highest on factor 2, consumer interest and environmental groups, and the two items that load the highest on factor 3, the press and TV, do not correlate highly with other items. We therefore attempted to combine these four items into two separate two-item scales. Only the scale combining consumer and environmental

Table C.24
Factor Structure of Confidence-in-Organizations Items[a]

Item	Organization	Factor 1	Factor 2	Factor 3	Factor 4	Factor 5
2-A	Organized religion	.07	.06	.13	.09	.66
2-B	Education	.21	.28	.41	−.09	.47
2-C	Medicine	.17	.05	.23	−.40	.45
2-D	The press	.00	.28	.69	−.21	.02
2-E	TV	.02	.07	.67	−.01	.18
2-F	Organized labor	.36	.06	.48	.25	.15
2-G	Major companies	.18	−.21	.07	−.38	.57
2-H	Banks and financial institutions	.18	−.18	.06	−.21	.68
2-I	Executive branch of federal government	.33	−.42	.16	−.55	.27
2-J	U.S. Supreme Court	.21	−.01	.32	−.65	.11
2-K	Congress	.42	−.12	.59	−.28	.22
2-L	E.P.A.	.77	.10	.10	−.11	.13
2-M	Consumer Product Safety Commission	.69	.36	.11	−.07	.08
2-N	Military	.52	−.27	.14	−.20	.42
2-O	Scientific community	.08	.09	.00	−.73	.17
2-P	Consumer interest groups	.15	.76	.18	−.05	.00
2-Q	Environmental groups	.21	.78	.16	−.06	.02

[a]Principal components, oblique rotation, tau-B correlation matrix, Connecticut combined sample (n = 690).

groups appears to be very useful, however (confidence in TV and the press were not highly correlated), and thus we used only this scale in our analysis. Table C.25 also gives informataion on this scale.

Government Support for Energy Technologies

We included five items in the survey (Question 36-A through 46-E) that were designed to assess people's attitudes toward government spend-

Table C.25
Reliability Analysis of Confidence-in-Organizations Scales

| | Item-Total Correlations[a] | | | |
| | Connecticut | | Arizona | |
Scale	General	Combined	General	Combined
Establishment Organizations				
Items: 2-B	.40	.39	.40	.39
2-C	.41	.42	.45	.45
2-G	.45	.45	.48	.48
2-H	.40	.42	.48	.47
2-I	.47	.49	.47	.48
2-J	.46	.45	.50	.47
2-K	.48	.46	.43	.41
2-L	.40	.42	.42	.41
2-M	.35	.36	.41	.39
2-N	.48	.48	.49	.50
2-O	.37	.35	.41	.41
Standardized-item alpha[b]	.72	.71	.70	.73
Number of cases	541	691	475	623
Consumer and Environmental Groups				
Items: 2-P	.80	.82	.79	.80
2-Q	.80	.82	.82	.83
Standardized-item alpha[b]	.70	.68	.68	.68
Number of cases	538	689	476	625

[a] tau-B.
[b] Computed using tau-B item correlations.

ing on energy technologies: ". . . rate how much, if any, 'the government' should pay for each of the following:"

A. Research and development costs for nuclear electric power.
B. The costs of operating and maintaining nuclear electric power plants.
C. Research and development costs for solar energy.
D. The costs of installing and operating solar energy devices.
E. The costs of installing energy conservation measures in private residences.

Although we had no particular reason to believe that all these items would be positively correlated, it turns out that they were. Reliability

Table C.26
Reliability Analysis of Attitudes Toward Government Spending on
Energy Technologies Scale

| | Item-Total Correlations[a] | | | |
| | Connecticut | | Arizona | |
Scale Items	General	Combined	General	Combined
36-A	.52	.51	.50	.51
36-B	.61	.60	.63	.63
36-C	.53	.54	.61	.61
36-D	.69	.69	.68	.70
36-E	.57	.57	.60	.58
Standardized-item alpha[b]	.73	.73	.75	.76
Number of cases	541	691	478	627

[a] tau-B.
[b] Computed using tau-B item correlations.

analysis indicates, moreover, that these five items yielded a reasonably good additive scale (see Table C.26).

Salience of Technological Issues

While attitude scales can measure what people think about certain things, they indicate neither how important these things are nor how likely the people being questioned are to change their opinions. Yankelovich, Skelly, and White (Keene and Sackett, 1981), being concerned about the latter of these problems, developed what they call a Mushiness Index that they claim measures the firmness of people's opinions. They have used the index to establish the "mushiness" of many domestic and foreign policy issues.

The index, applied separately in our survey to the safety of automobile travel, the safety of industrial chemicals, nuclear weapons, handguns, the safety of nuclear electric power, and the safety of commercial air travel, is comprised of four questions:

On a scale of 1 to 6, where "1" means that you and your friends and family rarely, if ever, discuss the following issues and "6" means that you and your friends and family discuss it relatively often, where would you place yourself?

On a scale of 1 to 6, where "1" means you could change your mind very easily on the following issues, and "6" means that you are likely to stick with your position no matter what, where would you place yourself?

On a scale of 1 to 6, where "1" means that the following issues affect you personally very little and "6" means that you really feel deeply involved in these issues, where would you place yourself?

On a scale of 1 to 6, where "1" means that you feel you definitely need more information on the following issues and "6" means that you do not feel you need to have any more information on them, where would you place yourself?

In addition to these "mushiness" questions, which applied specifically to each technology, we also asked five general questions that should be relevant to the salience of all technologies. Question 1 in our survey asked:

In general, would you say that recently you have been taking a good deal of interest in current events and what's happening in the world today, some interest, or not very much interest?

Question 25-A asked:

When you watch TV news and documentary shows do you pay a great deal of attention to issues such as the ones on technology we have been discussing; do you pay some attention; or don't you pay much attention to these issues?

Questions 26-A, 27-A, and 28-A asked similar questions about magazines, newspapers, and the radio.

Combining these general questions with the industry-specific "mushiness" items yielded salience scales with relatively low reliability coefficients (standardized-item alpha). Therefore we decided to look more carefully at the mushiness items alone.

Reliability and factor analyses (using principal components, oblique rotation, and matrices of tau-B correlations) indicated that answers to the question of whether the respondents felt that they needed more information on the subject did not correlate very highly with answers to the other three questions, nor did it correlate highly with a scale constructed of all four items. Therefore, we dropped this question from the "mushiness" scales. This left six rather short, three-item scales of salience, one for each technology. Table C.27 reports the results of a reliability analysis of these six scales. Although the coefficients of reliability are relatively low, they

Table C.27
Reliability Analysis of "Mushiness" Scales

| | Item-Total Correlations[a] | | | |
| | Connecticut | | Arizona | |
Technology	General	Combined	General	Combined
Automobile Travel				
Items: 39-A	.68	.69	.63	.62
40-A	.58	.57	.52	.52
41-A	.67	.69	.67	.67
Standardized-item alpha[b]	.62	.62	.54	.54
Number of cases	537	687	477	626
Industrial Chemicals				
Items: 39-B	.67	.70	.62	.67
40-B	.58	.58	.57	.54
41-B	.68	.70	.67	.70
Standardized-item alpha[b]	.63	.65	.57	.60
Number of cases	537	687	477	626
Nuclear Weapons				
Items: 39-C	.69	.70	.62	.62
40-C	.57	.57	.57	.55
41-C	.66	.68	.65	.67
Standardized-item alpha[b]	.62	.63	.56	.56
Number of cases	538	688	477	626
Handguns				
Items: 39-D	.74	.75	.70	.70
40-D	.50	.50	.51	.51
41-D	.71	.73	.71	.72
Standardized-item alpha[b]	.64	.64	.62	.62
Number of cases	538	688	477	626
Nuclear Electric Power				
Items: 39-E	.69	.70	.64	.65
40-E	.60	.59	.56	.55
41-E	.67	.68	.68	.70
Standardized-item alpha[b]	.64	.65	.59	.60
Number of cases	537	687	477	626

Table C.27 (continued)

| | Item-Total Correlations[a] | | | |
| | Connecticut | | Arizona | |
Technology	General	Combined	General	Combined
Air Travel				
Items: 39-F	.72	.71	.62	.62
40-F	.59	.59	.58	.57
41-F	.73	.72	.69	.70
Standardized-item alpha[b]	.83	.68	.66	.66
Number of cases	538	688	477	626

[a] tau-B.
[b] Computed using tau-B item correlations.

are somewhat higher than the much longer, nine-item scales we started with. Since the alpha coefficient of reliability depends in part, however, on the number of items in a scale (fewer items yield lower scores), these values are not unreasonable for three-item scales and are quite consistent across samples.

Next, we returned to the five items we had eliminated concerning respondents' interest in current events and how much attention they paid to issues concerning technology on TV and radio and in magazines and newspapers. Reliability analysis (Table C.28) shows that although the alpha

Table C.28
Reliability Analysis of Salience of Technology Scale

| | Item-Total Correlations[a] | | | |
| | Connecticut | | Arizona | |
Scale Items	General	Combined	General	Combined
1	.52	.52	.55	.57
25-A	.48	.48	.52	.53
26-A	.58	.62	.59	.61
27-A	.58	.58	.51	.57
28-A	.53	.53	.42	.45
Standardized-item alpha[b]	.64	.66	.60	.66
Number of cases	541	691	478	627

[a] tau-B.
[b] Computed with tau-B item correlations.

coefficients for this scale are rather low, they are at least consistent across samples.

Organizational Membership

We asked respondents (Question 63) which of the following organizations they belonged to: fraternal groups, service clubs, veterans' groups, political clubs, labor unions, sports groups, youth groups, school service groups, hobby or garden clubs, school fraternities or sororities, nationality groups, farm organizations, literary, art, or music groups, professional or academic societies, church-affiliated groups, discussion or study groups. Factor analysis (using principal components, oblique rotation, and a matrix of tau-B correlations) showed many small clusters of items but no single factor that included many of the items. Therefore, we eliminated four organizations (veterans' groups, labor unions, hobby or garden clubs, and farm organizations) that were either negatively or not highly associated with the other items and constructed an additive scale with the re-

Table C.29
Reliability Analysis of Organizational Membership Scale

| | Item-Total Correlations[a] | | | |
| | Connecticut | | Arizona | |
Organization	General	Combined	General	Combined
Fraternal groups	.29	.33	.31	.31
Service clubs	.32	.37	.37	.43
Political clubs	.23	.33	.17	.31
Sports groups	.46	.41	.48	.47
Youth groups	.36	.32	.35	.35
School service groups	.37	.36	.33	.34
School fraternities or sororities	.27	.30	.25	.30
Nationality groups	.24	.27	.24	.25
Literary, art, or music groups	.36	.37	.37	.39
Professional or academic societies	.47	.49	.42	.53
Church-affiliated groups	.49	.48	.57	.49
Discussion or study groups	.37	.38	.42	.44
Standardized-item alpha[b]	.61	.64	.66	.71
Number of cases	537	685	473	621

[a] tau-B.
[b] Computed with tau-B item correlations.

maining items. Table C.29 shows the item-total correlations (tau-B) and standardized-item alpha coefficient of reliability for that scale.

Socioeconomic Class

Question 53 asked respondents whether they considered themselves to be in the lower, working, middle, or upper social class. Most people listed themselves as being working or middle class (Table C.31).

Since the variation on this item was so small, we constructed an alternative socioeconomic class scale from Questions 48, on type of occupation; 59, on education; and 62, on income, collapsing 0, 1, 2, 3, and 4 years of education into a single category; under $1,000 and $1,000 to $2,999 income into a single category; and dividing occupational prestige

Table C.30
Income and Education

	Connecticut		Arizona	
	General	Combined	General	Combined
Income				
Less than $5,000	3%	2%	8%	7%
$5,000–$9,999	8	7	12	9
$10,000–$19,999	20	16	29	25
$20,000–$29,999	26	24	22	21
$30,000–$39,999	17	18	10	12
$40,000–$74,999	19	25	14	22
Over $75,000	7	8	5	6
Total	100%	100%	100%	100%
Number of cases	498	640	442	586
Years of Education				
Less than 7	2%	1%	3%	3%
7–9	10	8	10	8
10–12	41	35	43	32
13–15	19	17	21	19
16	14	18	12	16
More than 16	14	21	11	22
Total	100%	100%	100%	100%
Number of cases	540	690	474	623

Tau-B, income by state (general population): $-.16; p < .01$.
Tau-B, education by state (general population): $-.03$, n.s.

Table C.31
Socioeconomic Class

	Connecticut		Arizona	
	General	Combined	General	Combined
Question 53				
Lower class	2%	2%	1%	1%
Working class	35	31	43	34
Middle class	58	60	51	59
Upper class	5	7	5	6
Total	100%	100%	100%	100%
Number of cases	537	685	473	620
SES Scale[a]				
Mean	35.0	37.1	32.3	35.2
Median	35.0	37.4	32.3	36.1
Variance	66.2	74.0	77.8	98.0
Number of cases	486	628	429	573

Tau-B, SES by state (general population): $-.06$; $p < .05$.
[a] Education, income, and occupational prestige.

scores into 17 equal intervals. (We used the Hodge-Siegel-Rossi Prestige Scores [Davis, 1983: 337–349]). The final SES scale was the sum of these items. Table C.31 presents statistics on this scale. (Table C.30 shows the distribution of income and education in the four samples.)

Although the variance on the SES scale is greater than the variance on the single SES item, the scale suffers from the defect that there are many missing cases. (Many people, in particular, were reluctant to reveal their incomes.) Therefore, we used the single SES item (Question 53) rather than the SES scale in the analysis.

D

Statistics

Zero-Order Measures of Association for Ordinal Variables

Kendall's tau-B, Somers's D_{yx}, and Goodman and Kruskal's gamma, three measures commonly used to describe association between two ordinal variables, are all based on a comparison of the relative magnitudes of independent and dependent variable observations for all possible (n) pairs of analytic units. (This includes the comparison of every ith observation with every jth observation, every jth observation with every ith observation, and every observation with itself.) Such comparisons yield a count of concordant pairs (C), discordant pairs (D), pairs that are tied on the independent but not the dependent variable (T_i), pairs that are tied on the dependent but not the independent variable (T_d), and pairs that are tied on both variables (T_{id}). The sum of C, D, T_i, T_d, and T_{id} is n^2.

A pair is scored as concordant if observation X_i is greater than observation X_j and Y_i is greater than Y_j, or if X_i is less than X_j and Y_i is less than Y_j. If X_i is greater than X_j but Y_i is less than Y_j (or vice versa), the pair is scored as discordant. If no distinction can be made between the X_ith and X_jth observations, the pair is scored as tied on the independent variable; if no distinction can be made between the Y_ith and Y_jth observations, the pair is scored as tied on the dependent variable.

Gamma is then defined as:

$$\text{gamma} = \frac{C - D}{C + D}, \tag{1}$$

Somers's D_{yx} as:

$$D_{yx} = \frac{C - D}{C + D + T_d}, \tag{2}$$

and Kendall's tau-B as:

$$\text{tau-B} = \frac{C - D}{\sqrt{C + D + T_i} \sqrt{C + D + T_d}} = \sqrt{D_{yx}} \sqrt{D_{xy}}, \tag{3}$$

where D_{xy} is computed as D_{yx} with the order of independent and dependent variables reversed.

Gamma ignores tied pairs on both the independent and dependent variables. This is equivalent to saying that the relationship (gamma) among untied pairs is an unbiased estimate of the relationship among tied pairs. This assumption is probably not tenable, as measurement error (i.e., reversals of predicted order) is surely more likely among pairs that are close together on one or the other metric than among pairs that are far apart on both scales. (Tied pairs are so close together that their order cannot be determined with the measuring instrument.) In other words, if all pairs could be ranked with respect to each other (i.e., if there were no ties), gamma would probably be lower than it is when some ranks are tied. We have not used gamma in this analysis.

Somers (1962b) observed a striking similarity between Kendall's tau-B and the product-moment correlation coefficient, r, and between D_{yx} and the standardized regression coefficient. Although Somers was not willing to speak of tau-B or D_{yx} as being anything more than "ordinal analogs" of r and beta, Hawkes (1971) has shown that they are indeed something more: tau-B is the equivalent of r, and D_{yx} is the equivalent of beta, for the ordered case.

To see this, it is useful to note that r, like tau-B and D_{yx}, can also be derived from paired comparisons. The only difference in the case of r is that absolute, rather than relative, differences between observations are recorded. For computing tau-B, X_{ij} is scored $+1$ if X_i is greater than X_j; -1 if X_i is less than X_j; and 0 if there is no discernible difference between the two observations. For r, the absolute value of X_{ij} is calculated.

Given only this difference in measuring X_{ij} for the ordinal and interval cases, r and tau-B are computed by the formula:

$$\frac{\Sigma X_{ij} Y_{ij}}{\sqrt{\Sigma X_{ij}^2} \sqrt{\Sigma Y_{ij}^2}}, \qquad (4)$$

where the summations X_{ij}, Y_{ij}, X_{ij}^2, and Y_{ij}^2 are over all pairs of observations.

This formula for a generalized coefficient of correlation was first suggested by Daniels (1944). From it follows not only that tau-B and r are essentially the same measure, that they differ only in their measurement rules, but also, as Hawkes (1971) has shown, that a generalized measure of variation and covariation may also be stated for the ordinal and interval cases, the only difference between the two being the way observations for paired comparisons are scored. The variation of an ordinal or interval variable is computed by the formula:

$$\text{Var}(X) = \frac{\Sigma X_{ij}^2}{2n^2}, \qquad (5)$$

and the covariation by the formula:

$$\text{Cov}(X, Y) = \frac{\Sigma X_{ij} Y_{ij}}{2n^2}. \qquad (6)$$

In terms of variation and covariation, the formula for tau-B may be written as:

$$t_B = \frac{\text{Cov}(X,Y)}{\sqrt{\text{Var}(X)\,\text{Var}(Y)}}, \qquad (7)$$

and the formula for Somers's D_{yx} may be written as:

$$D_{yx} = \frac{\text{Cov}(X,Y)}{\text{Var}(X)}. \qquad (8)$$

Formulas for partial tau-B and partial D_{yx} are also available (Hawkes, 1971).

Variance and Variation

The variance of a distribution produced by measurement with an interval scale refers to how much that distribution is spread out around the mean and is defined, arithmetically, as:

$$S^2 = \frac{\displaystyle\sum_{i=1}^{n} (\overline{X} - X_i)^2}{n}, \tag{9}$$

where $\overline{X}$ is the mean of the distribution and n the number of measurements. The variance, like the mean, is a parametric measure; that is, it presumes the distribution it is measuring to be reasonably "normal" in shape.

Although Equations 5 and 9 give exactly the same numerical answers, they are conceptually different. (To avoid confusion, I have referred to the value computed by Equation 9 as the "variance" and that computed by Equation 5 as "variation.") Equation 9 calculates how spread out a distribution is around its mean; Equation 5 calculates how spread out or bunched up a distribution is in general. The distinction is important. The variance of a distribution, as described by Equation 9, is meaningful only if the distribution is unimodal and not skewed. The variation of a distribution, as described by Equation 5, on the other hand, makes no assumptions about the "shape" of the distribution. (Since "normality" need not be assumed, it is a nonparametric, descriptive measure.)

Since Equation 5 may be used with ordinal, as well as interval, data, it is also possible to calculate the "variation" of an ordinal variable. In this case the concept "variance" would be inappropriate (as it would make reference to the mean), but the concept "variation" is perfectly appropriate: it refers simply to how spread out or bunched up the distribution is. The maximum variation, which is equal to $1/2\,[(c-1)/c]$, where c is the number of categories into which the variable is divided (Hawkes 1971: 913), occurs when observations are distributed equally among all categories of the scale; the minimum (i.e., 0), when all observations fall into a single category.

Multivariate Analysis of Ordinal Data

Of particular relevance to our current research is the fact that a matrix of tau-B intercorrelations may be factor analyzed or used to compute multiple correlations and regression coefficients (Ploch, 1974). We took advantage of this in scale development (Appendix C) and in the data analysis reported in Chapters 5, 6, and 7.

Multiple tau-B is computed with the same formulas one would use to compute a multiple correlation (R), the only difference between the two measures being that the R is based on absolute differences between all pairs on the independent and dependent variables, whereas multiple tau-B is based only on the relative differences (i.e., $+1$, 0, or -1).

Unlike zero-order, partial, and multiple correlations, which have much the same interpretation in the two systems, regression coefficients have a somewhat different interpretation for ordinal variables than they have for interval variables. In the product-moment system, regression coefficients represent the amount by which each independent variable must be multiplied in order to produce the best least-squares prediction of the dependent variable. Such an interpretation is meaningless, however, for variables that lack equal-interval measurement. Therefore, the ordinal system of regression employs a standardized beta coefficient—standard, partial, Somers's D_{yx} (1962b)—that, like its product-moment counterpart, can be interpreted as a measure of the relative impact of each independent variable in the equation in accounting for the variation of the dependent variable (Ploch, 1974). Regression equations for ordinal variables, then, may be written as:

$$Y_{ij} = Dy_{1.23 \ldots k} X_{1ij} + Dy_{2.13 \ldots k} X_{2ij} + \ldots$$
$$+ Dy_{k.123 \ldots k-1} X_{kij}, \qquad (10)$$

where "Y_{ij} is the expected difference on variable Y for the ith and jth observation, the initial subscript on the independent variables has been added to identify the variable and the subscripts of D coefficients follow the usual conventions for partial regression coefficients by listing the independent variables also taken into account" (Hawkes, 1971: 916).

Statistical Significance of Measures of Relationship Among Ordinal Variables

The advantages of zero-order tau-B and regressions based on multiple tau-B and partial D_{yx} for our data are several: (1) we need assume only an ordinal level of measurement; (2) we can test all monotonic relationships directly without assuming linearity or transforming variables to achieve linearity; and (3) we are not bound by the parametric assumptions inherent in the product-moment system.

We do, however, pay a price for these advantages: the sampling distributions for multiple tau-B and standard partial Somers's D_{yx} are unknown. This means that we cannot test the statistical significance of these two measures, although we can test the statistical significance of zero-order tau-B with:

$$Z = \frac{C - D}{2(2n + 5)/9n(n - 1)}. \qquad (11)$$

Since the samples in our study are quite large, however (over 400), testing the statistical significance of relationships adds very little to the analysis. A tau-B of 0.10 is "statistically significant" for samples of this size even though it accounts for only 1 percent of the variation in the dependent variable. Such small relationships, although *statistically significant,* are of trivial substantive significance.

Criticisms

Nonparametric regressions based on zero-order tau-B correlations have not been without detractors. One of the more cogent and often-cited critics of the ordinal strategy, Kim, has shown quite convincingly that "the logic of ordinal prediction involves measurement assumptions that are not supported by the properties of the ordinal scale and that, in consequence, the ordinal partials cannot, in general, be clearly interpreted" (Kim, 1975: 293). What Kim does not show, however, although he does imply it, is that parametric statistics in no way compensate for measurement inaccuracies. Indeed, given the measurement inaccuracy common in survey research, product-moment partials can be interpreted with no more clarity than can partials produced by the ordinal system. This does not mean, however, that partials computed with either system are meaningless; it means only that they must be interpreted with caution and a certain degree of flexibility.

Given a choice between parametric and nonparametric statistics, Kim (1975; 294) argued that one should choose the parametric statistics, not because they are more accurate, but because this choice will tend to force social scientists to refine their measurements to approximate more closely the assumptions of the product-moment system. Although this strategy might be reasonable in the long run, it was not reasonable in our case. We had a set of survey data in hand, which had been gathered according to the best survey techniques available, that could not meet the measurement assumptions of the product-moment system, but needed analyzing nonetheless. In our case, the nonparametric, ordinal system seemed the better alternative if for no other reason than that it admits at the outset that our measurement was less than perfect and that the results of our analysis, therefore, should be taken as approximate rather than definitive.

Zero-Order Relationships Among Nominal Variables

Except for a few sociodemographic variables (such as religion) and one dependent variable (activist status), all of the variables in our study are interval, ordinal, or dichotomous, and thus can be analyzed with the ordinal-based system of statistics just described. A system of statistics for analyzing relationships among nominal variables (or variables of higher measurement level treated as nominal variables) is needed, however, to identify the factors associated with whether or not people are activists, and if they are activists, whether their actions are pro-benefits or pro-safety.

There are two measures, both developed by Goodman and Kruskal (1954), for measuring zero-order association between two nominal classifications. One measure, lambda-b, explains variation in the dependent variable by comparing the number of cases that fall in the modal category of the dependent variable within each category of the independent variable with the number of cases that fall in the modal dependent variable category without reference to the independent variable. Such comparisons ignore variations between non-modal categories, however, which means, among other things, that lambda-b will be zero (indicating no relationship) whenever the modal category on the dependent variable is the same for all categories of the independent variable even though some relationship exists between the independent and dependent variable.

Tau-b is sensitive to variations in all dependent variable categories. It is therefore a superior measure of association for two nominal variables even though it is less commonly used and is somewhat more complicated to compute than lambda-b. SPSS (Nie et al., 1975), for example, which we used for most of our analyses, includes lambda-b as one of the statistical options in the sub-program *CROSSTABS,* but does not include procedures for computing tau-b. (Neither does any other popular computer software package of which we are aware.)

The statistical significance of tau-b (Light and Margolin, 1971) for large samples is approximated with the formula:

$$\chi^2 = t_b (n - 1)(r - 1),$$

where r = number of categories in the independent variable, with d.f. = $(r - 1)(c - 1)$, where c = number of categories in the dependent variable.

References

Achen, C. H. (1982) *Interpreting and using regression.* Beverly Hills: Sage.

Baker, S. P., B. O'Neill, and R. Karpf. (1984) *The injury fact book.* Lexington, Mass.: Lexington Books.

Brannon, R. (1973) "Attitude and action: A field experiment joined to a general population survey." *American Sociological Review* 38:625–636.

———. (1976) "Attitudes and the production of behavior." In B. Seidenberg and A. Snadowsky, eds., *Social psychology.* New York: Free Press.

Brodeur, P. (1985) "The asbestos industry on trial." *New Yorker* 61 (June 10):49ff.

Brown, M. W. (1986) "Truth, precision and seductive numbers." *New York Times* (May 27):C3.

Buss, D., and K. Craik. (1983) "Contemporary worldviews: Personal and policy implications." *Journal of Applied Social Psychology* 13:259–280.

Carson, R. (1962) *Silent spring.* Boston: Houghton Mifflin.

Cipolla, C. M. (1978) *The economic history of world population.* 7th ed. Harmondsworth, England: Penguin.

Cohen, B. (1985) "Criteria for technological acceptability." *Risk Analysis* 5:1–3.

Cohen, B., and I. Lee. (1979) "A catalog of risks." *Health Physics* 36:707–722.

Combs, B., and P. Slovic. (1979) "Newspapers coverage of causes of death." *Journalism Quarterly* 56:837–843.

Costner, H. L. (1965) "Criteria for measures of association." *American Sociological Review* 30:341–353.

Daniels, H. E. (1944) "The relation between measures of correlation in the universe of sample permutations." *Biometrika* 33:129–135.

Davis, J. A. (1983) *General social surveys, 1972–1983.* Chicago: National Opinion Research Center.

Deutscher, I. (1966) "Words and deeds: Social science and social policy." *Social Problems* 13:235–254.

Diamond, S. (1985) "The disaster in Bhopal: Lessons for the future." *New York Times* 134 (Feb. 3):1Aff.

Dodge, W., and M. Grier. (1978) "Consultation and consensus in a new era in policy formulation?" Report of the Compensation Research Center of the Conference Board in Canada.

Douglas, M., and A. Wildavsky. (1982a) *Risk and Culture.* Berkeley: University of California Press.

———. (1982b) "How can we know the risks we face? Why risk selection is a social process." *Risk Analysis* 2:49–51.

Draper, J. H. (1971) *Citizen participation.* Toronto, Canada: New Press.

Dunlap, R. (1975) "The impact of political orientation of environmental attitudes and actions." *Environment and Behavior* 7:428–454.

DuPont, R. (1980) *Nuclear phobia—Phobic thinking about nuclear power.* Washington, D.C.: The Media Institute.

Echholm, E. (1986) "After accident at the Soviet station, nuclear power is questioned again." *New York Times* 135 (May 2):10A.

Ellul, J. (1964) *The technological society,* trans. J. Wilkinson. New York: Vintage.

Farhar, B., P. Weis, C. Unseld, and B. Burns. (1978) *Public opinion about energy: A literature review.* Golden, Col.: Solar Energy Research Institute.

Fischhoff, B., P. Slovic, and S. Lichtenstein. (1979) "Weighing the risks." *Environment* 21:17–20, 32–38.

Fischhoff, B., P. Slovic, S. Lichtenstein, S. Derby, and R. Keeney. (1981) *Acceptable risk.* Cambridge: Cambridge University Press.

Fischhoff, B., P. Slovic, S. Lichtenstein, S. Read, and B. Combs. (1978) "How safe is safe enough? A psychometric study of attitudes toward technological risks and benefits." *Policy Sciences* 9:127–152.

Fischhoff, B., S. Watson, and C. Hope. (1984) "Defining risk." *Policy Sciences* 17:123–138.

Fishbein, M., and I. Ajzen. (1975) *Belief, attitude, intention, and behavior: An introduction to theory and research.* Reading, Mass.: Addison Wesley.

Fishbein, M., and L. Newman. (1976) "Increasing attitude-behavior correspondence by broadening the scope of the behavioral measure." *Journal of Personality and Social Psychology* 33:793–802.

Fleming, D. (1972) "Roots of the new conservation movement." *Perspectives in American History* 6:7–91.

Freeman, L. C. (1965) *Elementary applied statistics.* New York: Wiley.

Gardner, G. T., A. R. Tieman, L. C. Gould, D. R. DeLuca, L. W. Doob, and J. A. J. Stolwijk. (1982) "Risk and benefit perceptions, acceptability judgments, and self-reported actions toward nuclear power." *Journal of Social Psychology* 116:179–197.

Goodman, L. A. (1972) "A modified multiple regression approach to the analysis of dichotomous variables." *American Sociological Review* 37:28–46.

———. (1978) *Analyzing qualitative/categorical data.* Cambridge, Mass.: ABT.

Goodman, L. A., and W. H. Kruskal. (1954) "Measures of association for cross classifications." *Journal of the American Statistical Association* 49:732–764.

Gori, G. B., and B. J. Richter. (1978) "The macro-economics of disease prevention in the United States." *Science* 200:1126.

Green, C. (1980) "Not quite Dr. Strangelove." Paper presented at the Conference on Energy and Planning, Craigie College, Ayr, Scotland, 27–29 May.

Green, C., and R. Brown. (1980) "Through a glass darkly: Perceiving perceived risks to health and safety." Research paper, School of Architecture, Duncan of Jordanstone College of Art, University of Dundee, Scotland.

Harding, C., and J. Eiser. (1984) "Characterizing the perceived risks and benefits of some health issues." *Risk Analysis* 4:131–141.

Harry, J., R. Gale, and J. Hendee. (1969) "Conservation: An upper-middle-class social movement." *Journal of Leisure Research* 1:246–254.

Hawkes, R. K. (1971) "The multivariate analysis of ordinal measures." *American Journal of Sociology* 76:908–926.

Hendee, J., W. Catton, L. Marlow, and F. Brackman. (1968) Wilderness uses in the Pacific Northwest: Their characteristics, values, and management preferences. USDA Forest Service Research Paper PNW–61.

Hohenemser, C., R. Kates, and P. Slovic. (1983) "The nature of technological hazard." *Science* 220:378–384.

Hornback, K. (1974) *Orbits of opinion: The role of age in the environment's attentive public, 1968–72.* Ph.D. diss., Michigan State University.

Howard, N., and S. Antilla. (1979) "What price safety? The 'zero-risk' debate." *Dun's Review* (September):48–53.

Hull, C. H., and N. H. Nie. (1981) *SPSS update 7–9.* New York: McGraw-Hill.

Kantrowitz, A. (1975) "Controlling technology democratically." *American Scientist* 63:505–509.

Kasper, R. (1980) "Perceptions of risk and their effects on decision making." In R. Schwing and W. Albers, Jr., eds., *Societal risk assessment: How safe is safe enough?* New York: Plenum.

Keene, H. K., and V. A. Sackett. (1981) "An editor's report on the Yankelovich, Skelly and White 'Mushiness Index.'" *Public Opinion* (April/May):50–51.

Kendall, M. G. (1962) *Rank correlation methods.* 3rd ed. New York: Hafner.

Kim, J. O. (1975) "Multivariate analysis of ordinal variables." *American Journal of Sociology* 81:261–298.

Kish, L. (1965) *Survey sampling.* New York: Wiley.

Kreitler, H., and S. Kreitler. (1976) *Cognitive orientation and behavior.* New York: Springer.

Krzywicki, L. (1934) *Primitive society and its vital statistics.* London: Macmillan.

Lewis, H. (1980) "The safety of fission reactors." *Scientific American* 242:53–65.

Lichtenstein, S., P. Slovic, B. Fischhoff, M. Layman, and B. Combs. (1978) "Judged frequency of lethal events." *Journal of Experimental Psychology: Human Learning and Memory* 4:551–578.

Light, R. J., and B. H. Margolin. (1971) "An analysis of variance for categorical data." *Journal of the American Statistical Association* 16:534–544.

Lipset, S. M., and W. Schneider. (1983) *The confidence gap: Business, labor, and government in the public mind.* New York: Free Press.

Liska, A. (1975) *The consistency controversy.* New York: Wiley.

Lobel, T. E. (1982) "The prediction of behavior from different types of beliefs." *Journal of Social Psychology* 118:213–223.

Lowrance, W. (1976) *Of acceptable risk.* Los Altos, Calif.: Kaufman.

McKechnie, G. E. (1974) *Environmental response inventory manual.* Palo Alto: Consulting Psychologists Press.

Marsh and McLennan Cos., Inc. (1980) "Risk in a complex society." Public opinion survey (June), New York, New York.

Mazur, A. (1977) "Science courts." *Minerva* 15:1–14.

———. (1981) *The dynamics of technical controversy.* Washington, D.C.: Communications Press.

Melber, B., S. Nealey, J. Hammersla, and A. Rankin. (1977) *Nuclear power and the public: Analysis of collected survey research.* Seattle: Battelle Human Affairs Research Centers.

Mitchell, R. (1980) "Public opinion and nuclear power before and after Three Mile Island." *Resources* (Resources for the Future newsletter, January–April): 5–8.

Morrison, D. E., and R. E. Henkel, eds. (1970) *The significance test controversy.* Chicago: Aldine.

Nader, R. (1965) *Unsafe at any speed.* New York: Grossman.

National Academy of Sciences/National Regulatory Commission. (1983) *Risk assessment in the federal government: Managing the process.* Washington, D.C.: National Academy Press.

National Center for Health Statistics. (1984) *Health, United States, 1984.* Washington D.C.: U.S. Gov't. Printing Office.

Nelkin, D. (1984) *Controversy: The politics of technical decisions.* Beverly Hills: Sage.

New York Times. (1986a) "Hearing set for air bags." 135 (Jan. 25):39A.

———. (1986b) "Worry about air control repairs." 135 (April 2):15A.

———. (1986c) "Reagan signs measure relaxing gun controls." 135 (May 20):16A.

Nie, N. H., C. H. Hull, J. G. Jenkins, K. Steinbrenner, and D. H. Bent. (1975) *Statistical package for the social sciences*. 2nd ed. New York: McGraw-Hill.

Nuclear Regulatory Commission. (1975) *Reactor safety study: An assessment of accident risks in U.S. commercial nuclear power plants*. Washington, D.C.: WASH 1400, NUREG–75/014.

Orcutt, G. H., H. W. Watts, and J. B. Edwards. (1968) "Data aggregation and information loss." *The American Economic Review* 58:773–787.

Ostheimer, J., and L. Ritt. (1976) "Environment, energy, and black Americans." Sage Research Paper 90–025.

Otway, H. (1975) "Risk assessment and societal choices." Research Memorandum 75–2. Laxenburg, Austria: International Institute for Applied Systems Analysis.

———. (1985) "Multidimensional criteria for technology acceptability." *Risk Analysis* 6:403–415.

Otway, H., and J. Cohen. (1975) "Revealed preferences: Comments on the Starr benefit-risk relationships." Research Memorandum 76–80. Laxenburg, Austria: International Institute for Applied Systems Analysis.

Otway, H., and M. Fishbein. (1977) "Public attitudes and decision making." Research Memorandum 77–54. Laxenburg, Austria: International Institute for Applied Systems Analysis.

Otway, H., and K. Thomas. (1982) "Reflections on risk perception and policy." *Risk Analysis* 2:69–82.

Otway, H., and D. von Winterfeldt. (1982) "Beyond acceptable risk: On the social acceptability of technologies." *Policy Sciences* 14:247–256.

Pearce, D. (1978) "The nuclear debate is about values." *Nature* 274:200.

Perrow, C. (1982) "Not risk but power." *Contemporary Sociology* 11:298–299 (book review).

———. (1984) *Normal accidents*. New York: Basic Books.

Ploch, D. R. (1974) "Ordinal measures of association and the general linear model." In H. Blalock, ed., *Measurement in the social sciences: Theories and strategies*. Chicago: Aldine.

Raiffa, H. (1980) Concluding remarks. In R. Schwing and W. Albers, Jr., eds., *Societal risk assessment: How safe is safe enough?* New York: Plenum.

Renn, O. (1981) "Man, technology, and risk: A study on intuitive risk assessment and attitudes towards nuclear power." Report Jül-Spez 115. Jülich, Federal Republic of Germany, Nuclear Research Center.

Robinson, W. S. (1950) "Ecological correlations and the behavior of individuals." *American Sociological Review* 15:351–357.

Rowe, W. (1977) *An anatomy of risk*. New York: Wiley.

Schnaiburg, H. (1973) "Politics, participation and pollution: The environmental movement." In J. Walton and D. Carns, eds., *Cities in change: Studies on the urban condition.* Boston: Allyn & Bacon.

Schwartz, S. (1968) "Words, deeds, and the perception of consequences and responsibility in action situations." *Journal of Personality and Social Psychology* 10:232–242.

Schwing, R. (1980) "Tradeoffs." In R. Schwing and W. Albers, Jr., eds., *Societal risk assessment: How safe is safe enough?* New York: Plenum Press.

Shribman, D. (1983) "Pushing for a nuclear freeze." *New York Times* 132 (Sept. 6): 10B.

Slovic, P. (1980) Personal communication. Eugene, Oreg.: Decision Research, Inc.

———. (1986) "Informing and educating the public about risk." *Risk Analysis* 5:271–274.

Slovic, P., and B. Fischhoff. (1983) "How safe is safe enough? Determinants of perceived and acceptable risk." In C. Walker, L. Gould, and E. Woodhouse, eds., *Too hot to handle? Social and policy issues in the management of radioactive wastes.* New Haven: Yale University Press.

Slovic, P., B. Fischhoff, and S. Lichtenstein. (1979) "Rating the risks." *Environment* 21:14–20, 36–39.

———. (1980) "Facts and fears: Understanding perceived risk." In R. Schwing and W. Albers, Jr., eds., *Societal risk assessment: How safe is safe enough?* New York: Plenum.

———. (1981) "Characterizing perceived risk." In R. Kates and C. Hohenemser, eds., *Technological hazard management.* Cambridge: Oelgeschlager, Gunn and Hain.

———. (1984) "Regulation of risk: A psychological perspective." In R. Noll, ed., *Social science and regulatory policy.* Berkeley: University of California Press.

———. (Unpublished.) "Perceived and acceptable risk: Further studies of expressed preferences." Eugene, Oreg.: Decision Research, Inc.

Somers, R. H. (1962a) "A measure of association for ordinal variables." *American Sociological Review* 27:799–811.

———. (1962b) "A similarity between Goodman and Kruskal's Tau and Kendall's Tau, with a partial interpretation of the latter." *Journal of the American Statistical Association* 57:804–812.

———. (1968) "An approach to the multivariate analysis of ordinal data." *American Sociological Review* 33:971–977.

Sowby, F. (1965) "Radiation and other risks." *Health Physics* 11:879–887.

Stallings, R. (1973) "Patterns of belief in social movements: Clarifications from an analysis of environmental groups." *Sociological Quarterly* 14:465–480.

Starr, C. (1969) "Social benefits versus technological risk." *Science* 169:1232–1238.

———. (1972) "Benefit-cost studies in sociotechnical systems." Committee on

Public Energy Policy, *Perspectives on Benefit-Risk Decision Making.* Washington, D.C.: National Academy of Engineering.

Starr, C., and C. Wipple. (1980) "Risks of risk decisions." *Science* 208:1114–1119.

Stolwijk, J. A. J., D. R. Deluca, L. C. Gould, L. W. Doob, G. T. Gardner, and A. T. Tiemann. (1980) "Program to investigate public perceptions of technological risk." Final Report to Northeast Utilities Company, Hartford, Conn.

Sullivan, J., and A. Fenn. (1976) *Role of people's councils in improving public participation in electric utility policy making.* Washington, D.C.: National Council for the Public Assessment of Technology.

Tognacci, L., R. Weigel, M. Wideen, and D. Verfnon. (1972) "Environmental quality: How universal is public concern?" *Environment and Behavior* 4:73–86.

Tversky, A., and D. Kahneman. (1974) "Judgment under uncertainty: Heuristics and biases." *Science* 185:1124–1131.

———. (1981) "The framing of decisions and the psychology of choice." *Science* 211:453–458.

Upton, A. (1982) "The biological effects of low-level ionizing radiation." *Scientific American* 246:41–49.

Vallois, H. V. (1960) "Vital estimates in prehistoric population as determined from archaeological data." In R. F. Heizer and S. F. Cook, eds., *The application of quantitative methods in archaeology.* Chicago: Quadrangle.

Vlek, C., and P. Stallen. (1979) *Persoonlijke Beoordeling van Risico's.* University of Groningen, Institute for Experimental Psychology.

von Winterfeldt, D., and W. Edwards. (1984) "Patterns of conflict about risky technologies." *Risk Analysis* 4:55–68.

Walker, C. A., L. C. Gould, and E. J. Woodhouse, eds. (1983) *Too hot to handle? Social and policy issues in the management of radioactive wastes.* New Haven: Yale University Press.

Webster, F. (1975) "Determining the characteristics of the socially conscious consumer." *Journal of Consumer Research* 2:188–196.

Weidenreich, F. (1949) *The shorter anthropological papers of Franz Weidenreich.* New York: Viking.

Weigel, R. (1977) "Ideological and demographic correlates of pro-ecology behavior." *Journal of Social Psychology* 103:39–47.

Weigel, R., and L. Newman. (1976) "Increasing attitude-behavior correspondence by broadening the scope of the behavioral measure." *Journal of Personality and Social Psychology* 33:793–802.

Whittemore, A. (1983) "Facts and values in risk analysis for environmental toxicants." *Risk Analysis* 3:23–33.

Wicker, A. (1969) "Attitudes versus actions: The relationship of verbal and overt behavioral responses to attitude objects." *Journal of Social Issues* 25:41–78.

Wilson, R. (1979) "Analyzing the daily risks of life." *Technology Review* 81:40–46.

Winner, L. (1977) *Autonomous technology.* Cambridge, Mass.: The MIT Press.

Woodhouse, E. J. (1982) "Managing nuclear wastes: Let the public speak." *Technology Review* 85:12–13.

———. (1983) "The politics of nuclear waste management." In C. A. Walker, L. C. Gould, and E. J. Woodhouse, eds., *Too hot to handle? Social and policy issues in the management of radioactive wastes.* New Haven: Yale University Press.

World Almanac and Book of Facts. (1986) New York: Newspaper Enterprise Assoc.

Wynne, B. (1983) "Redefining the issues of risk and public acceptance: The social viability of technology." *Futures* (February):13–32.

Zeisel, H. (1968) *Say it with figures.* New York: Harper.

Index

DATE DUE

Perceptions   215963